"Evil is more than a theodicy issue: it has the potential to purify our understanding and so to deepen our theological endeavors. By placing our experience of suffering within a broader theological context, *Evil and Creation* enhances our understanding of the doctrine of creation. The result is a rich variety of reflections on topics such as evolution, animal death, intellectual disability, Sabbath, and covenant."

Hans Boersma, Saint Benedict Servants of Christ Chair in Ascetical Theology, Nashotah House Theological Seminary

"Ever since Hume, 'the problem of evil' has widely been seen as the ultimate argument against religious faith: if our world is the creation of a God who is supremely just, supremely loving, and supremely powerful, how can it continue to be so much characterized by unwarranted suffering, and wounded so much by deliberate human malice? Since earliest times, literature has grappled with this question in various forms, the Bible and the Christian theological tradition have struggled to answer it, and philosophers secular and religious have continued to address it—without a consistent or conclusive response.

"This volume brings together a collection of biblical scholars, students of early Christianity, contemporary theologians, and thoughtful readers of literature who consider again aspects of the relationship of faith to our experience of evil, both individual and universal. The result is consistently informative, widely provocative, and often unsettling—redefining the boundaries of the questions we ask and putting into new light the answers we look for. It is a rich and significant contribution to our continuing search for long-term meaning in our history."

Brian E. Daly, SJ, Catherine F. Huisking Professor Emeritus, University of Notre Dame

"A very welcome collection of essays on the perennial problem of evil, or rather reflections, drawing upon the wide breadth of the Christian tradition, that offer theological responses to the existence of evil and suffering, and their place in creation, and deepen our understanding of the mystery of God and ourselves: a rich feast on which to be nourished!"

Fr. John Behr, Regius Chair of Humanity, University of Aberdeen

EVIL *and*

CREATION

Historical and Constructive Essays in Christian Dogmatics

STUDIES IN HISTORICAL & SYSTEMATIC THEOLOGY

H
S S
T

EVIL *and* CREATION

Historical and Constructive Essays
in Christian Dogmatics

Edited by **DAVID LUY, MATTHEW LEVERING,**
and **GEORGE KALANTZIS**

STUDIES IN HISTORICAL AND SYSTEMATIC THEOLOGY

LEXHAM PRESS

Evil and Creation: Historical and Constructive Essays in Christian Dogmatics
Studies in Historical and Systematic Theology

Print ISBN 9781683594345
Digital ISBN 9781683594352
Library of Control Control Number 2020943976

Lexham Editorial: Todd Hains, Lisa Eary, Abigail Stocker
Cover Design: Owen Craft
Typesetting: Danielle Thevenaz

The Chicago Theological Initiative (CTI) exists to promote ecumenical scholarship and spiritual friendship among theologians within the broader Chicagoland area.

CTI is committed to the creedal inheritance of catholic Christianity and equally committed to following the crucified and risen Christ in self-sacrificial moral life.

It fosters inter-confessional and inter-institutional collaboration for the sake of advancing the theological disciplines and enabling mutual edification among Christian scholars.

In obedience to the command of the incarnate Lord, CTI hopes for full visible and confessional unity among Christians, but pursues this goal through a ministry of friendship and of mutual encouragement along the path of witnessing through teaching and scholarship to the truth, love, and mercy of Jesus Christ.

In this sense, CTI's mission pertains fundamentally to the evangelization of the academy so that Christian scholarship will be able to perform its task of contemplating and handing on the mysteries of faith to the next generation.

CTI CHICAGO
THEOLOGICAL
INITIATIVE

CONTENTS

ACKNOWLEDGMENTS

—

This volume originated as a series of papers delivered in 2018 at the spring colloquium of the Chicago Theological Initiative, which took place in the Harbor House at Wheaton College. Chicago Theological Initiative is a cooperative venture involving a number of Chicago-area institutions. Accordingly, there are many people for us to thank and acknowledge. We are honored to have received financial assistance from the Carl F. H. Henry Center at Trinity Evangelical Divinity School. We are indebted especially to Thomas McCall (director) and Geoffrey Fulkerson (assistant director) for their willingness to include our colloquium as part of the Henry Center's Creation Project, which is funded by a generous grant from the Templeton Foundation. Without this funding, neither the colloquium nor this book would have been possible. In addition to acknowledging the Henry Center at Trinity, we must also express our thanks for the shared leadership and support provided by the Center for Scriptural Exegesis, Philosophy, and Doctrine at Mundelein Seminary and The Wheaton Center for Early Christian Studies at Wheaton College. We are grateful to Lexham Press for agreeing to publish this volume and especially for the work of Todd Hains in bringing it to completion. Finally, we wish to thank each of the exemplary scholars who contributed an essay for this volume.

ABBREVIATIONS

—

CCC	*Catechism of the Catholic Church*. U.S. Catholic Conference. New York: Doubleday Religion, 2003
CCSL	Corpus Christianorum: Series Latina. Turnhout: Brepols, 1977–
Civ.	Augustine, *De civitate Dei*
Comm. Eccl.	*Commentarius in Ecclesiasten*
Conf.	Augustine, *Confessionem libri XIII*
CSEL	*Corpus Scriptorum Ecclesiasticorum Latinorum*. Vienna: Tempsk, 1894–1900
Enchir.	Augustine, *Enchiridion*
GCS	Griechischen christlichen Schriftsteller der ersten drei Jahrhunderte
Gen. imp.	Augustine, *De Genesi ad litteram imperfectus liber*
Gen. litt.	Augustine, *De Genesi ad litteram*
Gen. Man.	Augustine, *De Genesis contra Manichaeos*
GNO	*Gregorii Nysseni Opera Online*
Hom. Eccl.	*Homiliae in Ecclesiasten*
Lib.	Augustine, *De libero arbitrio*
PG	Patrologia Graeca. Edited by Jacques-Paul Migne. 162 vols. Paris, 1857–86
PTA	Papyrologische Texte und Abhandlungen
SC	Sources Chrétiennes

Schol. Eccl.   *Scholia in Ecclesiasten*
Ver. rel.   Augustine, *De vera religione*

1

—

INTRODUCTION

Evil in Christian Theology

David Luy and Matthew Levering

The essays comprising this book consider evil in relation to the Christian doctrine of creation. A theological account of evil is not exactly the same thing as a response to the problem of evil, even if the former typically includes aspects of the latter. Some of the chapters in this book address the problem of evil (for example, chaps. 3, 7, 9), but the purpose of the collection as a whole is not to produce a theodicy. It is rather to reflect on the emergence of moral and physical evil from the standpoint of a particular doctrinal locus. In this introduction, we expand briefly on the nature of this task, calling special attention to the difference between a theological account of evil and a response to the problem of evil.

BEYOND THE PROBLEM OF EVIL

For ancients and moderns alike, the question of God is deeply intertwined with the riddle of evil. "At least in the western tradition," Herbert McCabe observes, "nothing so affects our attitude to God as our recognition of evil and suffering."[1] In the late modern West, evil happenings in the world may seem to awaken religious skepticism. For those living downstream of Voltaire and David Hume (and in the shadow of twentieth-century atrocities), the intrusion of evil appears to call traditionally Christian notions

---

1. McCabe first wrote these words in a work of 1987 titled *God Matters*, but the line is quoted here from Herbert McCabe, "Evil," in *The McCabe Reader*, ed. Brian Davies and Paul Kucharski (New York: T&T Clark, 2016), 85.

of God automatically into question.[2] The recorded experience of Christian saints across the centuries bears witness to an alternate possibility, however. The endurance of bitter suffering can serve to deepen rather than enervate religious commitment.[3] It is true, McCabe acknowledges, that suffering may cause us to "reject God as infantile, as unable to comprehend or have compassion on those who suffer and are made to suffer in his world." But it is also possible, he continues, that suffering may cause us to find, "as Job did, that it was *our view of God* that was infantile; we may in fact come to a deeper understanding of the mystery of God."[4]

The second response and existential posture described here by McCabe implies a *theological* construal of evil and suffering wherein the bitterness of affliction has been incorporated into the broader task of faith seeking understanding. Suffering relates to the experience of God here in two primary ways. First, it functions as a purifying agent. Existential trials bear a potent capacity to expose the superficiality of theological frameworks unable to prove their mettle in the face of calamity.[5] As Martin Luther (1483-1546) so often insisted, the true theologian is one whose religious commitments have been tested and steeled in the fires of affliction.[6] In this sense, suffering refines the church's theological understanding. At the same time, however, suffering can achieve significance for religious piety

---

2. For a helpful discussion of this general impulse, see David Bentley Hart, *The Doors of the Sea* (Grand Rapids: Eerdmans, 2005), 7-15.

3. Consider, for instance, the flood of devotional literatures known as the *ars moriendi*, prompted by high mortality rates in the medieval and early Reformation period. See Austra Reinis, *Reforming the Art of Dying: The Ars Moriendi in the German Reformation (1519-1528)* (Aldershot, UK: Ashgate, 2007). The same blossoming of devotional piety emerges in relation to many other periods of intense suffering in the history of the church. See, for instance, Nicholas Hope, *German and Scandinavian Protestantism 1700-1918*, Oxford History of the Christian Church (Oxford: Oxford University Press, 1999), 3-20.

4. McCabe, "Evil," 85, emphasis added.

5. This appears to be what McCabe means when he suggests that suffering may reveal to us that it is our conception of God that turns out to be immature. Job's friends are a classic example here. For more on the need to develop less superficial responses to evil, see Michel Barnes's essay of this book.

6. This is the fundamental meaning of Luther's often-quoted but frequently misinterpreted sentiment expressed in a table talk from 1531. "Sola autem experientia facit theologum" (*Tischreden* [Table Talk], vol. 1, *Tischreden aus der ersten Hälfte der dreißiger Jahr* [Weimar: H. Böhlaus Nachfolger, 1912], 16.13). The classic expression of this principle that affliction plays an essential part in the formation of the theologian appears in a preface Luther composed in 1539. For the standard English translation of this preface, see *Career of the Reformer IV*, ed. Helmut T. Lehmann and Lewis W. Spitz, Luther's Works 34 (Philadelphia: Fortress, 1960), 285-88.

only to the extent that it is itself understood theologically. Affliction on its own is at best ambiguous so long as it remains abstracted from a theological framework. One of the essential functions of Christian doctrine within the life of the church is that it gives direction to the way in which Christians reflect on their experiences of evil and suffering in the world. Doctrine supplies the decisive hermeneutical framework in relation to which suffering becomes endurable for the Christian, even if evil itself remains to some extent an impenetrable mystery.[7] A theological account of evil locates trial and affliction within a theological context, acknowledging that suffering also often quickens, purifies, and refines the church's theological understanding.

Such accounts are standard fare within the literatures of premodern Christian theology. Awaiting execution from his prison cell, Boethius (ca. 477–524) seeks consolation in his plight by reflecting on his experience in relation to a theological frame of reference (i.e., the mysteries of providence and divine eternality).[8] Likewise, Macrina (ca. 330–379) ponders the immaterial soul and the bodily resurrection in conversation with her brother Gregory as she anticipates her impending death.[9] In an exposition of Psalm 139 (138 in his Latin version), Augustine (354–430) situates earthly sorrow in more general terms by framing the volatility of human experience with a theological canvas.

> During this night, during this mortal life, human beings experience both light and darkness: the light of prosperity and the darkness of misfortune. But when Christ has come and made the soul his own dwelling through its faith, when he has promised a different light, when he has inspired and granted patience, when he has counseled men and women not to be too happy over prosperity lest they be crushed by adversity—then believers begin to treat the present world with detached indifference. No longer are they elated when

---

7. Most theologians from the tradition would deny that evil is the sort of thing that can ever become intelligible in any conventional sense of the term.

8. Boethius, *Tractates; The Consolation of Philosophy*, trans. H. F. Stewart, E. K. Rand, and S. J. Tester, Loeb Classical Library (Edinburgh: St. Edmundsbury, 1973).

9. Gregory, Bishop of Nyssa, *The Life of Saint Macrina*, trans. Kevin Corrigan (Eugene, OR: Wipf & Stock, 2005); Gregory, *On the Soul and the Resurrection*, trans. Catherine Roth, Popular Patristics 12 (Yonkers, NY: St. Vladimir's Press Seminary, 1993).

things chance to go well with them, nor are they shattered when things turn out badly. They bless the Lord in all circumstances, not only in abundance but also in loss, not only in health but also in sickness. The promise sung of in another psalm is kept in their lives: *I will bless the Lord at all times; his praise shall be in my mouth always* (Ps. 33:2/ 34:1).[10]

Notice here that Augustine is not advancing a theoretical explanation for why suffering exists in the world. His purpose is rather to recontextualize the experience of suffering by situating it within a theological context. For Christians indwelled by the Spirit of Christ and illuminated by the light of a glorious, eschatological promise, the volatile realities of this earthly life lose much of their bitter sting.

Johann Arndt (1555–1621) casts a similar vision. In his influential devotional text *True Christianity* (1610), Arndt writes:

A magnet draws a heavy piece of iron toward itself, and likewise a heavenly magnet, the love of God, ought to draw the burdens of our cross toward itself, so that it becomes light and easy. Why then should man's heart be troubled? Sugar makes bitter food sweet. How much then, ought the sweetness of divine love to make the bitter cross sweet? Because of this, the great patience and joy of the holy martrys arose, for God made them drunk by his love.[11]

The purpose of these theological meditations on suffering is pastoral. The reader or hearer is not summoned by Boethius, Nyssa, Augustine, or Arndt merely to adopt some new theoretical understanding of evil. The theological architecture these authors supply in the course of their examination of suffering is meant to evoke a new existential posture in relation to worldly vicissitude. In this respect, these premodern writers may be understood as seeking to outline a theological account of evil.

---

10. Saint Augustine, *Essential Expositions of the Psalms*, trans. Maria Boulding, OSB, ed. Boniface Ramsey, Works of Saint Augustine (Hyde Park, NY: New City, 2015), 192–93.

11. Johann Arndt, *True Christianity*, trans. Peter Erb, Classics of Western Spirituality (New York: Paulist Press, 1979), 128.

Does such reflection need to be recovered in modern theological inquiry? To be sure, the impulse to make theological sense of suffering remains a constant for many faithful Christians living today. Surely it would be wrong to imply that such impulses receive no assistance whatsoever from the contemporary theological guild.[12] Still, it has sometimes been the case in recent centuries that theological accounts of evil (as we term them) have been eclipsed by an abiding preoccupation with the so-called problem of evil. Susan Neiman has argued somewhat provocatively that the problem of evil is the defining theme of modern philosophy.[13] From the devastation of Lisbon's earthquake in 1755 to the atrocities of the Holocaust in the 1940s, modern philosophical discourse may be understood as a protracted struggle to rediscover a meaningful world after the collapse of the medieval synthesis. Since philosophy sprouts fundamentally from a "demand that the world be intelligible," the emergence of evil in the world may thus be construed primarily as philosophical challenge.[14] Radical evil evokes the grim possibility of a world governed by chaos.[15]

The challenge posed by evil in modern philosophical literature falls hardest on the classical Christian view, which insists even in the face of radical evil that Christians may affirm, on biblical and philosophical grounds, that the world is providentially ordered by a God who is maximally good, just, and powerful. For many critics, evil exposes such a notion as utterly absurd.[16] As such philosophical criticisms have proliferated, it is under-

12. See, for instance, Kelly M. Kapic, *Embodied Hope: A Theological Meditation on Pain and Suffering* (Downers Grove, IL: IVP Academic, 2017); J. Todd Billings, *Rejoicing in Lament: Wrestling with Incurable Cancer and Life in Christ* (Grand Rapids: Brazos, 2015); John S. Feinberg, *When There Are No Easy Answers: Thinking Differently About God, Suffering, and Evil* (Grand Rapids: Kregel, 2016). See also Katherine Sonderegger's provocative account of evil in *Systematic Theology*, volume 1, *The Doctrine of God* (Philadelphia: Fortress, 2015).

13. Susan Neiman, *Evil in Modern Thought: An Alternative History of Philosophy* (Princeton: Princeton University Press, 2002), 3.

14. Neiman, *Evil in Modern Thought*, 7.

15. This possibility is, of course, not a modern discovery. Rather, it is profoundly presented and engaged within Scripture itself. The "answers" given therein—for example, at the end of the book of Job, or to the despairing prophet Elijah, or in the Gospels, in which the cross and resurrection of Jesus Christ stand out as the yet-mysterious solution, rooted in the divine presence, care, solidarity, and love—are not philosophical answers to a philosophical problem but existential answers to an existential problem.

16. David Hume, *Dialogues Concerning Natural Religion: And Other Writings*, ed. Dorothy Coleman, Cambridge Texts in the History of Philosophy (Cambridge: Cambridge University Press, 2007). On page 74 of this text, Hume states the problem of evil in classic form. "Is [God]

standable that the collective attention of modern theology has likewise migrated to the philosophical problem of evil and its modern permutations for the purpose of mounting a defense. The migration of attention is not by itself a problem. It becomes detrimental, however, when an elevated preoccupation with the problem of evil causes theological accounts of evil to wither from neglect or lapse entirely into desuetude.

Another potential hazard of the shift arises when sustained preoccupation with the problematics of evil and suffering leads to a fundamental reconfiguration of the architecture of theology. Such is the case, we (David and Matthew) contend, for a number of recent theological proposals that seek to account for evil in the world by suggesting that the existence of evil is a necessary entailment of the act whereby God creates the finite order.[17] This approach seems to allow a preoccupation with evil to overwhelm the doctrine of God (his transcendent freedom) and the doctrine of creation (its original goodness). Even if the account succeeds at making evil intelligible to some extent, from a dogmatic perspective the possible gain comes at too steep a cost.

In a similar vein, some recent arguments in favor of universalism appear to rest on philosophical presuppositions concerning what God must do if he is to be vindicated in the final analysis as just and good. David Bentley Hart has recently outlined a sophisticated version of this position. He contends it becomes apparent in Fyodor Dostoevsky's *The Brothers Karamazov* that "even if something like Gregory of Nyssa's vision of the last things [whereby suffering exercises a purgative function for a redemptive economy in which all are saved] should prove true, it will still be a happiness achieved as the residue of an inexcusable cruelty." After all, Hart points out, it is God who willed to create a world—or, at least, he chose to allow the ongoing existence of a fallen world—in which temporal creatures

---

willing to prevent evil, but not able? then is he impotent. Is he able, but not willing? then is he malevolent. Is he both able and willing? Whence then is evil?"

17. See, e.g., Jürgen Moltmann, *The Trinity and the Kingdom: The Doctrine of God*, trans. Margaret Kohl (Philadelphia: Fortress, 1993); Moltmann, *God in Creation: A New Theology of Creation and the Spirit of God*, trans. Margaret Kohl (Philadelphia: Fortress, 1993); Marilyn McCord Adams, *Horrendous Evils and the Goodness of God*, Cornell Studies in the Philosophy of Religion (Ithaca, NY: Cornell University Press, 2000); Marilyn McCord Adams, *Christ and Horrors: The Coherence of Christology*, Current Issues in Theology (Cambridge: Cambridge University Press, 2006).

are subjected to all sorts of gruesome and horrific sufferings, often through no fault of their own. In order to justify the creation of such a cosmos with its incalculable number of torments, God must do more, says Hart, than simply resolve all things in a universal salvation at the end. Rather, God must reveal in the end that He has in fact actively rescued creatures from the consequents of sin and suffering, and that absolutely nothing is lost. Hart sums up, "If God is the good creator of all, he is the savior of all, without fail, who brings to himself all he has made."[18]

This position requires of the Creator God something that God has not, in Christ, specifically revealed that he will do. Because theologians, indeed all humans, are limited as creatures, we suggest theologians must not determine what the Creator God *must* do in order to vindicate his own goodness. Certainly, the problems Hart means to address should continue to command our theological attention, but even in the face of conceptual dissonance we must resist the temptation when faced with the problem of evil to impose a philosophical solution that, however plausible, exceeds what we can know or require of God on the basis of what God himself has revealed.[19]

With these concerns having been registered, we readily acknowledge that a response of some sort to the philosophical problem of evil remains an indispensable task. After all, Scripture itself and the theological tradition prepare for just such a response, though naturally the response implicit within these sources is rooted existentially in the self-revelation of God and includes an affirmation of God's personal presence and solidarity with sufferers. Without any response to the philosophical problem of evil, it will be impossible to demonstrate that the broader theological account of evil available among Christian thinkers might even possibly possess real intelligibility and value.[20] We freely admit the premise that a

---

18. David Bentley Hart, "The Devil's March: *Creatio ex nihilo*, the Problem of Evil, and a Few Dostoyevskian Meditations," in *Creation Ex Nihilo: Origins, Development, Contemporary Challenges*, ed. Gary A. Anderson and Markus Bockmuehl (Notre Dame: University of Notre Dame Press, 2018), 297–318, here 306, 318. Hart has also published a book-length defense of universalism: *That All Shall Be Saved: Heaven, Hell and Universal Salvation* (New Haven: Yale University Press, 2019).

19. For the varieties of Christian universalism see Michael J. McClymond, *The Devil's Redemption: A New History and Interpretation of Christian Universalism* (Grand Rapids: Baker Academic, 2018).

20. McCabe helpfully describes the problem of evil as an "impediment" that must be removed if a person is expected to consider the second existential posture as a rational possibility ("Evil," 85).

view rightly deemed to entail a logical contradiction should not be retained even if it proves stimulating or useful in other respects. Still, even as we acknowledge the importance of such inquiry, a response to the problem of evil is not the same thing as a theological account of evil. Whereas the effort to respond to the problem of evil removes an important obstacle to the embrace of doctrinal Christianity, a theological and biblical account seeks to make sense of suffering by incorporating it within the larger, existentially contextualized task of faith seeking understanding, in which a living relationship with Christ in the Holy Spirit conditions human reasoning about the justice, mercy, providence, and love of God.

If our suggestion is accurate that an abiding preoccupation with the philosophical problem of evil has sometimes distracted modern theologians from the task of formulating a theological account of evil, it is important for contemporary theological reflection to correct the imbalance. It will always remain a necessary task for Christian intellectuals to reflect on evil within the context of a prosecutorial trial in which Christianity sits as defendant. This was already a task taken up by Job, Jesus, Paul, and indeed all the biblical authors, though, of course, the prosecutors were not Humeans (though some were thoroughgoing skeptics of the kind found in the opening chapters of the Wisdom of Solomon). At the same time, theologians and pastors must always leverage the full resources of Christian doctrine—rooted in the living realities of faith—within a more synthetic attempt to make existential sense of suffering in theological and biblical perspective. These two tasks are not mutually exclusive, but should rather be affirmed as distinct and complementary moments within a fulsome account of theological inquiry.[21] Whereas the first moment considers the coherence of Christian theism primarily from the outside looking in, the second moment intentionally inhabits the intricate matrix of Christian dogma—a matrix of lived supernatural realities—and considers the world of experience (including the experience of evil and suffering) from the inside looking out. By embracing this second sort of inquiry, Christian

---

21. Eleonore Stump's incorporation of biblical narrative in relation to the problem of evil provides a helpful example of what such a complementary exercise might look like from the perspective of philosophical theology. See Eleonore Stump, *Wandering in Darkness: Narrative and the Problem of Suffering* (Oxford: Oxford University Press, 2010).

dogmatic inquiry, as a living work of faith, moves "beyond" the problem of evil, but without leaving the problem of evil entirely behind.

The essays in this book pursue a subset of this task by considering evil in relation to the doctrine of creation. Creation is by no means the only doctrinal reality pertinent to the larger task, but it surely occupies a position of fundamental importance. After all, the mystery of evil comes into focus when we consider the fact that evil has intruded a world created by the eternal and all-knowing God and declared by him to be "very good" (Gen 1:31).[22] It is also characteristic of the rich tradition of lament psalms to counterpose the outcries of human suffering with doxological meditations on God *as creator*. "I lift up my eyes to the hills—from where will my help come? My help comes from the LORD, who made heaven and earth," Psalm 121:1-2 proclaims. "My days are like an evening shadow," the afflicted one cries out in Psalm 102:11. "I wither away like the grass." "O my God," the psalmist pleads, "do not take me away at the midpoint of my life" (102:24) Here again, solace crests the horizon only when the sufferer turns to contemplation of the eternal God, who created this transitory world in which he presently languishes.

> Long ago you laid the foundation of the earth
>   and the heavens are the work of your hands.
> They will perish, but you endure;
>   they will all wear out like a garment.
> You change them like clothing, and they pass away;
>   but you are the same, and your years have no end.
> The children of your servants shall live secure;
>   their offspring shall be established in your presence.
>   (Ps 102:25-28)

In this, we discern an important truth that is clearly expressed in Psalm 75. The mystery of evil becomes endurable for the believer only in an experientially rich recognition of the fact that the teetering pillars of the earth are steadied in the end only by him who laid them in the first place (75:2-3).

---

22. All biblical citations are taken from the NRSV.

Part 1

—

EVIL *in*
EARLY CHRISTIAN SOURCES

2
—

JUDGMENT OF EVIL AS THE RENEWAL OF CREATION

Constantine R. Campbell

Look, I am making everything new. —Revelation 21:5

INTRODUCTION

This essay explores the relationship between the judgment of evil and the renewal of creation. With special reference to the apostle Paul, the essay examines the interrelationships between evil and the corruption of creation alongside judgment of evil and the restoration of creation. The essay also probes Paul's theological support as found in Genesis 2–3 and Isaiah 65–66, as well as various texts found within Second Temple literature. Returning to the New Testament, the essay then considers the voices of 2 Peter 3 and Revelation 19–22. While these texts have much in common with what we will find in Paul, they also raise the question of continuity versus discontinuity. In order to vanquish evil, will the new creation replace an old creation that needs to be destroyed? Or will the new creation constitute a restoration and renewal of the old created order? In other words, does the destruction of evil come at the cost of the destruction of all creation?

PAUL

Paul's eschatological vision includes the full sweep of creation, as all things in heaven and on earth will be renewed and centered around Christ. There is an inextricable link between the fate of humanity and that of creation, with the latter being subjected to decay because of the former. Just as humanity is gripped by suffering and death, so is the entire created order. It will only be released from its bondage to decay once humanity has been restored. This restoration can only occur in the wake of judgment.

FINAL JUDGMENT

The expectation of final judgment is a central theme of biblical eschatology, of Judaism, and, of course, for Paul. It is an indispensable feature of Paul's hope for the future, as he expects evil to be judged and justice to prevail. Ultimate justice constitutes the universal judgment of sin and evil. And it rights all wrongs.[1] According to Paul, God's wrath and anger are stored up for the disobedient, while glory, honor, and peace await those who do what is good (Rom 2:1–11; Eph 5:5–6; Col 3:5–7; 1 Tim 5:24–25). Judgment is viewed as reaping what has been sown—either destruction reaped from sowing according to the flesh, or eternal life reaped from sowing according to the Spirit (Gal 6:7–9). It also takes into account the role of conscience and exposes what is kept secret (Rom 2:14–16; 1 Cor 4:3–5). While all people begin as children under wrath by nature (Eph 2:1–3), believers are saved from God's wrath, since they have been declared righteous by the blood of Christ (Rom 5:8–10; 1 Thess 1:9–10; 5:9–10) and will be held blameless in the day of Christ (1 Cor 1:6–8; 1 Thess 3:13).

Anticipating objections to the contrary, Paul is adamant that God's judgment of the world is righteous (Rom 3:1–6; 9:19–24). The whole world is

---

1. In defining justice, it is useful to adopt the widely understood distinction of retributive and distributive justice. Perhaps the simplest way to distinguish between these two types of justice is to discern what is due a person in the face of injustice. If a person is a wrongdoer, they are due a just penalty—this is retributive justice. If a person, on the other hand, is the recipient of wrongdoing, they are due just recognition and compensation, for want of a better term. When a wrongdoer receives an appropriate penalty, retributive justice is achieved. When a recipient of wrongdoing receives appropriate restoration, protection, or compensation, distributive justice is achieved. See Nicholas P. Wolterstorff, "Justice and Peace," in *New Dictionary of Christian Ethics and Pastoral Theology* (Leicester, UK: Inter-Varsity Press, 1995), 16–17. According to the Bible, God is a God of justice and mercy. This understanding of God's character is inherited from the OT and upheld in the NT. Jesus is a preacher of eschatological justice, and the expectation of a coming judgment day shapes his own ministry and the NT framework for justice. Against the backdrop of the coming judgment, God's justice and mercy are seen profoundly in the death of Jesus, in which human sin is justly condemned. Thus, God is a just judge of sin, and yet mercifully grants the status of "just" to all in Christ. Those who are in Christ must also follow his example and bear unjust suffering, entrusting themselves to the one who judges justly. The expectation of final eschatological justice enables believers to forgo justice for themselves, all the while seeking distributive justice for others.

subject to his judgment (Rom 3:19), and all people will stand before the judgment seat of God to give an account of themselves to him (Rom 14:10-12). More specifically, Christ himself will judge the living and the dead (2 Tim 4:1-2; 4:8).

"PERSONAL" NEW CREATION

Before turning to Paul's use of the expression "new creation"—which only occurs in 2 Corinthians 5:17 and Galatians 6:15—we consider the Jewish background for the term. The Second Temple book that, according to Moyer Hubbard, best illuminates the perspective of the pre-Christian Paul is the book of Jubilees. The phrase "new creation" occurs twice in this book, in 1.29 and 4.26. Jubilees connects the new creation with the defeat of earthly and demonic powers that rage against Israel, and in this way is consistent with the main eschatological thrust of Second Temple apocalypses. Their picture of the future was that of "a completely transformed universe."[2]

Also related to Paul's "new creation" terminology is the Second Temple book Joseph and Aseneth, in which "creation and conversion become synonymous." Not only does the book offer a "vivid portrayal of conversion as new creation," but it is none other than the Spirit who effects this new creation. The Spirit's function in Joseph and Aseneth is to impart life.[3] The parallels here to Paul are self-evident.

In 2 Corinthians 5:16-17, Paul writes,[4]

> From now on, then, we do not know anyone from a worldly perspective. Even if we have known Christ from a worldly perspective, yet now we no longer know him in this way. *Therefore, if anyone is in Christ, he is a new creation*; the old has passed away, and see, the new has come!

The new creation here is, of course, the person *in Christ*—not the whole created realm, but a member within it. Rather than regard "anyone from a worldly perspective" (5:16a), Paul sees anyone who is *in Christ* (ἐν Χριστῷ)

---

2. Moyer V. Hubbard, *New Creation in Paul's Letters and Thought* (Cambridge: Cambridge University Press, 2002), 27, 36, 48, 53.

3. Hubbard, *New Creation in Paul's Letters and Thought*, 48, 73-74.

4. All translations are from the *Christian Standard Bible* (Nashville: Holman, 2017).

as *a new creation* (5:17a). This apparently means that "the old has passed away, while the new has come" (5:17b).

The language of "new creation" evokes the sense of realm contrast, in that the person in Christ now belongs under the realm of Christ.[5] This is how they are regarded as a new creation—being under the realm of Christ changes who they are, their allegiances, and their purpose for living.

In Galatians 6:14–16, Paul writes,

> But as for me, I will never boast about anything except the cross of our Lord Jesus Christ. The world has been crucified to me through the cross, and I to the world. *For both circumcision and uncircumcision mean nothing; what matters instead is a new creation.* May peace come to all those who follow this standard, and mercy even to the Israel of God!

Regarding the issue of circumcision and uncircumcision, neither status means anything in light of the cross of Christ. Paul will certainly "never boast about anything" apart from the cross (6:14) because any fleshly boast or status is made irrelevant by it. What matters instead "is a new creation" (6:15). This is the *standard* that is to be followed by all who desire peace, even for "the Israel of God" (6:16).

Paul does not elaborate on the meaning of this new creation, but he clearly refers to the person who, like him, has been crucified to the world (6:14). The notion of being raised with Christ is not mentioned here, but such a concept is implied by the new-creation language. The old has been crucified with Christ already. The person who is raised with Christ is therefore a new person and a new entity. Or, as Paul puts it, *a new creation.*

In Ephesians 2:8–10, Paul writes, "For you are saved by grace through faith, and this is not from yourselves; it is God's gift—not from works, so that no one can boast. *For we are his workmanship, created in Christ Jesus for good works*, which God prepared ahead of time for us to do." The element of new creation in this text is found at its end, referring to those who have been saved by grace through faith—"we are his workmanship, created in Christ Jesus for good works" (2:10a). People who have been saved by grace

---

5. Constantine R. Campbell, *Paul and Union with Christ: An Exegetical and Theological Study* (Grand Rapids: Zondervan, 2012), 117.

through faith are regarded as God's *workmanship*, or his "product" (ποίημα), having been "created in Christ Jesus."

The notion of new creation has been brewing since the beginning of the passage, where Paul describes his readers as "dead in your trespasses and sins" (2:1). These humans were spiritually dead. They were cut off from a relationship with God—the giver of life—because of their commitment to evil. But, Paul says, God "made us alive with Christ" (2:5). Thus, the transformation in view is not one of *reformation* but of spiritual *resurrection*. Those who were cut off from God—and were walking in the direction of eternal death—have been brought into a life-giving new relationship with their Creator, the source of all life. In this sense, the old person who was dead has been given new life, but no longer as that old person. Instead they are a new creation in Christ.

Moreover, such a new creation is brought about by God's work. This is plainly stated—"we are his workmanship" (2:10a)—but it is also woven throughout the passage. It is God who gives life to the spiritually dead (2:5); he raised them up with Christ (2:6a) and seated them in the heavens with him (2:6b). Because of these actions, Paul must insist that "you are saved by grace through faith, and this is not from yourselves; it is God's gift" (2:8). The argument of the whole passage leads inexorably to such a conclusion, since the spiritually dead are not able to save themselves. Only God has acted to bring about their spiritual resurrection.

All of this underscores the nature of the new creation: it is achieved by God's grace and crafted by his workmanship. But those who have been created in Christ Jesus have been fashioned "for good works" (2:10a). Though Paul carefully avoids the notion that their works might contribute to their salvation (2:8–9), he then insists on the right place for works in the life of the new creation. Good works have been prepared by God for us to do (2:10b)—or, literally, "for us to walk in" (ἵνα ἐν αὐτοῖς περιπατήσωμεν).

This walking imagery parallels the beginning of the passage, in which the spiritually dead "walked according to the ways of this world" (περιεπατήσατε κατὰ τὸν αἰῶνα τοῦ κόσμου τούτου). The rhetorical effect of this parallelism is to show that the "walking dead" have been recreated to be the "walking living," no longer slavishly following the ways of the world but now walking in the good deeds that God has prepared. This also underscores the nature of the new creation: while it is achieved by

God's grace and crafted by his workmanship, it is oriented to a new way of living and serving.

This new creation is also oriented toward the future, as revealed in 2:7 — "so that in the coming ages he might display the immeasurable riches of his grace through his kindness to us in Christ Jesus." While this verse is sometimes passed over as less significant for the overall argument of the passage, it could be argued that it is, in fact, its high point. Being saved by grace is not the ultimate good here, nor is walking according to good deeds. Rather, being fit to participate *in the coming ages*, and witnessing *the immeasurable riches* of God's grace, is the ultimate good. This is the true high point of the passage and the ultimate end to which all those who have been saved by grace are destined.

The new-creation texts of 2 Corinthians 5:16-17, Galatians 6:14-16, and Ephesians 2:8-10 show that for Paul the new creation begins with redeemed humanity. By their participation in Christ—the new man—believers participate in the new creation ahead of time. They are new and renewed; the old has passed away, the new has come.

"COSMIC" NEW CREATION

While the language of "new creation" is reserved for humanity in Paul's usage, the concept of a *cosmic* new creation is abundantly evident.

In Colossians 1:15-16, Paul writes,

He is the image of the invisible God,
the firstborn over all creation.
For everything was created by him,
in heaven and on earth,
the visible and the invisible,
whether thrones or dominions
or rulers or authorities—
all things have been created through him and for him.

A key passage regarding the relationship of Christ to the created order; we observe his preeminence over it as its creator (1:16), sustainer (1:17), and telos (1:16). There is clearly an intimate and intricate connection between creator and creation that characterizes the nature of creation from its beginning to its future.

Here we do not see two created orders—an "old" creation waiting to be replaced by a superior, new creation—but rather a renewed creation is envisaged through the lens of reconciliation. Everything was created by him (1:16) and everything is reconciled through him—*whether things on earth or things in heaven* (1:20). The renewal of the created order is, then, one of reunification, reconciliation, and peace-making through the blood of Christ shed on the cross. Thus the "new" created order is a better version of the old, but it is not discontinuous from it. There is no sense in which one is scrapped and replaced with the other.

In Ephesians 1:9-10, Paul writes,

He made known to us the mystery of his will, according to his good pleasure that he purposed in Christ as a plan for the right time *to bring everything together in Christ, both things in heaven and things on earth in him.*

While the language of new creation is not found in this text, the created realm is in view as everything is brought together in Christ, "both things in heaven and things on earth" (1:10). We do not observe a replacement of an "old" creation with a new one, but rather the existing creation is unified, or "summed up" (ἀνακεφαλαιόω) in Christ. In this sense, the creation is renewed by virtue of its realignment to Christ.

It is within the context of this renewed, united creation that those predestined according to God's purpose will enjoy their inheritance (1:11). This in turn leads those who hope in Christ to *bring praise to his glory* (1:12). Thus, we see that the eschatological blessings of inheritance and the eschatological goal of glory are set in the arena of the united creation that finds its recapitulation in Christ.

In Romans 8:18-23, Paul writes,

For I consider that the sufferings of this present time are not worth comparing with the glory that is going to be revealed to us. *For the creation eagerly waits with anticipation for God's sons to be revealed.* For the creation was subjected to futility not willingly, but because of him who subjected it in the hope that *the creation itself will also be set free from the bondage to decay into the glorious freedom of God's children.* For we know that *the whole creation has been groaning together with labor pains until now.* Not only that, but we ourselves who have the Spirit as the firstfruits we also groan within ourselves, eagerly waiting for adoption, the redemption of our bodies.

This is an extremely important text for understanding Paul's view of creation and new creation—or, perhaps better, the renewal of creation. He begins by discussing glory in 8:18, which is going "to be revealed in us." The glorious destiny of human beings is tied to the rest of creation, which "waits with anticipation for God's sons to be revealed" (8:19). Because of the fall of humanity, creation "was subjected to futility" (8:20) in the hope that it would "be set free from the bondage to decay" in relation to "the glorious freedom of God's children" (8:21). Like the children of Israel in Egypt, creation is now in slavery, but, as N. T. Wright expresses, it "is on tiptoe with expectation, longing for the day when God's children are revealed, when their resurrection will herald its own new life."[6] Creation has been suffering as a result of humanity's fall and will be restored from bondage in concert with God's children.[7] In this respect, creation's *groaning* is likened to that of *labor pains* as it eagerly awaits the arrival of the promised children of God.

By implication, the renewed creation will be the arena that the promised children of God will inhabit with their redeemed bodies. It seems that resurrected human beings will require a renewed creation in which to live. Whatever part of creation Paul envisages here (e.g., the earth, the heavens, etc.), it appears that resurrected people will remain in the arena of creation. They will not somehow supersede the created realm. Instead, their renewed creaturely status will be matched by the renewed creation.

In Romans 8, there is no hint that Paul imagines that the "old" creation will pass away in favor of a "new" creation. The passage clearly depicts a single creation that is, in the first instance, subjected to futility and will be set free from bondage in the future.

---

6. N. T. Wright, *Surprised by Hope: Rethinking Heaven, the Resurrection, and the Mission of the Church* (New York: HarperOne, 2008), 103.

7. William H. Dumbrell, *The Search for Order: Biblical Eschatology in Focus* (Grand Rapids: Baker, 1994), 277.

CONCLUSION

Judgment is a fundamental component of Paul's eschatological vision. It is the future event that will determine all subsequent reality for humanity, dividing all people toward their eternal destinations. While all humans are born under wrath, Christ saves those who have been made righteous by his blood. But even these will not escape the scrutiny of God's judgment, giving an account for the deeds done in the body.

Above all, judgment is concerned with putting the world to rights. Though its implications for individuals are stressed in several contexts, Paul is clear that its wider implications shape the destiny of the whole world. With Christ as Lord over all creation, judgment is the necessary means of expressing his rule. It is how Christ will exert righteousness and peace over all, by the bringing to account all evil and injustice. In the end, judgment is ultimately concerned with the eradication of evil and the final establishment of righteousness and peace. It is a necessary precursor to the promised renewal of creation.

It is clear that, while creation is the arena in which God works for the salvation of humanity and its glorification, it is not merely the arena for such activity—it is, in fact, the object of it, as God will restore, renew, and recenter the creation in concert with humanity. This is in keeping with Jewish apocalyptic expectation, as Richard Bauckham points out: "Personal eschatology was not for the most part divorced from historical and cosmic eschatology, since the hope of individuals was to share in the corporate future of God's people in God's kingdom and in the cosmic future of new creation for the world."[8] First Enoch offers a strong example of this connection. In the Book of the Watchers, there is a striking corollary of the judgment and destruction of sin and the restoration of the original pristine state of creation, as Grant Macaskill points out. Also in the Epistle of Enoch, the restored creation parallels judgment. As evil is purged from the earth, the righteous are healed and will no longer be threatened by it.[9]

---

8. Richard Bauckham, *The Fate of the Dead: Studies on the Jewish and Christian Apocalypses*, Supplements to Novum Testamentum 93 (Leiden: Brill, 1998), 1.

9. Grant Macaskill, *Revealed Wisdom and Inaugurated Eschatology in Ancient Judaism and Early Christology*, Supplements to the Journal for the Study of Judaism 115 (Leiden: Brill, 2007), 40–41.

This restoration of creation will be characterized by unification around Christ, since God has planned to bring everything together in Christ, things in heaven and on earth (Eph 1:9–10; Col 1:20). Each believer is already regarded a new creation in Christ (2 Cor 5:17; Eph 2:10), and in this sense, redeemed humanity forms the firstfruits of the cosmic new creation to come.[10] According to James Ware, "In the apostle's thought, the hope of the resurrection of the dead and of the renewed creation is not marginal to the faith, but the central feature and content of Christian hope."[11]

GENESIS 2-3

Paul's belief that the fate of creation is inextricably tied to that of humanity no doubt arises from Genesis 2–3. The Second Temple Jewish literature that likewise affirms such a connection is also indebted to Genesis. First, the man is formed "out of the dust from the ground" (Gen 2:7), just as every tree grew out of the ground (2:9), and every wild animal and every bird of the sky were likewise formed out of the ground (2:19). The man has a common bond with all vegetation and wildlife, since they are alike formed out of the ground.

The Lord God placed the man in the garden of Eden "to work it and watch over it" (2:15). He was given responsibility to name each living creature (2:19–20). Together with his helper, who is formed out of the man himself, *and not out of the ground* (2:21–23), the man is at once part of the created order while also over it. This unique relationship sheds some light on why the fate of humanity is so significant for the rest of creation; there is an organic oneness between humanity and the rest of creation, but there is also a priority and dignity afforded to humanity.

---

10. The relationship between newly created individuals and the cosmic new creation is mediated by the Spirit. As Beale indicates, "the Holy Spirit is what causes us to be existentially linked with the new world to come. ... Believers have begun to participate in the new creation through the Spirit's regenerating work, who has resurrected them and created them as a new creation." See G. K. Beale, "The Eschatology of Paul," in *Studies in the Pauline Epistles: Essays in Honor of Douglas J. Moo*, ed. Matthew S. Harmon and Jay E. Smith (Grand Rapids: Zondervan, 2014), 204. See also Petrus J. Gräbe, " 'And He Made Known to Us the Mystery of His Will ... ': Reflections on the Eschatology of the Letter to the Ephesians," in *Eschatology of the New Testament and Some Related Documents*, ed. Jan G. van der Watt, Wissenschaftliche Untersuchungen Zum Neuen Testament 2/315 (Tübingen: Mohr Siebeck, 2011), 266.

11. James P. Ware, "Paul's Hope and Ours: Recovering Paul's Hope of the Renewed Creation," *Concordia Journal* 35, no. 2 (March 2009): 132.

The drama of the fall in Genesis 3 has at its core the overturning of this relationship between humanity and the rest of creation. The serpent rebels against this order by challenging and seeking to subvert the man and woman's dominion. By misquoting and directly contradicting God, the serpent misleads the woman to misuse an item within the created garden—the forbidden fruit of the tree of the knowledge of good and evil. The overturn of relationship between humanity and creation is seen in the serpent's misleading the woman, the woman's following the serpent's misleading, and the man and the woman's transgression against creation by partaking of the forbidden fruit.

The ensuing enmity between humanity and the rest of creation is then codified through the curse of God. The serpent will be cursed more than any animal, eating dust all its days, and there will be hostility between the serpent and the woman, its offspring and hers—"He will strike your head, and you will strike his heel" (3:14-15). While the *protoevangelion* is typically understood to point forward to Christ's defeat of the Satan, we may also note its relationship to the topic at hand: the offspring of the woman will put down the rebellious element of the created order. By striking the serpent's head, Christ will reconcile creation to himself.

To the man God says,

> The ground is cursed because of you. You will eat from it by means of painful labor all the days of your life. It will produce thorns and thistles for you, and you will eat the plants of the field. You will eat bread by the sweat of your brow until you return to the ground, since you were taken from it. For you are dust, and you will return to dust. (3:17-19)

Because of human sin against God and against creation, "the ground is cursed because of you" (3:17). The curse focuses on the relationship between nature and humanity. The man's prefall vocation was to work and to watch over the garden of Eden. But now, expelled from the garden (3:24), his work will be perverted. It will be painful, as the object of his work will make it more difficult for him, producing thorns and thistles. This enmity between the man and creation does not, however, lead to divorce, since he will himself return to the ground. We are reminded that he is but dust (see 2:7), to which is connected the ominous addendum, "and you will return to dust" (3:19). In this way, man and the ground can only be reconciled through death.

If we consider the curse of the ground in reverse, we may glimpse the trajectory of God's unfolding plan of salvation and recreation. Painful labor will cease. The enmity between humanity and the rest of creation will come to an end. Instead of remaining in the ground as dust, humanity will be raised from the grave. In this way, Genesis 2–3 sets the terms for the unfolding biblical hope of redemption. While this is an eschatological hope, "it also remains an earthly hope. The biblical idea of redemption always includes the earth," as George Eldon Ladd puts it.[12]

ISAIAH 65–66

The themes established in Genesis 2–3 resonate throughout the entire biblical tradition. But in relation to the renewal of creation in particular, the eighth-century prophet Isaiah is of preeminent importance. Isaiah looks to the deliverance of creation from corruption and expresses this through natural terms. As Ladd summarizes,

> The wilderness will become fruitful (Isa. 32:15), the desert will blossom (Isa. 35:2), sorrow and sighing will flee away (Isa. 35:10). The burning sands will be cooled and the dry places be springs of water (Isa. 35:7); peace will return to the animal world so that all injury and destruction is done away (Isa. 11:9); and all this results because the earth becomes full of the knowledge of God (Isa. 11:9).[13]

The final and climactic chapters of Isaiah's prophecy offer, according to Hubbard, "the classic expression of new creation in the biblical tradition."[14] Isaiah 65–66 resonates with themes found in Genesis 2–3, depicting a new creation in which the earth and humanity are restored to their intended glory. Indeed, in these chapters Yahweh will create a new heavens and a new earth (Isa 65:17), with a Jerusalem that will be a joy and a delight to her people (65:18). The perils of human death will be overturned (65:20), and they "will fully enjoy the work of their hands" (65:22). Human work

---

12. George Eldon Ladd, *The Presence of the Future: The Eschatology of Biblical Realism*, rev. ed. (Grand Rapids: Eerdmans, 1974), 59.

13. Ladd, *Presence of the Future*, 61–62.

14. Hubbard, *New Creation in Paul's Letters*, 16.

will no longer consist of painful toil as we wrestle against an antagonistic, accursed creation. With the restoration of creation, work will once again be a joyous expression of our participation in that creation.

Strikingly,

"The wolf and the lamb will feed together,
and the lion will eat straw like cattle,
but the serpent's food will be dust!
They will not do what is evil or destroy
on my entire holy mountain,"
says the LORD. (Isa 65:25)

This depicts not only the cessation of hostilities within the created order, but shalom—the wolf and the lamb feed *together*, the lion will eat straw like cattle, *instead of* eating cattle. The serpent, however, retains its lowly position as a dust eater. But the practice of evil will cease, and destruction itself will be destroyed on Yahweh's holy mountain.

However, Isaiah 66 makes clear that judgment on Yahweh's enemies must accompany such restoration of the created order.

You will see, you will rejoice,
and you will flourish like grass;
then the LORD's power will be revealed to his servants,
but he will show his wrath against his enemies.
Look, the LORD will come with fire—
his chariots are like the whirlwind—
to execute his anger with fury
and his rebuke with flames of fire.
For the LORD will execute judgment
on all people with his fiery sword,
and many will be slain by the LORD. (Isa 66:14–16)

Yahweh's people will flourish as they witness his power, but his enemies will suffer his wrath. He will execute universal judgment, leading to the destruction of many. As all remaining humankind comes to worship Yahweh, they will see the dead bodies of those who have rebelled against him (66:23–24).

Isaiah's eschatological vision is one of a new heavens and a new earth with a glorious new Jerusalem at its center, from whence Yahweh will reign with glorious and unchallenged power. The glory of this scene involves the reversal of the effects of humanity's fall and creation's curse. The created order is brought to harmony and evil is vanquished.

As we consider the contributions of Genesis 2–3 and Isaiah 65–66, alongside the Jewish literature that likewise draws on these texts, we are better able to apprehend Paul's conception of the connection between the judgment of evil and the renewal of creation. But of course Paul is not the only New Testament theologian to address this issue. Indeed, his exposition—especially that found in Romans 8—might be seen in tension with the outlook expressed in 2 Peter 3 and Revelation 19–22. As such, the remainder of this essay will seek to address this apparent tension by considering those important texts.

2 PETER 3

Toward the end of Peter's fiery second letter, he offers the ultimate solution that will bring to an end all false teaching, false prophecy, and all the wickedness of the earth. The day of the Lord will come like a thief, and "on that day the heavens will pass away with a loud noise, the elements will burn and be dissolved, and the earth and the works on it will be disclosed" (2 Pet 3:10). Indeed, "the heavens will be dissolved with fire and the elements will melt with heat. But based on his promise, we wait for new heavens and a new earth, where righteousness dwells" (3:12–13). In order for righteousness to dwell on the earth, a new heavens and a new earth must first come. Indeed, the present heavens and earth "are stored for fire, being kept for the day of judgment and destruction of the ungodly" (3:7). That is, for evil to finally be vanquished, the earth in which it currently reigns must be undone.

Peter's language of a new heavens and a new earth obviously derives from the Isaianic vision of the same. But Peter's depiction seems much more discontinuous than Isaiah's and, indeed, Paul's. This is an issue to which we must return, but for now we ought to apprehend Peter's strong language of *dissolution*—"the heavens will be dissolved with fire and the elements will melt with heat" (3:12). Isaiah depicted the new heavens and new earth in very earthly terms—with the wolf alongside the lamb and

Yahweh reigning from Zion—implying, at least conceptually, some degree of continuity between old and new. In fact, Isaiah offers no hint that the old will be destroyed and replaced. But Peter views a new heavens and earth that will *replace* the old heavens and earth once the old have been destroyed through fire.

Peter's strong language of discontinuity can be accounted for by his apocalyptic overtones. Peter is known for his frequent use of apocalyptic imagery in both letters, and given the stark contrasts commonly found in apocalyptic literature, Peter's sharp discontinuity between old and new need not be pressed beyond rhetorical effect. Indeed, Peter (in both letters) draws on the imagery of Noah's flood, which stands as Peter's model as he considers God's judgment of sin and his work of new creation (1 Pet 3:20; 2 Pet 3:6). In that judgment, the earth was "destroyed" through the flood, but the new world that emerged through water was in fact a renewal of the old. The old was dissolved through water, but the new shares some continuity with it, being located on the same planet, subject to the same rules of physics, chemistry, and inherent design. Indeed, it was even made of the same materials. Given Peter's fondness for the flood imagery, it is likely that his conception of the new heavens and new earth replacing the old follows a similar pattern. The old will be dissolved—not by water, but by fire (since Yahweh promised not to wipe out the earth again through flood; Gen 9:11)—and the new will exhibit some degree of continuity with it. In this way, Peter echoes 1 Enoch. When the flood typology is used as a paradigm for the final judgment in the Apocalypse of Weeks, it undergirds the idea that a remnant will be delivered from judgment, just as with the flood, thus allowing continuity as well as discontinuity.[15]

Thus, Peter's striking discontinuity is just that—striking rhetoric. It does not necessarily mean that his eschatological vision is at odds with Isaiah and Paul. His stress on discontinuity represents the radical extent to which creation must be purified in order to eradicate evil. As Paul Williamson states, "While Peter speaks of destruction, using the image of a cosmic conflagration, he is primarily describing the destruction of sin and corruption. Creation is not being eradicated: it is being radically cleansed."[16]

---

15. See Macaskill, *Revealed Wisdom and Inaugurated Eschatology*, 42.

16. Paul R. Williamson, *Death and the Afterlife: Biblical Perspectives on Ultimate Questions*, New Studies in Biblical Theology 44 (London: Apollos, 2017), 181.

REVELATION 19-22

After the fall of Babylon the Great in chapter 18, the book of Revelation depicts the celebration of a vast multitude in heaven—because God has judged the notorious prostitute who corrupted the earth (19:1-2). With this judgment secure, it is now time for the marriage of the Lamb (19:7-9). But just as the reader is led to expect the imminent wedding banquet, instead comes the terrifying image of a warhorse, with its rider who judges and makes war with justice (19:11). He wears a robe dipped in blood and leads the armies of heaven (19:13-14). From his mouth comes a sharp sword, with which he strikes the nations. He tramples the winepress of the fierce anger of God (19:15). The armies of the earth wage war against the rider but quickly lose the battle, and the beast and its false prophet are thrown in to the lake of burning sulphur, while the rest are killed by the rider's sword as the birds of the air devour their flesh (19:19-21).

The ancient serpent, the devil, is then bound for a thousand years and thrown into the abyss (20:2-3). After he is released, he is thrown into the fiery lake of sulphur along with the beast and the false prophet for eternal torment (20:10). Then comes judgment day, as Death and Hades give up their dead and each one is judged according to their works (20:13). Anyone whose name is not found in the book of life is thrown into the lake of fire (20:15).

It is only after this complete victory over and absolute destruction of evil that John utters the words, "Then I saw a new heaven and a new earth; for the first heaven and the first earth had passed away, and the sea was no more. I also saw the holy city, the new Jerusalem, coming down out of heaven from God, prepared like a bride adorned for her husband" (Rev 21:1-2). The new Jerusalem is the bride who has been prepared for the wedding banquet of the Lamb. From then on, God's dwelling place is with his people, and death will be no more (21:3-4). The Alpha and the Omega is making everything new and freely gives to the thirsty from the spring of the water of life (21:6). But in the new Jerusalem there is no place for evildoers, whose place is in the fiery lake of sulphur (21:8). Evil has been completely vanquished and is not able to detract from the beauty and splendor of the new Jerusalem. Nothing unclean will ever enter it (21:27). The tree of life is in the middle of the city, providing healing for the nations, and there will no longer be any curse (22:2-3).

From the sequence of events, and from explicit references in Revelation 19–22, it is clear that evil must be judged and vanquished in order for the new heaven and earth to be established. There is no place for evil within this new creation. The effects of the fall of humanity and the curse on creation will have been completely undone. Their only vestige will be seen in the need for restoration and healing.

Revelation's vision of the new heaven and new earth is strongly discontinuous with the old—in parallel with 2 Peter 3, and somewhat in tension with Isaiah and Paul. Most striking is the statement that "the first heaven and the first earth had passed away" (21:1). But this, like Peter's language of dissolution, is best treated as apocalyptic indulgence for rhetorical effect: "When John tells us that 'the first heaven and the first earth had passed away,' he speaks not of the dissolution of the universe, but of its radical transformation," Williamson says.[17] In fact, there are several indicators of continuity that support this rhetorical understanding of the "passed away" statement.

First, the new Jerusalem comes down out of heaven, resulting in God's dwelling with humanity (21:2–3). While the author does not say that the coming down out of heaven is *to the earth*, this is implied and is so understood by most interpreters. It certainly would have been so understood by John's original readers. Second, the nations of the earth are drawn to the new Jerusalem (21:24), implying continuity with the world known to John and his readers.

Third, the new Jerusalem has at its center the tree of life, the leaves of which offer healing to the nations (22:2). This tree of life points of course to the tree of life of Genesis 2:9, which stood at the center of the garden of Eden. After the fall, the man and woman are expelled from the garden so that they will not have access to this same tree (Gen 3:22–23). Thus, this important symbol stresses continuity with the original creation. It is a symbol of restoration. Now that sin and evil have been vanquished and humanity has been restored, the tree of life may once again stand in the center of the arena in which God and humanity dwell together. If the new heaven and earth were entirely new, and the old had literally passed away, the tree of life would not carry such significance.

---

17. Williamson, *Death and the Afterlife*, 181.

Nevertheless, the presence of the tree of life in the new Jerusalem also implies some level of discontinuity, for it speaks to the absence of that other tree that stood alongside it in the middle of the garden of Eden—the tree of the knowledge of good and evil. Its absence from the middle of the new Jerusalem is a striking difference compared to the garden. While its absence from the city is not explained, we may infer that it has no place there because evil has been vanquished from creation, and there is now not even the possibility of its return. Only the tree of life remains.

Thus, we conclude with Williamson:

> Just as with the individual's "new creation," so with the cosmic: the old has passed away and the new has come—not by obliteration and replacement, but by purging and renewal; what John describes in Revelation 21 is creation renewed, a radical transformation, a new world order, involving a newness in quality rather than a newness in time.[18]

CONCLUSION

We began with the apostle Paul and considered his relationship to four other key biblical voices—Genesis, Isaiah, Peter, and Revelation. These representative voices demonstrate the interwoven relationship of evil to the created order, which can be distilled down to two simple points: (1) evil has corrupted creation; and (2) the glory of the new creation will be assured by the permanent absence of evil.

According to Paul, judgment of evil will be universal, and it will be just. The judgment to come cannot be escaped, but believers will be counted blameless in Christ. Their security in Christ is assured by the fact that Christ himself has been appointed judge of the living and the dead. Ultimately, however, judgment is about putting the world to rights. There is a single creation that will be renewed and restored. Thus, judgment is concerned with the eradication of evil and the establishment of righteousness and peace within creation. With N. T. Wright, "*God the creator intends at the last to remake the creation,* righting all wrongs and filling

---

18. Williamson, *Death and the Afterlife*, 181.

the world with his own presence." The salvation of humanity is tied to this renewal of creation, in keeping with Jewish expectation, because, again with Wright, "The main problem standing in the way both of the original purpose of creation and (now) of its renewal and restoration is the failure of humankind to act as God's imagebearers in the world. God must therefore put humans to rights in order to put the world to rights."[19] Thus it is no surprise that redeemed believers are described as new creations since, for Paul, the new creation begins with redeemed humanity.

To understand Paul, we noted the connection between sin and creation found in the Hebrew Scriptures, with special reference to Genesis 2–3 and Isaiah 65–66. The ground is cursed because of man's sin, but the *protoevangelion* points to the crushing of the rebellious element of the created order and its subsequent restoration. The fall of humanity and the effects of the curse will be overturned in the new creation. And in order for the new creation to flourish, evil must be judged and destroyed.

All of these points are echoed and affirmed in the fellow New Testament voices of 2 Peter 3 and Revelation 19–22. While this is so, these texts also raise the question of whether the old creation will be destroyed and replaced, or whether—with Paul—the old will be renewed and restored.

RENEWAL, NOT REPLACEMENT

This essay has argued for the renewal—rather than the destruction and replacement—of creation on the grounds that imagery and language that appears to support new-for-old replacement must be understood rhetorically rather than literally. J. Richard Middleton accounts for the biblical imagery of cosmic destruction as "describing momentous events and realities that cannot be adequately conveyed in ordinary descriptive prose." Such biblical imagery does not point to "the annihilation of the cosmos, but rather a new world cleansed of evil."[20]

This approach makes better sense of the clear elements of continuity between old and new. It makes better sense of *resurrection*, which gives new life and form to old bodies, rather than replacing the old with

---

19. N. T. Wright, *Paul and the Faithfulness of God* (Minneapolis: Fortress, 2013), 926, italics original.

20. J. Richard Middleton, *A New Heaven and a New Earth: Reclaiming Biblical Eschatology* (Grand Rapids: Eerdmans, 2014), 121, 125.

something entirely new. The disciples did not find a discarded old body of Jesus in the tomb while a new one was walking around in Jerusalem. The resurrected Jesus has the same body as the crucified Jesus, though it has been transformed. As Ware states, "Jesus' resurrection is the ultimate affirmation of creation and its goodness."[21] Finally, the restoration of creation makes better sense of who God is. As Jürgen Moltmann states, "There are not two Gods, a Creator God and a Redeemer God. There is one God. It is for his sake that the unity of redemption and creation has to be thought."[22]

JUDGMENT OF EVIL AS THE RENEWAL OF CREATION

Judgment of evil, and its ultimate destruction, is the necessary precursor to the renewal of creation. Just as the original prefall creation was free from sin and therefore uncorrupted, so the postjudgment creation will be free from sin and therefore restored. In the end, "the human heart, human society, and all of nature must be purged of the effects of evil, that God's glory may be perfectly manifested in his creation," as Ladd puts it.[23]

But the biblical picture reveals more than simple renewal too, in two important respects. First, unlike the original creation, the renewed creation will contain *no possibility of the presence of evil*. The tree of the knowledge of good and evil will not be found in the new Jerusalem. There will never be another fall. Second, the renewed creation will be more than a mere restoration. It is enhanced beyond the original. Instead of one man and one woman dwelling peacefully with God, there will be a multitude. Instead of a garden, there will be a city. Instead of a garden protected from the world outside, the city gates will be open to the nations. Instead of being lit by sun and moon, the glory of God will illuminate the city. In this sense, the eschaton is understood as "the completion

21. Ware, "Paul's Hope and Ours," 137.

22. Jürgen Moltmann, *The Coming of God: Christian Eschatology*, trans. Margaret Kohl (Minneapolis: Fortress, 1996), 259.

23. Ladd, *Presence of the Future*, 59–60.

of the act of creation."[24] In the words of Jürgen Moltmann, "The end is much more than the beginning."[25] "The true creation is not behind us but ahead of us."[26]

---

24. Julia S. Konstantinovsky, "Negating the Fall and Re-constituting Creation: An Apophatic Account of the Redemption of Time and History in Christ," in *When the Son of Man Didn't Come: A Constructive Proposal on the Delay of the Parousia*, ed. Christopher M. Hays in collaboration with Brandon Gallaher, Julia S. Konstantinovsky, Richard J. Ounsworth, OP, and C. A. Strine (Minneapolis: Fortress, 2016), 110.

25. Moltmann, *Coming of God*, 264.

26. Jürgen Moltmann, *Ethics of Hope*, trans. Margaret Kohl (Minneapolis: Fortress, 2012), 129.

3
—
QOHELETH AND HIS PATRISTIC SYMPATHIZERS ON EVIL AND VANITY IN CREATION

Paul M. Blowers

"Vanity of vanities, says the Preacher, vanity of vanities! All is vanity" (Eccl 1:2; 12:8).[1] These disquieting words of Qoheleth settle like a cold fog not only over Hebrew and Jewish wisdom literature but over the whole of canonical Scripture. They are enshrined in the list of the Bible's classic hard sayings. The terminology of vanity sounds troubling enough, but as one of Ecclesiastes' recent commentators, Antoon Schoors, emphasizes, the Hebrew *hebel* carries the strong sense of utter absurdity. "Absurdity of absurdities! All is absurdity" has a shrill ring to it, but it is altogether true to Qoheleth's purpose. Shoors observes,

> "Absurd" is to be understood in the sense of this word in existentialist philosophy: it refers to a disparity between two phenomena which are thought to be linked by a bond of harmony or causality but which are actually disjunct or even conflicting. Absurdity means that one sees that ideas, visions, convictions do often not tally with reality as it is experienced.[2]

Those ideas, visions, and convictions, of course, are the inherited standards of Israel's monotheistic faith, including the principle that the Creator has

---

1. Unless otherwise noted, Scripture quotations follow the RSV.
2. Antoon Schoors, "Theodicy in Qohelet," in *Theodicy in the World of the Bible*, ed. Antii Laato and Johannes C. de Moor (Leiden: Brill, 2003), 375; also Schoors, *Ecclesiastes*, Historical Commentary on the Old Testament (Leuven: Peeters, 2013), 20, 38–47.

dignified the creation as good (e.g., Gen 1:4), and the Deuteronomic promise that the righteous and sinners will receive just retribution from God,
proof positive of a secure and consistent moral order. In Qoheleth's view,
all this has already broken down.

While many modern critical interpreters thus lump Ecclesiastes
into the projected genre of "skeptical wisdom" literature in the Bible,
ancient Christian interpreters had their own robust opinions on what to
make of the Preacher's grim worldview. Rather remarkably, given that
Ecclesiastes caught some severe criticism among the rabbis, there was
little questioning of its canonical status in early Christian tradition. Even
Theodore of Mopsuestia (ca. 350–ca. 428), who was accused by the Council
of Constantinople of 553 of disparaging Job as an exotic work in the genre of
Greek tragedy, and the Song of Songs as an irrelevant nuptial rhapsody, still
held to the usefulness of Ecclesiastes.[3] Meanwhile, I will not take the time
to survey the various hermeneutical approaches to the book in the limited
number of extant patristic commentaries and homilies. These ran a gamut
from literal to spiritual modes of interpretation. Instead, I want to focus
on how the Preacher's dour musings specifically on evil and vanity were
registered and reworked by patristic interpreters within a late ancient
philosophical and theological climate where issues of providence, evil,
and human free will remained very much alive and well.

THE DILEMMA OF FATHOMING EVIL IN
PATRISTIC THOUGHT AND IN ECCLESIASTES:
PRELIMINARY CONSIDERATIONS

The premise of my essay is that most of the patristic interpreters of
Ecclesiastes whom we will be considering were little interested in extrap-
olating from the Bible a novel theory of evil, and of course the Bible was
only too happy not to offer them one. Much of the spadework of theorizing
evil had been done by the philosophers they most admired. One certainly
need not look very far for patristic thinkers East and West in late antiquity
who enthusiastically embraced and reworked Neoplatonic ideas of evil as

---

3. For the indictments against Theodore's views here, see the *Acts of the Council of Constantinople of 553*, Session 4, §§72–80, trans. Richard Price, Translated Texts for Historians 51 (Liverpool: Liverpool University Press, 2009), 1:262–67.

"nonbeing" and as the privation of the good, and much has been written on Neoplatonism's impact on patristic understandings of evil, especially in Athanasius (ca. 296/298–373), the Cappadocian Fathers, Augustine, and later Dionysius the Areopagite (fl. 500 AD), Maximus the Confessor (ca. 580–662), and John the Scot (ca. 815–ca. 877). The attraction for Christian writers clearly lay in a philosophical model that denied evil genuine ontological status in the cosmos (thereby exonerating the Creator of introducing it into the world) while, on the moral level, allowing that evil, as a void of the good, could positively fill that void in the form of an illusion. I am reminded of Athanasius's claim, reasserted by Gregory of Nyssa (ca. 335–ca. 395), that every human creature is, together with Adam, the true "inventor" (εὑρήτης) of evil, *imagining* it as a viable moral option and thus granting it a counterfeit existence and intelligibility.[4] Indeed, the Adamic fall set in motion a pattern of reinventing evil again and again, generation after generation, even though there were clear differences, especially after Augustine, over the dynamics of the legacy from Adam.

On the face of it, patristic approaches to the origins and perpetuation of evil in the world would seem to have been on a collision course with Qoheleth, whose vision of evil and vanity begins and ends with the assumption that human existence has essentially been rigged from the outset. Whether an Epicurean (as Clement of Alexandria [ca. 150–ca. 215] thought),[5] or a skeptic, or a cynic, or a freethinker, or a pious agnostic, or some hybrid thereof, the Preacher is rather obviously a determinist, although some modern exegetes contend that he projects this divine determinism as benevolent since it has definite advantages for lowly human beings, who cannot possibly control the conditions of their existence.[6] What is more, Qoheleth never shows explicit interest in something like the primordial Adamic fall, even if his language of human toil and final resolution into dust shows reminiscences of the curse on humanity in

---

4. Athanasius, *Contra gentes* 7; *De incarnatione* 5, ed. Robert Thomson (Oxford: Oxford University Press, 1971), 18, 146; Gregory of Nyssa, *De virginitate* 12 (GNO 8/1:298–99).

5. Clement of Alexandria, *Stromateis* 5.90.2 (GCS 15:385).

6. See, e.g., Norbert Lohfink, *Qoheleth: A Continental Commentary*, trans. Sean McEvenue (Minneapolis: Fortress, 2003), 16, arguing that the Preacher's "image of an eternal cycle structuring the cosmos is not, as almost all commentators suggest, an image of despair, but rather it is completely positive. It means the participation of beings in continuous Being."

Genesis 3 (see Eccl 2:22–23; 3:20; Gen 3:19).[7] His determinism is not such that he believes God has forced moral evil on humanity. On the contrary, God ostensibly created humanity morally upright, but human beings have, as he says, "sought out many devices" (Eccl 7:29). The important thing here is that Qoheleth himself does not let humans morally off the hook in a situation where fate appears to rule the day. The moral order is *not* already tilted in favor of vice, even though it appears that "there is not a righteous man on earth who does good and never sins" (Eccl 7:20).

So why would Qoheleth's treatment of evil and vanity in the world be appealing to patristic commentators, despite the New Testament's almost total ignorance of the book? A good clue comes in the fact that several Greek Christian commentators, including Basil of Caesarea (330–379), Didymus the Blind (ca. 313–ca. 398), Evagrius Ponticus (345–399), and Olympiodorus of Alexandria (sixth century) followed Origen's (ca. 184–ca. 253) imitation of a Platonic philosophical curriculum in labeling Ecclesiastes a book of "physics" (τὰ φυσικά), preceded by Proverbs as a book of "ethics" and followed by Song of Songs as a book of "epoptics," or theological mysteries.[8] Jerome (ca. 347–420) follows suit in the Latin tradition.[9] The distinction may seem odd since Ecclesiastes itself has a strong ethical dimension, and Olympiodorus was quick to add that there is "physics" in Proverbs just as there is "ethics" in Ecclesiastes.[10] But Origen, echoed by Jerome, had already specified the close relation of ethics and physics in this scheme of growth in wisdom, indicating that physics focuses on the things of nature so as to help the disciple judge the vanity of empirical reality in order ascetically to spurn it and rise to the essential and the eternal.[11] This thoroughly befits the ethos of "physics"

---

7. On this point, see Katharine Dell, "Exploring Intertextual Links between Ecclesiastes and Genesis 1–11," in *Reading Ecclesiastes Intertextually*, ed. Katharine Dell and Will Kynes (New York: Bloomsbury T&T Clark, 2014), 6–11.

8. See especially Origen, *Commentarius in Canticum* prologue 3.1, 6 (SC 375:128, 132); Basil, *Homilia* 12.1 (PG 31:388A); Evagrius, *Scholia in Proverbia* 247 (SC 340:342); Olympiodorus, *Comm. Eccl.* (PG 93:477C–480A). For a helpful analysis of some major Greek patristic commentators on Ecclesiastes, see Marc Hirschman, "The Greek Fathers and the Aggada on Ecclesiastes: Formats of Exegesis in Late Antiquity," *Hebrew Union College Annual* 59 (1988): 137–55.

9. Jerome, *Comm. Eccl.* 1.1 (CCSL 72:250).

10. Olympiodorus, *Comm. Eccl.* (PG 93:477C)

11. Origen, *Commentarius in Canticum* prologue 3.1, 6 (SC 375:128, 132); see also Jerome, *Comm. Eccl.* 1.1 (CCSL 72:250).

in Hellenistic philosophy, which virtually never focused on the science of natural phenomena at the exclusion of ethics and theology.

Indeed, the kind of "physics" exhibited in Ecclesiastes matched the object of what some of the book's patristic commentators conceived and practiced as "natural contemplation" (θεωρία φυσική; *contemplatio naturalis*), a sapiential discipline in which, especially from the fourth century on, bishops sought to train lay audiences in ecclesiastical context, and which, in monastic communities, elders regularly prescribed for their disciples.[12] Natural contemplation treated the "natural world" not just as an architecture of spiritual and material structures, ontologically speaking, but as a revelatory economy, in which the ultimate intelligibility of those structures was thoroughly bound up with the moral "history" of the creatures who inhabited them. Qoheleth too had little interest in the native "design" of the cosmos as such, focusing instead on how human beings, in the predictable but fateful contingencies of life, and in the face of the raw *givenness* and inexorability of evil "under the sun" (Eccl 1:3, 9, 14; 2:11, 17, 18, 19, 20; 3:16; 4:1, 3, 7, 15; 5:13, 18; 6:1, 12; 8:9, 15, 17; 9:3, 6, 9, 11, 13; 10:5) were to eke out some kind of purposeful and consequential existence.

As we shall see, however, patristic commentators wanted to press the issue of the providential divine pedagogy operative through this cosmic scheme of things, in which context the overriding question was not where evil and vanity originated but how they were to be observed, confronted, managed, and surmounted. Qoheleth's dialectical style, standing in tension with the dignity of corporeal creation and its enslavement to vanity, worked well to the purposes of "natural contemplation" as a heuristic exercise. And though some of the commentators saw Proverbs as the great work of Solomonic maxims, Ecclesiastes itself strung together abundant maxims (see 12:9–10),[13] together with memorable catchphrases ("vanity of vanities," "chasing after wind," "under the sun," etc.), which worked with particular didactic effect for the strongly ascetically oriented commentators such as Didymus the Blind and Evagrius.

---

12. On the scope of natural contemplation, see my *Drama of the Divine Economy: Creator and Creation in Early Christian Theology and Piety* (Oxford: Oxford University Press, 2012), 322–35; also Joshua Lollar, *To See into the Life of Things: The Contemplation of Nature in Maximus the Confessor and His Predecessors* (Turnhout: Brepols, 2013).

13. A number of modern critical scholars of Ecclesiastes see the book as a collection of maxims, or *mashals*. See Schoors, *Ecclesiastes*, 9–10, on this approach.

EVIL AND VANITY IN ECCLESIASTES:
THE SHAPE OF PATRISTIC INTERPRETATION

As I noted, Qoheleth's patristic interpreters did not explore a theory of evil per se behind the profuse language of vanity and toil, going with the flow of the Preacher's presentation of vanity as everywhere oppressing the "natural" life of humanity. In his homilies, however, Gregory of Nyssa estimates that Qoheleth, being the "Ecclesiast" who preaches for the benefit of the church and the faithful, had already intuited a basically Christian-Neoplatonic conception of evil. He already understood that being has become a slave to nonbeing through the delinquency of human freedom.[14] Commenting on the phrase "Wisdom excels folly as light excels darkness (Eccl. 2:13)," Gregory writes:

> I think it is appropriate that he uses the analogy of light in the discernment of the good. Since darkness is in its own nature unreal (for if there were nothing to obstruct the sun's rays, there would be no darkness), whereas light is of itself, perceived in its own essence, he shows by this analogy that evil does not exist by itself, but arises from deprivation of anything which is prior to it. What is perceived as essentially opposed to good, is not; for what in itself is not, does not exist at all; for evil is the deprivation of being, and not something existing. Thus the difference is the same between light and darkness and between wisdom and folly.[15]

By attributing to Qoheleth an identification of being, good, and wisdom in their opposition respectively to nothingness, evil, and folly, Gregory indeed signals that the ontology of evil sits only in the background of the Preacher's essay on the vanity that permeates empirical existence and obscures the Creator's purposes in and for the world.

So what is this vanity? There is a fairly broad consensus in patristic exegesis of the language of vanity in Ecclesiastes that it as an extended lament over the futility of human striving rather than a direct indictment of the created order in and of itself.[16] The earliest full extant commentary, Gregory Thaumaturgus's (ca. 213–ca. 270) *Metaphrasis on Ecclesiastes*,

---

14. Gregory of Nyssa, *Hom. Eccl.* 1 (GNO 5:279–80); *Hom. Eccl.* 2 (GNO 5:301).
15. Gregory of Nyssa, *Hom. Eccl.* 5 (GNO 5:356); see also *Hom. Eccl.* 7 (GNO 5:406–7).
16. The term *vanity* appears nearly forty times in Ecclesiastes' twelve chapters.

which takes the form of an amplified paraphrase of the work, sets the pace of later commentaries by downplaying divine responsibility for the world's vanity and accentuating the sad rhythms of existence into which creatures (animate and inanimate) have devolved. Here we see the first evidence of a Christian platonizing of Qoheleth that becomes pervasive: human beings are bound to futility precisely because they have fixated on transitory things instead of aspiring to higher and enduring realities.[17] Thaumaturgus perhaps learned from his teacher Origen, whose *Commentary on Ecclesiastes* is unfortunately lost. Thaumaturgus further augments the moral meaning of Qoheleth's "vanity" and especially the phrase "striving after wind" (1:14 et al.), which the Septuagint literally translates "choosing the breeze" (προαίρεσις πνεύματος), by speaking of the "strange and foul spirit" (πνεύματος ἀλλοκότου καὶ μυσαροῦ) and utter "absurdity" (ἀτοπία) that have descended on human affairs.[18] Gregory of Nyssa, who certainly knew Thaumaturgus's *Metaphrasis*, spends a significant part of his first *Homily on Ecclesiastes* waxing eloquent on "vanity" as an indicating of the futility and pointlessness of life.

One can certainly understand why Thaumaturgus, and many later patristic interpreters who followed suit, endeavored to highlight the *moral* crisis of vanity. Were Qoheleth simply neutrally or scientifically describing creaturely existence as a grand charade, a faux reality, his essay would degenerate into an impious mockery. Fortunately, early Christian commentators recognized that the Preacher himself argued dialectically, inserting into his grim reflections certain signals of the overriding wisdom and benevolence of the Creator, and of the underlying integrity of his handiwork, such as could still be conducive to human thriving. An abiding question, however, is whether, for these commentators, "vanity" or futility in itself is principally a *punitive condition* imposed by the Creator "from above"—such as Paul seemed to interpret it in Romans 8:19–25, describing the subjection of creation to vanity as corruptibility and decay in anticipation of eventual transformation—or else principally an *epistemic and*

---

17. See Gregory Thaumaturgus, *Metaphrasis in Ekklesiasten* 1.3 (PG 10:989A); also the analysis in John Jarick's excellent translation with commentary, *Gregory Thaumaturgos' Paraphrase of Ecclesiastes* (Atlanta: Society of Biblical Literature, 1990), 9–10.

18. Gregory Thaumaturgus, *Metaphrasis in Ekklesiasten* 1.14–15 (PG 10:989C–D); also Jarick, *Gregory Thaumaturgos' Paraphrase*, 21–23.

existential dilemma "from below," a crisis of subjectivity whereby neither the wise person nor the fool has sure access to God's providential wisdom and all are called to live perennially in pious ignorance despite the shadow of futility.

Patristic interpreters desired to accommodate and integrate both of these perspectives. Origen, in his treatise *On First Principles*, early on makes an explicit connection between Qoheleth's vanity and the vanity described by Paul in Romans 8:19-25. He takes the Preacher's repeated phrase "under the sun" as signaling that God's punitive but remedial subjection to vanity begins with the sun itself as an embodied creature, and with all the heavenly bodies, who, in a kind of cosmic ministry, "groan" together with human beings in the *hopeful* waiting period until their "glorious" and "bodily" redemption arrives (Rom 8:21, 23).[19] Elsewhere Origen even places words on the sun's mouth, to admonish pagans that *helios* is not to be worshiped since it is subjugated to the same vanity as all other beings:

> Why do you call me god? There is one true God. And why do you bow down to me? ... Why do you wish to worship someone who worships? For I, too, bow down to God the Father and worship him. And in obedience to his commands I am subjected to vanity because of the One who subjected me in hope. And though I am now clothed with a corruptible body, I shall be set free from the bondage of corruption for the glorious liberty of the children of God (cf. Rom. 8:20-21; Wis. 9:15).[20]

This treatment of the sun and planets as living beings, capable of experiencing such a subjection to vanity, provided fodder for Origen's posthumous critics attacking his cosmology and eschatology, especially Jerome.[21]

---

19. Origen, *De principiis* 1.7.5, Greek and Latin text ed. and trans. John Behr, *Origen: On First Principles*, Oxford Early Christian Texts (Oxford: Oxford University Press, 2017), 128-31. Also see Origen, *Commentarii in evangelium Joannis* 1.17.98-99 (GCS 10:21); *Commentarii in Romanos* 7.2, ed. Caroline Hammond Bammel, *Der Römerbriefkommentar des Origenes: Kritische Ausgabe der Übersetzung Rufinus* (Freiburg im Breisgau: Herder, 1998), 3:567-68.

20. Origen, *Exhortatio ad martyrium* 7 (GCS 2:9), trans. Rowan Greer, *Origen: Exhortation to Martyrdom*, Classics of Western Spirituality (New York: Paulist Press, 1979), 46 (slightly altered).

21. See Jerome, *Epistula* 124.4 (to Avitus) (CSEL 56:99-101).

Jerome himself, once again appealing jointly to Qoheleth and Paul, conceives vanity on a kind of axis stretching between futility and "glory":

> "Vanity of vanities," says Ecclesiastes, "all is vanity" (1:2). If what
> God creates is summarily very good, then in what way is everything
> "vanity," and not just "vanity" but "vanity of vanities"? Just as the
> Song [of Songs] is exhibited as the surpassing Song among all Songs,
> so too the "vanity of vanities" is shown to be the magnitude of vanity.
> Such is what is described in the Psalms: "and yet every living man is
> the sum total of vanity" (Ps. 38:6[39:5]). If the living man is "vanity,"
> then the dead man is "vanity of vanities." We read in Exodus that
> the face of Moses was glorified to the point that the sons of Israel
> could not look on it (Ex. 34:30-35). The Apostle Paul speaks of that
> glory which is no glory in comparison with the glory of the gospel:
> "For what was glorified in this case is not [now] glorified because
> of an exceeding glory" (2 Cor. 3:10). Therefore we are able in this
> way to say that the heavens, earth, seas, and everything contained
> within this circle [of creation] is good per se, but compared with
> God it is like nothing.[22]
>
> Those things that are seen are temporal, while those things that
> are unseen are eternal; or—because "the creation has been sub-
> jected to vanity and it groans and is in labor and waits for the reve-
> lation of the sons of God" (Rom. 8:22-23), and "now we understand
> in part and we prophesy in part" (1 Cor. 13:9)—all is vanity until
> what is perfect comes.[23]

Here Jerome seems clearly to be pushing back against a hyperplaton-
izing of Qoheleth and Paul alike. Even though worldly vanity is to yield
to an exceeding eschatological glory, this must not be construed as the
purely material and corporeal creation eventually giving way fully to the
spiritual. The key lies in Paul's vision of ever greater degrees of glory, such
that the relative dignity or subsidiary glory of the whole creation is transcended by a superior state of perfection, in comparison with which the

---

22. Jerome, *Comm. Eccl.* 1.2 (CCSL 72:252), my translation.
23. Jerome, *Comm. Eccl.* 1.2, trans. Richard Goodrich and David Miller, Ancient Christian
Writers 66 (New York: Newman, 2012), 36.

world now appears vain and paltry. Jerome goes even further, applying this scheme to God's progressive revelation. From the Preacher's statement that "a generation goes, and a generation comes, but the earth remains forever" (Eccl. 1:4) Jerome deduces, "The earth stands until the synagogue gives way and the whole church comes in. When the gospel has been proclaimed in all the earth, then the end will come."[24] By this account, if vanity is a punitive condition of creation, it would seem to belong only to the age of reprobation under the law, which has already begun to be transcended with the advent of Christ.

Gregory of Nyssa takes a position on vanity as the punitive but remedial condition of creation that compares favorably with elements in both Origen and Jerome. Gregory has no qualms about considering vanity endemic to the corporeal realm and to the life of sense experience, which, in the larger scheme of things, is "unreal" (ἀνύπαρκτος) and "insubstantial" (ἀνυπόστατος).[25] But like Jerome, Gregory is fiercely defensive of the corporeal order itself as a divine creature and as useful as a vector toward its Creator's goodness and beauty, so long as human subjectivity does not become desirously fixated on its distractions.[26] Augustine provides yet another variation. His Old Latin text of Ecclesiastes 1:2 reads not *vanitas vanitatum* "vanity of vanities," but *vanitas vanitantium*, "vanity of the vain," or as Edmund Hill translates it using a neologism, "vanity of the vanitators." Those who commit vanity infest the corporeal creation. "Because," writes Augustine, "if you remove the vanitators, who chase after the last and least things as if they were the first and foremost, [the] body [*corpus*] will not be vanity, but in its own class it will manifest beauty [*pulchritudinem*], though of the least and lowest degree, without any deception."[27]

---

24. Jerome, *Comm. Eccl.* 1.4, trans. Goodrich and Miller.

25. Gregory of Nyssa, *Hom. Eccl.* 1 (GNO 5:281–84).

26. Gregory of Nyssa, *Hom. Eccl.* 1 (GNO 5:284).

27. Augustine, *Ver. rel.* 21.41 (CCSL 32:212), trans. Edmund Hill, *The Works of Saint Augustine: A Translation for the 21st Century*, 1.8:55; also Augustine, *Expositio quarundam propositionum ex epistula apostoli ad Romanos* 53.10, Latin text ed. and trans. Paula Fredriksen Landes, *Augustine on Romans*, SBL Texts and Translations 23 (Chico, CA: Scholars Press, 1982), 24.

VANITY AS A DIVINE TUTORIAL

Having examined vanity as a punitive condition, let us look at the other side of the equation, vanity as an epistemic and existential crisis—even a religious crisis—seeking resolution. The rhythms and repetitions of mortal existence create a sad liturgy of banality and futility in Qoheleth's sermon. Physical nature has only a fleeting beauty and seems to operate according to tedious cycles (Eccl 1:5-10). There is nothing new under the sun (1:3, etc.). Earthly pleasures are not ultimately satisfying (2:1-11). Fate seems to have a lock indiscriminately on the destiny of the wise and the foolish alike, the righteous and the sinner (2:14-17; 5:10; 6:1-7; 7:15; 8:14; 9:1-3). Even wisdom or knowledge gained is vexing for the one who acquires it (1:13-18).

For not a few of Qoheleth's patristic sympathizers, however, this stark picture brilliantly unfolds a much deeper revelatory economy, especially since, through a prosopological reinterpretation, it is Christ himself who is the true Ecclesiast, the true Preacher, speaking through this work, even if the historic Solomon is allowed at times to have his own say. Origen, and much later Olympiodorus, see Solomon ("son of David") as a *typos* of Christ, but Gregory of Nyssa, Evagrius, and Jerome all treat Jesus Christ as the true "author" of the sermon, at least, Jerome insists, on the "spiritual" level of interpretation.[28] With Christ as the Preacher, the landscapes of vanity in Ecclesiastes suddenly and radically change, becoming a grand divine tutorial in the quest for authentic wisdom, virtue, and transformation.

Gregory of Nyssa is a veritable master of describing this conversion. For him it is not just the transcendent Logos speaking through the Preacher to draw the distracted denizens of earth toward heavenly beauty. When, for example, the Preacher intimates that he gave his heart "to seek out and examine by wisdom concerning all things that happen under heaven" (Eccl 1:13), this is Christ describing his incarnational descent to investigate from the inside the vanity, the "crooked things," of the fallen world, so that he could set them aright and restore all of creation to its completeness.[29] What is more, Christ the Ecclesiast is his own philosopher of nature and being, uncovering from beneath the vanity the permanence and integrity

---

28. Gregory of Nyssa, *Hom. Eccl.* 1 (GNO 5:279-80); Evagrius, *Schol. Eccl.* 1 (SC 397:58); Jerome, *Comm. Eccl.* 1.1 (CCSL 72:250).

29. Gregory of Nyssa, *Comm. Eccl.* 1 (GNO 5:280; *Comm. Eccl.* 2 (GNO 5:298-300, 303-5).

of the divine Good which contradicts and undermines the evil that is non-being. So the phrase "[there is a time] to rend and to mend" (Eccl. 3:7) is the Ecclesiast instructing us to be torn away from evil's illusion and united to the Good, which can even be understood in an ecclesial sense as being united with the church.[30]

Interestingly, Gregory perceives Christ the Ecclesiast, in his meditation on "times and seasons" (Eccl 3:1–8), as giving insight into the mystery of time itself, and especially the way in which spatio-temporal extension (διάστημα) conditions created things and the human experience thereof.[31] Gregory adds here to his considerable treatment of διάστημα in earlier works, but the message from the Preacher confirms for him that διάστημα profoundly constrains human knowledge of God while simultaneously sustaining its pursuit. In close connection, Gregory views Christ the Ecclesiast as laying out the staggering vanity of human language and communication. His maxim that "all words are laborious (ἔγκοποι)" (Eccl 1:8) actually cuts two ways. It indicates how the words that truly convey spiritual benefit are arduous, but also that all words intrinsically are at a total loss to convey the transcendent triune God.[32] Later, with his projection of "a time to keep silence and a time to speak," Christ for Gregory is reinforcing that, given the poverty of language and its dependence on diastemic conditions, silence is appropriate in the recognition that spoken words can never reach to God's adiastemic nature, but speech is appropriate, as it has been in Scripture, to express the wonders of what God has done in his extraverted action toward creation.[33] The Ecclesiast thus validates insights into the nature of human language that were crucial in Gregory's battle with the neo-Arian nominalist Eunomius.

Didymus the Blind and Evagrius, who commented on Qoheleth primarily for audiences of ascetics or monastics, were drawn to the fact that Christ as the true Ecclesiast often spoke not just with straightforward

---

30. Gregory of Nyssa, *Comm. Eccl.* 7 (GNO 5:406–8).

31. Gregory of Nyssa, *Comm. Eccl.* 6 (GNO 5:374–6); *Comm. Eccl.* 7 (GNO 5:412). For analysis, see also Alden Mosshammer, "Time for All and a Moment for Each: The Sixth Homily of Gregory of Nyssa on Ecclesiastes," in *Gregory of Nyssa: Homilies on Ecclesiastes: An English Version with Supporting Studies*, ed. Stuart Hall (Berlin: Walter de Gruyter, 1993), 249–76.

32. Gregory of Nyssa, *Hom. Eccl.* 1 (GNO 5:291–94).

33. Gregory of Nyssa, *Hom. Eccl.* 7 (GNO 5:409–16).

moral admonitions but also in riddles or seeming contradictions in order to reveal the deeper meaning of vanity and its implications for progress in the spiritual life. Didymus has a strong penchant for clarifying what the Preacher has intentionally made obscure. For instance, he assumes that the maxim "Who can set in order the one whom [God] has made crooked" (Eccl 7:13 LXX) is to be taken in a moral sense and cannot mean that God makes anyone morally crooked but that he reveals their crookedness after the fact.[34] For Didymus, the Ecclesiast confirms this in 7:29 when he states, "God made humanity upright, and human beings sought out many *devices*," λογισμούς in the LXX, an interesting turn of phrase since λογισμοί, for ascetical commentators such as Didymus and Evagrius, is a loaded term that names those idle distractions, those vanities of the mind, that perennially hijack diligent souls from their contemplative vision.[35]

Evagrius, in his *Scholia [Notes] on Ecclesiastes* (a commentary genre well suited to Qoheleth's maxims and enigmatic sayings), takes quite seriously that Christ the Ecclesiast is teaching physics or the contemplation of nature as well as the higher pursuit of *theologia*. The former itself is a certain vanity, since the inhering principles or λόγοι of all created things become "vain" in themselves once one has risen to knowledge of the Trinity.[36] Evagrius takes special note of the dictum in 1:13 that God has placed in human beings an "evil distraction" (περισπασμὸν πονηρὸν), and is quick to point out that "evil" here really must mean *painful* (ἐπίπονον) or else, if it has a moral sense, simply that God has *permitted* evil to vex human beings.[37] When God's implanting of "distraction" in humans comes up again in 3:10, Evagrius presumes this to mean that God has allowed them to become diverted by the objects of sense so that the more mature may press toward the contemplation of the deeper purposes or *logoi* of creation and by the "eternity" (3:11) that God has also implanted in human

---

34. Didymus, *Comm. Eccl.* 212.12 (PTA 16:51).

35. Didymus, *Com. in Eccl.* 231.13 (PTA 16:121–25).

36. Evagrius, *Schol. Eccl.* 2 (SC 397:58–60).

37. Evagrius, *Schol. Eccl.* 4 (SC 397:62). Help comes from 2:26, where the Ecclesiast specifies that God has given the *sinner* "distraction of adding and gathering, to give to the one who is good before God," which Evagrius ties to Prov 8:28, the dictum that "he who increases his wealth with interest and excess gathers it for him who has empathy for the poor" (*Schol. Eccl.* 14, SC 397:78).

beings.[38] Indeed, where the Ecclesiast describes God "distracting" human beings with the "merriment of their hearts" (5:19), Evagrius presumes this to be an inversion bespeaking the rapturous delight of a higher knowledge (γνῶσις).[39]

In a different vein, Evagrius shares Gregory of Nyssa's apprehension about the vanity of human language for communicating higher or divine realities. The Ecclesiast instructs against loquacity and rash speech and on economy in using words (Eccl 5:1-6). Perhaps recalling his mentor Gregory Nazianzen (329-390), Evagrius understands this as a warning against thoughtlessly theologizing and the need for discipline in speaking of the divine, or speaking to the divine in prayer, since words are fraught with mental representations (νοήματα) that cannot reach God.[40]

MOURNING THE VANITIES

Let me bring this vain paper of mine to a close by a musing of my own after examining how Qoheleth's patristic sympathizers dealt with his enigmatic reflections on vanity in the cosmos, both as a punitive condition and as an epistemic and existential crisis. Patristic commentators drew a wide variety of moral and spiritual lessons from Ecclesiastes, but I am struck by the sustained interest among them in the pathos of mourning as a particularly worthy and commendable human response to vanity's grip on nature, on human culture, and on individual human pursuits. The Preacher had of course warned of laughter as itself a foolish distraction (περιφορά; Eccl 2:2), which Basil of Caesarea and others took to mean a frivolousness wholly foreign to Jesus' own teaching.[41] More importantly, however, the Preacher had set in contrast the due seasons of "weeping" and "laughing," and of "mourning" and "dancing" (3:4), and patristic interpreters could not imagine this merely as a contrasting of grief over material losses and joy over success in life.

It seems obvious enough that weeping and mourning would simply mirror the self-enclosed futility of the world that Qoheleth projects. But

---

38. Evagrius, *Schol. Eccl.* 15 (SC 397:80-82); see also *Schol. Eccl.* 40 (SC 397:134).

39. Evagrius, *Schol. Eccl.* 44-45 (SC 397:140).

40. Evagrius, *Schol. Eccl.* 35 (SC 397:116); see also Gregory Nazianzen, *Orationes theol.* 1.3-5 (SC 250:76-84).

41. Basil, *Regulae fusius tractatae* 17 (31:961A-965A).

as Gregory of Nyssa sees it, this is no superficial melancholy. Coming from Christ the Ecclesiast, the same Christ whose second Beatitude pronounced blessedness on those who mourn (Matt 5:4), this particular breed of grieving looks much more like a primal, Adamic lament, informed by the realization that paradise is all gone now, evaporated behind us, and that the present vanity of existence includes the specter of "shortness of life, its painfulness, its beginning with tears and its end in tears, pitiable childhood, dementia in [old] age, unsettled youth, the constant toil of adult life, burdensome marriage, lonely celibacy, the troublesome multitude of children, sterile childlessness, miserliness over wealth, the anguish of poverty."[42] Gregory echoes here his reflections on grief in his early treatise *On Virginity* (a theme on which Michel Barnes has written two eloquent essays).[43] Grieving is the converse of loving, and it bespeaks the tragedy in which we live, exemplified especially well in the case of the married couple who, in the seemingly promising intimacy of marriage, fall into mourning as the honeymoon subsides and the harsh realities of lost bliss, infertility, child-rearing, and prospective widowhood begin to set in.[44] As Gregory clarifies in his homily on the second Beatitude, we are all called to a healthy sort of mourning over our nature and over the "deceitfulness of life" (ἀπάτη τοῦ βίου)[45] which in his view also serves to reinvigorate our desire for God.

Monastic commentators, meanwhile, were drawn to Qoheleth's image of the "house of mourning" (Eccl 7:4), which in the LXX version is better translated "house of compunction" since the word here for mourning is πένθος, the verbal form of which Jesus uses in the second Beatitude to bless those who mourn (Matt 5:4); and yet πένθος is also pervasively used in

---

42. Gregory of Nyssa, *Hom. Eccl.* 6 (GNO 5:387), trans. Stuart Hall and Rachel Moriarty, *Gregory of Nyssa: Homilies on Ecclesiastes* (Berlin: de Gruyter, 1993), 108–9. See also Gregory's *Homiliae in Beatitudinibus* 3 (GNO 7/2:106), observing the sheer "deceitfulness of life" (ἀπάτη τοῦ βίου).

43. Michel René Barnes, " 'The Burden of Marriage' and Other Notes on Gregory of Nyssa's *On Virginity*," in *Papers Presented to the International Conference on Patristic Studies Held at Christ Church, Oxford, Thirteenth Conference, 1999*, ed. M. F. Wiles and E. F. Yarnold, Studia Patristica 37 (Leuven: Peeters, 2001), 12–19; Barnes, "What Have I Become, My Sweetest Friend? Death and Its Passions in the Early Church" (unpublished paper for the Chicago Theological Initiative, Wheaton College, IL, 16 March 2016).

44. Gregory of Nyssa, *De virginitate* 3 (GNO 8/1:257–66).

45. Gregory of Nyssa, *Homiliae in Beatitudinibus* 3 (GNO 7/2:106).

Greek monastic literature for deep sorrow over sin. Didymus understands the "house of mourning" in just this way, and Evagrius sees this compunction as humanity's very goal, which results in the enjoyment of abundant spiritual goods.[46] They thereby reset the context from one of grieving over the futility of life to one of repentance and consciousness of sin, though the two contexts are hardly incompatible and actually thoroughly intersect. Typically all full and uninterrupted rejoicing is deferred, then, to the time of the eschatological healing of creation, when all the tears of past vanity and sin are wiped away.

What we see here further confirms the pattern of patristic interpretation of Ecclesiastes as a book of physics and as a study guide for the contemplation of nature, into which is already integrated the concerns of ethics and spiritual growth, all as preparatory for *theologia* (knowledge of and union with God). Cutting through the harsh skepticism of the book, patristic interpreters understood the Ecclesiast to be depicting nature not as a static system of being but as the theater of the dynamic and turbulent relation between Creator and creation, a dramatic stage on which human beings simultaneously thrive and languish, experiencing the divine Wisdom but also habitually succumbing to evil's illusion. Even if Ecclesiastes shows little interest in a primordial fall of creatures, patristic commentators assumed that the world it described was ontologically good but tragically lapsed, compromised by a host of vanities which the benevolent Creator was nonetheless using to discipline his creatures but also to instruct them in the direction of the new world inaugurated in Jesus Christ.

Such an approach to Qoheleth may, at the end of the day, be quite unsatisfying to contemporary higher-critical scholarship fixated on locating the book within Hebrew and Jewish wisdom literature; but for many of its patristic interpreters, the acknowledgment of Christ as the true Ecclesiast radically broadened the book's purview and redefined the character of its wisdom and its maxims for mundane existence.

---

46. Didymus, *Comm. Eccl.* 197–8 (PTA 16:7–11); Evagrius, *Schol. Eccl.* 55 (SC 397:156).

4

—

PROBLEM OF EVIL

Ancient Answers and Modern Discontents

Paul L. Gavrilyuk

This essay aims to bring out the differences between the approaches to the problem of evil in antiquity and our time. By design, the essay sketches out a picture of a large-scale transformation. Any painting with broad brushstrokes is bound to dissatisfy at the level of details. As someone who appreciates fine-grained historical contextualization of complex theological ideas—of the kind afforded by other papers at this symposium—I would be the first to acknowledge that the task of providing a master narrative is a very precarious affair. Admittedly, master narratives are not a popular sport nowadays. For some (present audience excluded), such narratives are inherently "oppressive." In other words, master narratives are a part of the problem of evil rather than its solution, and as such should be consigned to deconstruction. While such demolition work might in some cases be necessary, a dirge for all master narratives is not merely premature, but inevitably self-defeating.

Aside from the general skepticism about master narratives, one might doubt whether any narrative that assumes a shift in premodern and modern sensibilities is on the right track. I think that the transition needs to be handled with care and that this question cannot be answered in the abstract. The argument of this paper is that there are indeed some significant points of discontinuity between premodern and modern times. What those are has to be discovered inductively by considering vast amounts of complex evidence.

In what follows I offer, in part 1, an account of the web of beliefs and existential attitudes that have shaped the premodern Christian accounts for the problem of evil. Then, in part 2, I chart the transformations of this web of beliefs and attitudes in modernity and beyond. While I wear the hat of an Orthodox patristic theologian most of the time, I do not have a plan here for returning the prodigal children of modernity into the house of patristic wisdom. To state the obvious, such a return is a historical impossibility. The sacred canopy of patristic theodicy cannot provide a complete cover for all our present-day struggles. This essay, then, has a more modest purpose of beginning a sort of a transhistorical conversation.

THE PROBLEM OF EVIL IN GREEK
PHILOSOPHY AND PATRISTIC THOUGHT

There was no shortage of solutions to the problem of evil in antiquity. Consider, for example, the wealth of insight afforded by Greek tragedy. The tragic poets locate evils variously in the will of the gods, in human ignorance and proclivity to be carried away by violent passions, and in the mysterious workings of fate (*tyche, moira, ate*) and necessity (*ananke*). Tragedy invites its spectators to become reconciled with the reality of suffering by admitting its inevitability. "Suffering for mortals is nature's iron law," declares Euripides.[1] In the final scene of *Oedipus the King*, with the king of Thebes now blind and expelled from his city, Sophocles has the choir recite the following piece of folk wisdom: "Therefore, while our eyes wait to see the destined final day, we must call no one happy who is of mortal race, until he hath crossed life's border, free from pain."[2] To expect a life devoid of suffering is to set oneself up for a major disappointment and to deny the central feature of the human condition, namely, mortality. The best thing to do is to admit with Aeschylus the law of Zeus "that man must learn by suffering [*pathei mathos*]."[3] Life is a tragedy in which we are both

---

1. Euripides, *Hippolytus* 208. Euripides was probably drawing on the following pessimistic comment of Theognis, *Elegies* 425–428, widely debated by later thinkers: "For man the best thing is never to be born,/ Never to look upon the hot sun's rays, / Next best, to speed at once through Hades' gates/ And lie beneath a piled-up heap of earth."

2. Sophocles, *Oedipus the King* 1581–84.

3. Aeschylus, *Agamemnon* 177. See William Chase Greene, *Moira: Fate, Good, and Evil in Greek Thought* (Cambridge, MA: Harvard University Press, 1944), 99–100.

actors and spectators. As actors we undergo *pathos*, as spectators we can hope that the *pathos* of others will have a cathartic impact on us.[4]

The Stoics agreed with the tragic poets that suffering could become a valuable *paideia*, a lifelong learning experience. It was futile, they argued, to regard unavoidable misfortunes as intrinsically evil. While a true philosopher could not control many external things that happened to her, she could control some, if not all, of her responses to adversities. In order to train the soul how to respond properly, a philosopher needed to realize that evil lies not in external misfortunes, but in human intentions that are contrary to reason: it is evil to inflict pain, but not to endure it.[5] On this account, "no evil could befall a good man."[6] Genuine evil was ruled out from the life of the true philosopher by redefining what counts as evil and by changing one's attitude accordingly. The Stoics also maintained that the soul-making telos of putative evils can be appreciated when life is considered as a whole. Many ancients found this noble doctrine hard to swallow and followed the advice of Epicurus: maximizing life's pleasures by minimizing and avoiding pain.

Plato was the first Greek philosopher to see clearly that evil cannot be attributed to the gods. In the *Republic*, he formulates this principle in causal terms: "For the good things we must assume no other cause than God, but the cause of evil we must look for in other things and not in God."[7] Since Plato was hesitant to ascribe to God infinity or omnipotence, his answer to the problem of evil's ultimate origin was far from consistent. In *Timaeus*, he attributes imperfections of embodied beings to the creative agency of the lesser gods and to the limitations of the receptacle (*hypodoche*), later to be known as matter (*hyle*).[8] In *Theaetetus*, Plato even hints in passing at

---

4. See Aristotle, *Poetica* 6 (1449b27).

5. A. A. Long, "The Stoic Concept of Evil," *The Philosophical Quarterly* 18 (1968): 329.

6. Seneca, *On Providence* 1.3.

7. Plato, *Republic* 379C (trans. Greene, *Moira*, 298). See also Plato, *Timaeus* 30A.

8. Plato, *Timaeus* 40-42, 50-51. For patristic critique of the Platonic idea that some things were created by lesser gods, see Augustine, *Civ.* 12.25, who also denies that angels had any part in creation. According to Philo, *On the Confusion of Tongues* 35.179, some imperfections in creation are precisely attributable to angelic participation in the original creation. See H. A. Wolfson, *Philo* (Cambridge: Harvard University Press, 1948), 1:273. For an illuminating discussion of Platonic theodicy, see Peter Harrison, "Purpose, Design and the Intelligibility of Nature," 4 (unpublished paper). For a review of different competing theories of Plato's theodicy, see Harold Cherniss, "The Sources of Evil according to Plato," *Proceedings of the American Philosophical Society* 98 (1954): 23-30.

the necessity of ontological dualism: "It is impossible that evil will cease to exist: for there must always be something contrary to the good [*hypernantion ti to agatho*]."⁹ Plato did not develop this idea, but rather emphasized that the material world was beautiful, good, and ordered to the degree to which it reflected the realm of the eternal forms.

Building on Plato's vision, Plotinus placed matter at the very bottom of the hierarchy of forms, as that which was completely unbounded, measureless, and formless (*apeiron, ametron, aneideon*). It followed that matter was a "privation of the good" (*steresis tou agathou*) and, worse still, "evil in itself" (*to kakon to auto*), or even "the primary evil" (*proton kakon*).¹⁰ Fighting with what he considered to be gnostic distortions of his most sublime teaching, Plotinus argued that the material world was a beautiful, good, even if ultimately imperfect reflection of the intellectual universe.¹¹ For some of his critics, the tension in his teaching between the absolute evil of matter and the beauty of the material cosmos remained unresolved.¹²

Early Christian authors were careful not to impose any one solution to the problem of evil as binding on the church at large. More generally, in the history of Christian doctrine theodicy has never reached the level of dogmatic precision attained by the doctrines of the Trinity and incarnation. Nevertheless, patristic authors shared an impressive number of common assumptions regarding the problem of evil, in part by holding to theistic ontology and in part by excluding the rival metaphysical systems of Marcion, the gnostic teachers, Mani, and most philosophers.

The general assumptions of patristic authors may be summarized as follows. Shared commitment to monotheism ruled out all forms of ontological dualism, although weaker forms of dualism were always in the air under different guises: Manichaean, Platonic, apocalyptic, and so on. In other words, early Christian thinkers taught that God was omnipotent with far greater precision and consistency than their philosophical

---

9. Plato, *Thaetetus* 176a; see also Plotinus, *Enneads* 1.8.6, 2.4.5.

10. Plotinus, *Enneads* 1.8.4; see a similar point attributed to Platonizing Celsus in Origen, *Contra Celsum* 4.66.

11. Plotinus, *Enneads* 1.8.3-5. See Denis O'Brien, *Théodicée Plotinienne, Théodicée Gnostique* (Leiden: Brill, 1993).

12. See Edward B. Costello, "Is Plotinus Inconsistent on the Nature of Evil?," *International Philosophical Quarterly* 7 (1967): 483-97; John M. Rist, "Plotinus on Matter and Evil," *Phronesis* 6 (1961): 154-66.

counterparts among the pagans. The benevolent and almighty Creator of
the early Christian apologists tolerated no eternal antipodes, be it another
divine agent, or matter, or the realm of darkness and chaos. Unlike pagan
Platonists, orthodox patristic authors refused to locate the origin of evil in
matter.[13] The doctrine of *creatio ex nihilo* drove home the point that God's
goodness and power were limited neither by matter nor by anything else.

Early Christian heresiologists had little patience with the speculations
of the gnostics, who located the origin of evil in the cosmic drama of the
gods. The world was neither an afterthought of an incompetent committee
of gods, nor the result of Sophia's fall from the Pleroma. Irenaeus of Lyons
(ca. 130–ca. 202), Tertullian of Carthage (155–240), Origen of Alexandria,
Basil of Caesarea, and Augustine of Hippo, among others, concurred with
the Neoplatonists that God was not the author of evil.[14]

Nurtured on the biblical account of creation and having rejected ontological dualism, the orthodox Christians held that the omnipotent and
benevolent God created everything good. It followed that evil could not be
among the things originally created, and in this limited sense it was nonbeing. Following the Neoplatonists, Christian theologians explained that
evil was a privation of the good (*steresis, privatio boni*) similar to the way in
which darkness was the absence of light.[15] Evil was not a substance, since it
was parasitic on the good, depending on the good for its existence.[16] Pseudo-
Dionysius, following Proclus, proposed that evil was beyond nonbeing, since
evil was not merely the privation of the good, but also the negative force
destructive of the good.[17] The Areopagites' arguably more precise language

---

13. Tertullian, *Adversus Hermogenem* 9–11; Athanasius, *Contra Gentes* 6; Athanasius, *De incarnatione* 2; Augustine, *Conf.* 7.7.5.

14. Origen, *Contra Celsum* 6.53–55; Tertullian, *Adversus Marcionem* 2.9; Basil of Caesarea, *Homily Explaining That God Is Not the Cause of Evil* 3–5; Augustine, *Lib.* 1.2.4.10. Only a fragment of Irenaeus's letter to Florinus, titled *On the Sole Sovereignty* or *That God Is Not the Author of Evil* survives in Eusebius, *Historia Ecclesiae* 5.20.

15. Plotinus, *Enneads* 2.4.5, 10; see also Athanasius, *Contra Gentes* 7.4–5.

16. Augustine writes in *Enchir.* 8.27: "God judged it better to bring good out of evil than to permit any evil to exist." J. F. Shaw, trans., *The Enchiridion* (Whitefish, MT: Kessinger, 2010). See also Augustine, *Enchir.* 14.96; *Conf.* 7.7.18; Athanasius, *Contra Gentes* 4.4, 7.3; *De incarnatione* 4.5; John of Damascus, *De fide orthodoxa* 4.20. This point is emphasized by G. R. Evans, *Augustine on Evil* (New York: Cambridge University Press, 2000).

17. Pseudo-Dionysius, *Divine Names* 4; Proclus, *De malorum subsistentia* 38.7–11, discussed in Carlos Steel, "Proclus on the Existence of Evil," *Proceedings of the Boston Area Colloquium in Ancient Philosophy* (Lanham, MD: University Press of America, 1986), 95.

was not followed by the majority of the fathers, who continued to teach that evil was the corruption, perversion, and destruction of the good.[18]

Within the framework of Christian theism, the belief that evil was nonbeing did not lead to the conclusion that evil was a grand illusion (as it did, for example, in Buddhism). On the contrary, Christianity from the very beginning was characterized by a keen sense that evil was real, powerful, and all-pervasive.[19] Hence, the insight that evil was nonbeing was bound to provide a partial answer and generate more questions, such as: If God is not the author of evil, then who or what is? What feature of creation could be causally connected to evil without at the same time implicating God the Creator?

The general line of response to these perplexing questions was that the free agency of rational creatures accounted for the actualization of evil. The Creator could not be held responsible for the free evil choices that rational creatures made, since God did not bring about or causally determine these choices, but only permitted them to be made.[20] The reason for this permission, while ultimately somewhat mysterious, had to do with first allowing a genuine (as opposed to merely apparent) exercise of the freedom of choice as something intrinsically good and valuable, and second with the divine intention of ultimately drawing good out of all evil.[21] The obscurity of divine intention was no sign of divine failure; rather, it was a sign of the human failure to comprehend God's ways and to consider divine intentions with a mind undistorted by evil. In addition, God could bring about evil in the form of physical suffering, when it served the divine purpose of admonishing, converting, chastising, punishing, teaching, and healing those who were turned away from God.[22]

---

18. Augustine, *De natura boni* 4.

19. A Syrian ascetic master known as Pseudo-Macarius/Symeon ingeniously stated that while evil is very real for humans, in the sense of being an ever-threatening power of temptation living in one's heart, evil in this sense is not real for God, on whom it does not have a similar cognitive grip. See *Spiritual Homilies* 16.5–6.

20. Augustine problematized this claim in *Lib.* 1.2.4: "We believe that everything which exists is created by one God, and yet that God is not the cause of sin. The difficulty is: if sin goes back to souls created by God, and souls go back to God, how can we avoid before long tracing sin back to God?"

21. Origen, *Contra Celsum* 7.68, points out that God permits evil, but does not order evil by his will. See also Lactantius, *De ira dei* 13; Augustine, *Civ.* 1.8–29, 11.18.

22. Tertullian, *Adversus Marcionem* 2.13–15; Origen, *Contra Celsum* 6.56. See Hans Schwartz, *Evil: A Historical and Theological Perspective* (Minneapolis: Fortress, 1995), 103.

In addition to these philosophical considerations, the biblical narrative framework was indispensable for addressing the problem of evil. Salvation history, from creation to eschaton, offered the most comprehensive theodicy in narrative form. The creation account was relied on to support the claim that God was not the author of evil. The fathers drew on Genesis 3 and the story of the watchers in Genesis 6:1–4 to construct their theories of human and angelic fall respectively.[23] All patristic authors agreed that evil was causally connected to the misuse of free will, although their accounts of the fall differed considerably. Space permits me to only lightly scratch the surface of the three distinct patristic accounts. For Tatian (ca. 120–ca. 180) and Irenaeus the first sin was a thoughtless act of an innocent, yet inexperienced, childlike creature. For Origen the fall was a pretemporal noetic catastrophe that brought about the soul's imprisonment in the material world. Augustine's complex and comprehensive theory of the original sin locates the root of evil in the disorder of the will, for which no efficient cause can be found, but only deficient cause, located in the inclination of the will toward self-absorption and ultimately nothingness.[24] These theories share a common but differently expressed conviction that evil resides in the ultimately unanalyzable inclination of the free rational agent who mysteriously prefers the finite goods of creation to the infinite good of the Creator.[25]

It may be noted that while free choice could account for the existence of moral evil, the cause of natural evil was still left largely unexplained. This problem was resolved in different ways. Some fathers replied that human choice of evil had tragic and far-reaching consequences for the rest of creation. Others argued that "natural evil" was a misnomer: strictly

---

23. Gary Anderson, *Genesis of Perfection* (Louisville, KY: Westminster John Knox, 2001); Annette Yoshiko Reed, *Fallen Angels and the History of Judaism and Christianity: The Reception of Enochic Literature* (New York: Cambridge University Press, 2005).

24. Tertullian, *De exhortatione castitatis* 2.4–5; Augustine, *Lib.* 3.17, 48; *Ver. rel.* 12.23. See also Augustine, *Civ.* 13.14: "Hence from the misuse of free will there started a chain of disasters: mankind is led from that original perversion, a kind of corruption at the root, right up to the disaster of the second death, which has no end." Translated by Henry Bettenson, *Augustine: Concerning the City of God* (London: Penguin Books, 1984), 523. See David Ray Griffin, "Augustine and the Denial of Genuine Evil," in *The Problem of Evil: Select Readings*, ed. Michael L. Peterson (Notre Dame: University of Notre Dame Press, 1992), 197.

25. Athanasius, *Contra Gentes* 7.3–5; Athanasius, *De incarnatione* 15; Augustine, *Conf.* 7.18.

speaking, all evils were unnatural.[26] Augustine proposed that such disasters as fires and hurricanes represented the working of natural forces that were inherently good, but could be misdirected so as to harm humans.[27] Others speculated, drawing on the Stoic view mentioned earlier, that natural disasters were not evil at all, because no evil intention was involved.[28] Still others deferred to the universal religious insight that natural disasters were a form of divine punishment for human disobedience. God sent natural disasters to admonish, correct, restrain, and mete out retribution for sin.[29] Origen hinted more imaginatively, if rather vaguely, that natural disasters were a part of the demonic revolt against God.[30] On this analysis, natural evil was reducible to moral evil in its demonic form. Despite their considerable differences, these accounts of natural evil shared one general point in common: the ethical categories of moral corruption and sinfulness blended with the ontological categories of physical corruptibility, disorder, and death.

The narrative framework of salvation history offered more than just an explanation of evil's origin. Human history was presented as a series of God's redemptive acts, which culminated in the divine incarnation. God's assuming of human nature was interpreted as a new creation, as God's restoration of his image and likeness in human beings, as the God-man's victory over the powers of sin, corruption, death, and the realm of the demonic. The fruits of this victory, abundantly available in the sacramental life of the church, would be most fully manifest in the eschaton. The hope of the resurrection of the dead and the orientation of life toward the final judgment expanded the horizon of "the bigger picture" theodicy. Many early Christians endured persecution, torture, and martyrdom with the hope of attesting by their deaths to the power of Christ's resurrection

---

26. John of Damascus, *De fide orthodoxa* 4.20: "Evil is no more than a negation of good and a lapse from what is natural to what is unnatural, for there is nothing that is naturally evil." Translated by Frederic H. Chase, *Saint John of Damascus* (New York: Fathers of the Church, 1958), 386.

27. Augustine, *Civ.* 11.22.

28. Plotinus, *Enneads* 1.4.4–13; 1.8.4; 4.4.44.

29. Lactantius, *De ira dei* 17; Basil, *De fide orthodoxa* 4.19.

30. Origen, *Contra Celsum* 4.65. See John M. Rist, "Beyond Stoic and Platonist: A Sample of Origen's Treatment of Philosophy (*Contra Celsum* 4.62–70)," in *Platonismus und Christentum* (Münster: Aschendorff, 1983), 233–34.

and the reality of eternal life. The apocalyptic narrative, its awe-inspiring features notwithstanding, also functioned as a theodicy: the punishment of the wicked and the rewarding of the righteous manifested the ultimate triumph of the justice and goodness of God, and brought clarity into a world often fraught with moral confusion.

The common core of patristic theodicy may be somewhat schematically reduced to the following five points:

1. God is not the author of evil.

2. God prevents, permits, and draws good out of evil.

3. Ontologically evil is nonbeing, that is, a privation, corruption, and perversion of the good.

4. The misuse of angelic and human free will is the cause of evil.

5. Salvation history provides a narrative framework, which answers the question of how God draws good out of evil.

THE PROBLEM OF EVIL IN
MODERNITY: MAIN SHIFTS

Let me begin with two cautionary notes. I take any answer to the problem of evil to be essentially contested. Modern answers to the problem of evil are as variegated as the ancient ones. What hope, then, does one have for finding some semblance of a common tune in such a cacophony of voices? I take the common tune to be the framework beliefs and points of emphasis in dealing with the problem of evil, rather than material answers themselves. Nevertheless, even the framework beliefs need to be approached with great care: it would be wrong to impose on them any artificial uniformity.

My second cautionary note is that I take the boundaries between premodernity and modernity to be porous. What this means is that modern views about the problem of evil have not replaced premodern views altogether. In many cases, modern views have succeeded in pushing earlier views from the center stage to the periphery. However, most answers to perpetual questions are subject to the boomerang effect: they return in different ages under different guises. The problem of evil is no exception.

After these cautionary notes, we may identify six major shifts that have shaped the approaches to the problem of evil in premodernity and modernity.

1. With the exception of philosophical skeptics, most premodern thinkers were relatively confident that the problem of evil could be solved, at least theoretically, while they admitted that the eschatological solution was in the hands of God. The ancients may have disagreed on just what the solution was—Job clearly refused to accept all facile explanations of his pious friends—but most of them were confident that a convincing explanation was in principle available. Patristic authors insisted that the revelatory framework was necessary for articulating a comprehensive answer to theodicy and simultaneously found themselves baptizing select philosophical insights.[31] As the writings of Augustine on evil make especially clear, this revelatory framework presupposed a fundamental reorientation of one's worldview and a reordering of the self. A premodern theodicist was not an autonomous entity sitting in judgment of God's design. On the contrary, such a theodicist was a dependent creature seeking to align all of her thoughts and desires with the will of God.[32]

The contemporary discussion of theodicy is conducted quite differently. To most present-day readers, the book of Job raises more questions than it provides answers. A few optimistic voices aside, modern thinkers tend to approach theodicy as a great mystery.[33] For example, Paul Fiddes observes:

> Much of human suffering is apparently meaningless in itself, and because we experience suffering as senseless we are driven into silence and numbness of spirit; we are paralyzed by it in our will and emotions. We cannot use suffering actively to promote what is life-giving, making something out of it. There is thus no hope of learning from suffering, or using it to overcome what has caused it.[34]

---

31. Origen, *Contra Celsum* 4.65.

32. On this point, see Kenneth Surin, *Theology and the Problem of Evil* (Eugene, OR: Wipf & Stock, 1986), 1–38.

33. Among the optimists are Alvin Plantinga, *God, Freedom, and Evil* (Grand Rapids: Eerdmans, 1977), and John Hick, *Evil and the God of Love* (San Francisco: Harper & Row, 1978). Most other contemporary thinkers concede that theodicy may remain an unsolvable problem.

34. P. Fiddes, *The Creative Suffering of God* (Oxford: Clarendon, 1992), 146.

Fiddes continues that it is the meaning that believers find in the story of God's suffering on the cross that liberates them from the meaninglessness of their own suffering. Not all contemporary Christian theologians would concur with Fiddes's solution. However, they would agree that no one solution offers a comprehensive answer.

2. The ancients were more preoccupied with the metaphysical problem of evil's origin; contemporary thinkers more acutely feel and more frequently discuss the problem of seemingly unfair distribution of suffering. For example, for the Neoplatonists and Augustine, the answer to the question *unde malum* was a cornerstone of a comprehensive theodicy. For the present-day theodicists, the metaphysical problem of evil's origin often recedes into the background, and the question of why bad things happen to good people takes center stage.[35]

Early Christian theologians were more concerned to uphold the intellectual integrity of the claim that God was not the author of evil. The contemporary observers instead tend to focus on cases of gratuitous and horrendous evil. The claim of Platonizing metaphysicians that evil is a nonbeing generally leaves most modern students of the problem of evil unimpressed. A prevailing contemporary view seems to be that to condemn evil to nothingness is to dissolve, rather than to resolve, an age-old problem.[36] The premodern Christian thinkers embraced the proposition that evil is nonbeing with the same readiness with which our contemporaries, both Christian and non-Christian theodicists, seem to dismiss it.

3. The polemical context within which the problem of evil is discussed has changed considerably too. In premodernity, the main alternatives to monotheism (and the associated theistic view) were polytheism and dualism. In the web of polytheistic beliefs, to the extent to which those could be said to form a coherent whole, evil was due to bad luck, the alignment of the stars, or the workings of some malicious god. On a popular level, different forms of fatalism are still with us, if we take into account the enduring popularity of psychics and the questionable comfort that millions still derive from consulting their horoscopes. On a less popular

---

35. I have in mind the title of Harold Kushner's best-selling book *When Bad Things Happen to Good People* (New York: Schocken Books, 1981).

36. See H. J. McCloskey, *God and Evil* (The Hague: Martinus Nijhoff, 1974), 31.

level, deterministic explanations are peddled as the latest achievements of natural science and medicine. While serious metaphysical dualists of the Manichaean or Cathar bent are hard to come by today, some rather peculiar and watered-down versions of dualism have survived in the teachings of Mary Baker Eddy and the musings of some New Agers. It seems that the intellectual niche previously occupied by dualism now has a new tenant: protest atheism. While doubts about the divine realm were a theoretical possibility already in the time of the psalmist—"The fool says in his heart: there is no God" (Pss 14:1; 53:1)—the number of people who were prepared to entertain the same idea publicly in premodern times was admittedly quite small. The Epicureans had a very unpopular reputation of being covert atheists, despite the fact that they were professed polytheists who denied divine providence. Even the long-suffering Job could doubt God's justice, but not his existence. Most ancients would have found Hans Küng's dictum that the problem of evil is "the rock of atheism" largely incomprehensible. Our contemporaries, on the contrary, naturally resonate with Stendhal's bon mot: "God's only excuse is that he does not exist."

To be sure, protest atheism itself comes in different forms. As one possibility, consider the existential agony with which Ivan Karamazov rejects the harmony of the divine plan in the face of the atrocious suffering of children in Dostoevsky's famous novel. For Ivan, no prospect of future bliss or punishment could possibly outweigh the dark irrationality of evil. As a result, Dostoevsky's hero rejects the world and the Creator's plan as absurdly cruel. Ivan's rebellion was joined by a chorus of modern thinkers, including twentieth-century French existentialists Albert Camus and Jean-Paul Sartre. Atheism as a response to evil had next to no existential grip on our premodern ancestors. They could very well be disappointed in particular institutions that offered solutions to the problem of evil, but they were far less inclined to abandon God.

4. In premodernity, the trilemma of divine goodness, omnipotence, and the existence of evil was addressed by limiting the scope of genuine evil to sin and by insisting that God includes all evil into his redemptive purposes and turns it into good. By contrast, contemporary theodicists are more prepared to modify the divine attributes in classical theism than to question the possibility of gratuitous evil. In his bestselling

book, *When Bad Things Happen to Good People,* Rabbi Harold Kushner proposes that God is not powerful enough to resist the forces of natural evil,
such as hurricanes, tornadoes, and diseases.[37] According to Kushner, God
has limited resources for coping with the forces of chaos in the universe.
Process thinkers offer a more philosophically refined version of this thesis,
arguing that God develops with the world. Process theologians build the
limitations of divine power and other attributes into the nature of God.

In contrast to process theologians, open theists approach the problem
of evil not as a trilemma but as a quadrilemma, including also the attribute
of divine omniscience. Open theists reject any deterministic accounts of
divine foreknowledge in order to safeguard genuine human freedom. The
resultant version of theism is arguably more compatible with revelation,
although equally fraught with difficulties of a purely philosophical character (coherence) and religious character (Is a God who does not know the
future worthy of worship?).

Some Jewish and Christian theologians who study the Holocaust propose a reconsideration of the traditional understanding of divine attributes and divine action in light of the tragedy. They argue that divine
omnipotence and divine omnipresence cannot be approached in the same
manner "after the Holocaust." While their approaches differ considerably,
the common theme is that God's permission of horrendous evils requires
a different understanding of God.

Most kenotic theologians (considerable differences among them notwithstanding), in contrast, propose that a limitation of any divine perfection is not an inherent defect of the divine nature, but a function of the
divine will.[38] In other words, evil is permitted not because God is by nature
incapable of preventing it, but because God chooses to limit his ability to
destroy evil. The kenotic models of God's interaction with creation often
include similar limitations of divine omniscience and other divine perfections. The common denominator in process theism, open theism, and

---

37. Harold Kushner, *When Bad Things Happen to Good People* (New York: Schocken Books,
1981).

38. John Polkinghorne, ed., *The Work of Love: Creation as Kenosis* (Grand Rapids:
Eerdmans, 2001). For a recent assessment of different kenotic theories from the standpoint
of Chalcedonian Christology, broadly conceived, see C. Stephen Evans, ed., *Exploring Kenotic
Christology: The Self-Emptying of God* (New York: Oxford University Press, 2006).

kenoticism is the impulse to modify classical theism in order to account for the reality of evil. Most premodern Christian thinkers were not prepared to make such an accommodation.

In addition, many contemporary theodicists question the traditional theistic concepts of divine immutability and impassibility. They propose instead that God suffers compassionately with and for humanity. For them God, to use Alfred North Whitehead's oft-quoted statement, is "a fellow-sufferer who understands." For Jürgen Moltmann and other proponents of the theology of the cross, the cross is first of all a symbol of God's self-identification with the God-forsaken humanity.[39] For the premodern Christian authors, in the incarnation God makes human nature his own in order to transform its experiences. The experiences of suffering and death that are involuntary for most humans are rendered redemptive and free when they are transformed by the Logos. The patristic emphasis is not on the Logos suffering with us, although this aspect of the divine incarnation is not neglected, but on the Logos incarnate overcoming the limitations of suffering and death.

5. In the premodern theories of atonement, the fundamental problem is not suffering or gratuitous evil, but rather humanity's sin and alienation from God. In these theories, humanity's sinful condition is cashed out in different terms: as a transgression of the covenant, as missing the mark, as a burden, as a debt, as a state of captivity, as a disease, as a crime meriting capital punishment, as a failure to love, and so on. Correspondingly, God intervenes through Christ in order to offer sacrifice, to defeat the power of the demonic, to restore health to dying humanity by deifying it, to pay the moral debt in satisfaction of God's violated honor, to propitiate God's just wrath against the unrighteous, and to inspire all by an example of true love, to name the most influential possibilities. For modern theodicists, in contrast, God is on trial and stands in need of justification. God becomes reconciled to unjustly suffering humanity by becoming a fellow sufferer. This shift of emphasis has led some theologians to speak of the "abandonment of atonement," as traditionally understood.[40]

---

39. Jürgen Moltmann, *The Crucified God* (Minneapolis: Fortress, 1993).

40. Colin Grant, "The Abandonment of Atonement," *King's Theological Review* 9 (1986): 1–8.

6. The traditional metanarrative of creation, fall, redemption, and eschaton has been questioned by historians, natural scientists, and postmodern philosophers on different grounds. While many patristic theologians allegorized the stories of creation and the fall, much of early Christian theology depended on some version of the claim that there was a causal link between Adam and Eve's behavior in the garden and the subsequent drama of human history. For most of our contemporaries, be they ethicists, biologists, or historians, the claim that the first human transgression has radically changed the original harmony of all creation has lost much of its explanatory power.[41]

In late antiquity the sobering Augustinian doctrine of original sin put all doubts about the possibility of undeserved suffering to rest. According to this doctrine, all humanity, because of its implication in Adam's transgression, justly deserves nothing more than the perpetual pains of hell, from which some are rescued by God's unmerited grace. Since the Enlightenment the clouds of moral doubt have begun to gather over Augustine's doctrine, with the result that only a few contemporary Christian theologians would be prepared to defend this doctrine in its classical austerity. Contemporary theodicists point out that since humanity cannot be held collectively guilty before God, the rather facile explanation that horrendous evils are all forms of divine punishment or providential testing is not very compelling.

As I mentioned earlier, in our time other narrative frameworks are competing for the dominant position once occupied by the Christian master narrative of salvation history. Natural scientists have proposed a master narrative beginning with the Big Bang, continuing with the appearance of life and neo-Darwinian evolution, and eventually resulting in the heat death of the universe. In the hands of Richard Dawkins and his followers, Neo-Darwinism has acquired the status of an alternative worldview, which purports to account for the extraordinary waste and atrocious suffering in nature by postulating a complex interaction of blind chance (random mutation of genes) and equally purposeless necessity of the laws

41. See the remark of Joseph F. Kelly, *The Problem of Evil in the Western Tradition: From the Book of Job to Modern Genetics* (Collegeville, MN: Liturgical Press, 2002), 59: "People brought up on evolutionary concepts, on the belief that all life forms struggle for survival, usually against other life forms, see Augustine's theory [that once the world had been perfect and that we had lived in harmony with all creation] as something fantastic."

of nature (natural selection).[42] Ironically, one may discern in the cosmodicy of neo-Darwinism a resurgence of the Greek prephilosophic view that misfortunes are brought about by a mixture of chance and necessity.

Another metanarrative, which has gripped the minds of billions in the twentieth century, is Marxism. This theory offers what could be called a socio-dicy, that is, a theory of how to fix the world's evils by building a perfectly just society of the future. Marxist theory removes the center of the spiritual battle from the individual human heart (as in Christian asceticism) and relocates this battle in the sphere of large-scale historical events and social institutions. Karl Marx famously postulated that class struggle is the driving force of history. Having stigmatized Christian eschatology as an opium for the people, he proposed his own secular eschatological vision instead. The Marxist plan of world improvement includes a violent revolution, a godless apocalypse in which the force of the absolute good, the proletariat, would rise against the force of the absolute evil, the capitalists, to bring about communism. As a political project, Marxist ideology, when put in practice, has led to the loss of over fifty million lives, when we total up the victims of Stalin's gulags, Mao's Cultural Revolution, and other experiments of this sort. Some Western intellectuals seem to be undeterred by these disastrous experiments, as theories of justice with Marxist features continue to be a popular sport in the academy.

The other twentieth-century project of radical world improvement was Hitler's Third Reich, which also offered a (perverse) analysis of the causes of evil and a deadly solution for how to set things right. The self-inflicted horrors of the twentieth century should have taught us that nontrivial, comprehensive world improvement is exceptionally difficult to achieve without the bringing about of terrible evils. Tragically, some politicians remain undeterred by the lessons of the past.

The six major shifts identified here are meant to serve as rough indicators of the "climate of opinion" that colors our reception of premodern Christian approaches to the problem of evil. Theologically, my analysis is not intended as a paean to theologically happier times, nor as a jeremiad

---

42. Charles Darwin wrote: "I am inclined to look at everything as resulting from designed laws, with the details whether good or bad, left to the working out of what we may call chance." Quoted in Harrison, "Purpose, Design and the Intelligibility of Nature," 19.

about the present state of theology. Rather, I want to emphasize that we are dealing with a dynamic picture.

To add a seventh postmodern twist to the story, perhaps the greatest evil of postmodernity is that it recognizes no evil, or to be more precise, the prevailing postmodern sensibility is to treat evil not as a feature of external reality, but as a function of private judgment. As a countercurrent to this widespread relativistic tendency, which reduces all truth claims to power claims, there is an equally strong tendency to treat certain social taboos of the present-day Western society as radical evils that demand regular sacrifices of scapegoats and vast amounts of money to run the institutions that address them. We might not be able to save ourselves from all our contradictions, but at least we might see them more clearly when we treat the problem of evil afforded by a horizon larger than modernity.

The task of contemporary theology is to combine the penetrating patristic analysis of the dynamics of moral evil with modern sensitivity to cases of horrendous and undeserved suffering. Such a synthesis holds promise of becoming more existentially compelling than any nonreligious answer currently on offer. Nevertheless, even if most objections to the traditional theistic account of evil were put to rest, there is much about this problem that is bound to remain shrouded in mystery, at least on this side of the eschaton.

5
—

AUGUSTINE AND
THE LIMITS OF EVIL

From Creation to Christ in the Enchiridion

Han-luen Kantzer Komline

INTRODUCTION

Some years ago, Horton Davies bemoaned the tendency of contemporary theologians to jump to Christology to address the problem of evil. Davies attributed to them the view "that it is not in natural theology amenable to reason, but in the revelation of God in Christ and in His Incarnation, Cross and Resurrection, that faith is warranted and sustained despite sin, suffering, doubt and death." In Davies's view, such theologians had "discarded too rapidly" the more "traditional" responses to the problem of evil offered "by Augustine, Aquinas and Calvin."[1]

Davies's assessment raises two questions, one descriptive and one normative. First, how persuasive is the implied contrast between "traditional" approaches to the problem of evil, such as Augustine's, and christological approaches? Is it right to contrast Augustine's approach to the problem of evil with christological approaches?[2] Second, how should one evaluate

---

1. Horton Davies, *The Vigilant God: Providence in the Thought of Augustine, Aquinas, Calvin, and Barth* (New York: Peter Lang, 1992), 1.

2. The issue of the role of Christology in Christian approaches to the problem of evil calls to mind John Hick's classic critique of Augustine, which includes the point that his account of evil suffers from the "impersonal" character of his thinking. See Hick, *Evil and the God of Love* (New York: Harper & Row, 1966), 59. For a defense of Augustine's teaching on evil against the critiques of Hick, see Rowan Williams, "Insubstantial Evil," in *On Augustine* (New York:

strongly christological approaches to the problem of evil? Is it true that
Christology is insufficient to address the problem of evil?

Considering Augustine's approach to the problem of evil in his *Enchiridion*
sheds light on both questions.[3] While Augustine engaged the problem of evil
throughout the course of his career and other texts would perhaps be more
obvious choices, Augustine's *Enchiridion* is the ideal basis for a sketch of his
views.[4] Since it stems from around the year 421, this work allows us to consider Augustine's perspective on evil as a mature thinker, and its synthetic
presentation of the whole of the Christian faith provides an opportunity to
observe how Augustine relates evil to other Christian doctrines.

In this work, we see that Augustine discusses the problem of evil by
establishing theological boundaries around it.[5] His primary concern is not
evil itself but rather the limits of evil recognized by the Christian faith.[6]

Bloomsbury, 2016), 79–105. Davies echoes Hick in his conclusion when he writes of Augustine,
"His mistake—and not only his—was to consider the nature and activity of God in terms of
substance and power rather than in personal categories." Thus a tension emerges between
Davies's introduction, where he expresses dissatisfaction with the christological focus of
contemporary approaches, which he opposes to Augustine's, and the conclusion, where he
faults Augustine for treating the doctrine of evil in an impersonal way. It is precisely the
strongly christological character of Augustine's mature account that enables him to evade
concerns about the "impersonal" character of his approach.

3. On the theme of evil in Augustine's corpus more generally, see Hermann Häring,
"Malum," in *Augustinus-Lexikon*, ed. Andreas E. J. Grote, vol. 3 (Basel: Schwabe AG, 2004),
especially the bibliography found in columns 1119–21.

4. For other treatments of evil in the *Enchiridion*, see Wolfraum Kinzig, "Die Lehre vom
Bösen in Augustins *Enchiridion*," in *Rhetorik des Bösen*, ed. Paul Fiddes and Jochen Schmidt
(Würzburg: Ergon, 2013); G. R. Evans, *Augustine on Evil* (Cambridge: Cambridge University
Press, 1982), 166–68. Among Augustine's early works, *On Order* and *On the Free Choice of the
Will* receive frequent attention when it comes to the theme of evil, while among his later
works *Confessions* and *City of God* figure prominently in the discussion.

5. While not working primarily with the *Enchiridion*, Rowan Williams makes a related
argument in different terms in "Insubstantial Evil," 79–105. The present essay confirms
Williams's conclusion that Augustine's privative view of evil needs to be seen in connection
to how Augustine understands God's own self-sacrificial loving. His views on evil cannot be
separated from his theology.

6. William Babcock argues that in *On the Free Choice of the Will*, Augustine personalizes
and historicizes the problem of evil, moving it from an abstract philosophical plane to a
concrete moral one. Evil becomes, in Augustine's hands, a moral issue, a matter of sin and
punishment. See "Sin and Punishment: The Early Augustine on Evil," in *Augustine: Presbyter
Factus Sum*, ed. Joseph T. Lienhard, Earl C. Muller, and Roland J. Teske (New York: Peter Lang,
1993), 235–48; and, in a similar vein, Robert M. Cooper, "Saint Augustine's Doctrine of Evil,"
Scottish Journal of Theology 16, no. 3 (1963): 256–76. The mature Augustine reframes the issue
of evil once again. In the *Enchiridion* we see that Augustine portrays evil not just as a mysterious metaphysical problem, or even just as a pernicious moral problem, but as the object of
God's removal and negation. Evil is not only sin and punishment; it is the reason for divine

Giving an account of these limits requires moving beyond natural theology to address evil not only in relation to creation but also in relation to Christ. This approach delivers rewards that speak in favor of leaning on Christ in formulating a Christian response to the problem of evil.

To see how this is the case, we will begin by considering Augustine's account of the limits of evil in the *Enchiridion*, both epistemic and ontological. We will then examine the practical implications of considering the problem of evil from a christological angle. This analysis in place, we will be in a position to evaluate the normative question of a christological approach to the problem of evil. How important is a christological perspective? Is it necessary? Is it sufficient? These questions will be addressed in the conclusion.

THE EPISTEMIC LIMITS OF EVIL

In the *Enchiridion* Augustine describes limits as pertaining to evil both with respect to what it is, and with respect to our ability to know it. We turn first to the epistemic limits. The epistemic limits of evil Augustine treats in the *Enchiridion* fall into three major types: (1) limits of epistemic ability—that is, limits on how much we *can* know about evil; (2) limits of epistemic responsibility—that is, limits on how much we *should* know about evil; and (3) limits of epistemic hesitancy—that is, limits on how much we *claim* to know, or not to know, about evil.

Limits of the first type, pertaining to how much we *can* know about evil, stem both from what is objectively true about evil by Augustine's lights and from what we are capable of subjectively. As is well known, Augustine described evil as a privation of the good (*privatio boni*).[7] Given that, strictly

---

sacrifice and expiation. The mature Augustine situates evil theologically, as well as morally and metaphysically. As Henry Chadwick writes, in Augustine "the retributive emphasis is ultimately overlaid by the remedial." See Chadwick, *Studies on Ancient Christianity* (Burlington, VT: Ashgate, 2006), 162. Eventually Augustine's main concern becomes thinking about sin and evil in terms of how they are undone, not just in terms of how they are done. He wants to think about divine agency in redeeming sin, not just human agency in committing it.

7. *Enchir.* 3.11 (CCSL 46:53): "quid est autem aliud quod malum dicitur, nisi priuatio boni?" See also *On Free Choice* 3.13.36; *Civ.* 14.11; *The Nature of the Good* 3.23. Unless otherwise noted, English translations come from Augustine, "The Enchiridion on Faith, Hope, and Charity," trans. Bruce Harbert, in *On Christian Belief*, Works of Saint Augustine (Hyde Park, NY: New City, 2005). Latin citations are from M. Evans, ed., "Enchiridion ad Laurentium de fide et spe et caritate," CCSL 46:49–114.

speaking, evil has no substance of its own for Augustine, to give an account of the inherent meaning or content of evil is by definition impossible; evil has no independent meaning or content. The reality of evil entails that it can only be known by way of relation to the good, by harsh verbs. How does it distort, corrode, rupture, deprive? This is the most we can describe, not the "it" that does these things. So much for the obscurity of evil as object of human knowledge.

Augustine also dedicates considerable attention in the *Enchiridion* to the limitations of the epistemic subject. Both ignorance and error plague her efforts to find the truth.[8] Thus finitude and feebleness, as well as the peculiarities of the object of such "knowing," restrict what can be known about evil. Limits of epistemic ability, then, beset a person from both subjective and objective poles.

Within the domain of those things that *can* be known about evil, there is an even smaller set: those things that *should* be known about evil. We ought not know everything that we can know. Augustine provides a number of guidelines for discerning what falls within our epistemic responsibility.

In introducing the work as a whole, Augustine had already set some parameters for the discussion that followed; these overarching parameters apply to the issue of epistemic responsibility with respect to evil. The request that had prompted the writing of the *Enchiridion* itself implied a need for prioritizing. Laurence, who had petitioned the work, sought Augustine's help in determining what was essential to the Christian faith and what was not. He wanted to know where he should focus his attention. Note the element of adjudication entailed in the questions the work was to address "what we should seek above all [*maxime*], what we should chiefly [*principaliter*] avoid because of the various heresies there are ... what should be held first [*primum*] and last [*ultimum*] ... what is a sure and suitable foundation [*fundamentum*] of Catholic faith." Augustine's overarching answer to the questions of adjudication stated at the beginning of the work applies as much to human epistemic responsibility with respect to evil as it does to other theological topics. The main thing is this: "how God is to be worshiped."[9]

---

8. Augustine, *Enchir.* 5.17.
9. Augustine, *Enchir.* 1.4 (CCSL 46:49–50); 1.2 (CCSL 46:49).

Applying this bedrock principle to the problem of evil, Augustine writes, "We must know the causes of good and evil insofar as is necessary to enable us to travel along the road that leads to the kingdom."[10] Not everything is needful when it comes to what we ought to know about evil. We require only enough to continue progressing in the life of worship and faith.

What does this entail concretely? Augustine provides examples over the course of the work. Toward the beginning of the *Enchiridion*, he observes that there is much that *can* be known about the created world: "the properties and number of the elements, the movement and order and phases of the stars, the shape of the heavens, the kinds of animals, fruits, stones, springs, rivers, and mountains and their natures, the measurement of time and space, the indications of imminent storm and hundreds of other such things." Christians, however, should not conclude that all of this knowledge is required of them: "We do not need to inquire into the nature of things [*natura rerum*] as did those whom the Greeks call *physikoi*." Rather, "for a Christian it is enough to believe that the cause of created things [*rerum creatarum causam*] ... is nothing other than the goodness of the creator who is the one true God, and that there is nothing that is not either himself or from him, and that he is a Trinity."[11] So long as they understand the goodness of God, human beings need neither number the stars in the heavens, nor inquire into the "nature" of the evil found on earth. Comprehending God's goodness suffices for worship.

Augustine also names God's omnipotence as creating a kind of outer boundary of human responsibility to know about evil. Just as people ought to content themselves with knowing enough about evil to be confident that it does not threaten God's goodness, so it behooves them to reflect sufficiently on evil to align their understanding of it with belief in God's omnipotence. From the twin affirmations of God's goodness and God's omnipotence, according to Augustine, certain conclusions about evil follow.

For one, if God is good and omnipotent, we must conclude, according to Augustine, that "the fact that there are not only good things but evil ones is good [*bonum est*]." If God is good, then his permission of evil is good. If his permission of evil is good, then the direct result of this permission—that

---

10. Augustine, *Enchir.* 8.23 (CCSL 46:63).

11. Augustine, *Enchir.* 3.9 (CCSL 46:52–53).

not only good things but also evil things exist—must also be good. If no
good were to result, why would an omnipotent God permit evil? Augustine
insists on this point: "If we do not believe this, the very beginning of our
profession of faith is endangered, in which we confess our belief in one
God the almighty Father."[12]

Second, if God is good and omnipotent, then God can bring good out of
evil. Even more specifically, God can make an evil will good. Here Augustine
appeals to the precedent of creation. Surely the God who called the planets into being *ex nihilo* can gather the unwilling by making them willing,
breathing love into a voluntary void. Therefore Augustine asks, "Who is
so irreligious and foolish as to say that God cannot turn to good [*in bonum*]
any of the evil wills [*malas ... voluntates*] of men he wishes, when and where
he wishes?"[13]

As these two examples show, Augustine is persuaded that what we
should believe about evil must operate within certain theological constraints. Yet, so long as those constraints are respected, the Christian need
not feel undue pressure to speculate or take positions. Augustine's rhetorical question with regard to another issue applies equally as well to the problem of evil: "What need is there to affirm or deny ... opinions, or to define
them with care, when no harm is done by being in ignorance of them?"[14]
Sometimes ignorance is admissible. In fact, there are cases in which knowledge is more "harmful" than ignorance. In such cases ignorance is prefera-
ble, not only to error, but also to knowing. "There are some things of which
ignorance [*nescire*] is better than knowledge [*scire*]."[15] When it comes to
good and evil, too much knowledge is a bitter fruit.

While he places limits on what we can and should know about evil,
Augustine also underscores the importance of restraining agnosticism.
The academics epitomize the ironies of extreme skepticism. According to
them, "every error [*error*] is thought to be sin [*peccatum*], which they claim

---

12. Augustine, *Enchir.* 24.96 (CCSL 46:100).

13. Augustine, *Enchir.* 25.98 (CCSL 46:100); see also 24.97.

14. Augustine, *Enchir.* 15.59 (CCSL 46:81). Augustine himself provides a case study of when
ignorance is to be preferred to saying something false about the problem of evil. Augustine
is contentedly agnostic on whether misinterpretation of things perceived through sense
perception (that is, in the material world) counts as sin: "I do not know whether these and
other similar occurrences are also to be called sins" (7.20 [CCSL 46:60]).

15. Augustine, *Enchir.* 5.17 (CCSL 46:57).

can only be avoided by the avoidance of all assent." Yet, by withholding all assent, they are themselves guilty of error, which error—Augustine cheekily observes—"itself proves that they are alive, since nobody who is not alive can err," thus making them doubly mistaken.[16] The epistemic paralysis of the academics in the face of perceived evil (in the form of allegedly mistaken assent) in fact perpetuates evil by undermining faith. This kind of radical skepticism must be resisted. The light of faith both enables and demands assent. With respect to evil, this entails that "we must in no way doubt that the only cause of the good things that come our way is the goodness of God, while the cause of our evils is the will of a changeable good falling away from the unchangeable good."[17] There is a limit, says Augustine, even to the limits that can be placed on human ability and responsibility to know evil. Christians therefore need to strike a balance between being overly ambitious and overly cautious when it comes to their epistemic responsibilities concerning evil.

THE ONTOLOGICAL LIMITS OF EVIL

To consider the ontological limits of evil is to continue further along the trajectory we have been following in investigating the epistemic limits that pertain to evil, according to Augustine. As discussed above, the epistemic obscurity of evil in Augustine's account is in part a function of the fact that evil itself is a privation of the good, lacking inherent ontological integrity.[18] Thus, to identify the ontological limits of evil, which in turn impact the epistemic limits of evil, one must look beyond evil itself. One must concretize the abstract definition of evil as the privation of good by asking, "Privation of what good?" The best one can do to pinpoint what evil "is" is to identify what it is "against." Evil is always against something.

---

16. Augustine, *Enchir.* 7.20 (CCSL 46:60–61).

17. Augustine, *Enchir.* 8.23 (CCSL 46:63).

18. Augustine's emphasis on the privative character of evil in no way entails that he denies the reality of evil. Evil is a parasite, but to leech off the good it must be more than a phantom. Hence, it is misleading to describe evil as "an illusion" in his view or "no more than a deceiving appearance." See Evans, *Augustine on Evil*, xi. Häring helpfully observes that "with the formula *privatio boni* Augustine never understood evil in a domesticated way as pure absence, but rather as an extremely potent opposition to God and goodness." See "Malum," 1112. On the seriousness of evil in Augustine's privative account, see also Donald A. Cress, "Augustine's Privation Account of Evil: A Defense," *Augustinian Studies* 20 (1989), especially 112–13, where he argues against the idea that evil is "illusory" or "unreal" for Augustine.

The effort to define this something leads us to the two ontological limits of evil Augustine discusses in *Enchiridion*. Evil has a whence, to which it is opposed, as well as a whither, which opposes it.

These limitations obtain in a metaphysical sense as well as being repeated over and over again in every specific instance of evil that is existentially experienced. The original, metaphysical cause of evil, according to Augustine, is voluntary defection from the unchangeable good: "The cause of our evils is the will of a changeable good falling away from the unchangeable good." This whence represents a boundary both in terms of the when and the what of evil. On the one hand, evil has a starting point. For this reason, Augustine speaks of "the first [*primum*] evil that affected the rational creation, the first privation [*prima privatio*] of good."[19] There was a time when evil was not. On the other hand, the whence of evil also makes clear that evil is always parasitic on the good. Evil is contingent and relies on that which it opposes and undermines to be what it "is." Negativity is the what of evil, which means that behind every evil stands a limit of goodness it negates.

These metaphysical implications of the whence of evil pertain as well to concrete instances of evil one may observe in the course of daily living. Epidemics break out, and wounds result from injuries; the whence of evil acts as a chronological limit on what evil is. Moreover, illness deprives of health, while wounds deprive of wholeness.[20] As health is that from which sickness detracts, so good is the ontological limit of evil, both in terms of chronology and in terms of the structural negativity of evil.

There can be a new wellness on the other side of illness that interrupts health. This is the second ontological limit of evil Augustine considers in the *Enchiridion*. Evil also has a whither, an endpoint the Christian may hope for, in Christ's work of redemption. This christological whither serves as a limit on evil in two ways.

First, Christ's work exposes the limits of human freedom under sin. It does this by way of contrast. The perverse reality is that by their very (mis)use of free choice, human beings have damaged their ability to choose freely. Once sin is "committed by free choice, sin is the victor and free

---

19. Augustine, *Enchir.* 8.24 (CCSL 46:63).
20. Augustine, *Enchir.* 3.11.

choice is also lost" in the sense that human beings become unable to "do good by the free choice of [their] own will." Human beings continue to possess a kind of freedom in that they may still elect to do what gives them pleasure, but this kind of freedom does not ring true. By comparison to the freedom found in Christ, it is clear that this freedom is woefully limited: under this kind of freedom, one "will not be free to act justly," and "joy ... in doing good" is out of reach. This contrast makes clear that under sin, "the whole human race lay prostrate in evil, or rather was wallowing in evil, and hurtling from evil to evil."[21]

But Christ's work demarcates the limits of evil not only by helping us understand the limits imposed by sin but also by setting us free from these limits. By Christ's death, the human being "is liberated from evil [*liberatur a malo*]," loosed from the demeaning and life-depriving bonds of sin, not for a life of absolute autonomy but for a life of genuine freedom in obedient service to God. In Christ we are "set free from ruin," not because we have earned this freedom but despite the fact that we have forfeited it.[22] Christ's *merciful* choice undoes the consequences of our "evil use of free choice."[23]

In this way, in his person Christ halts the evil we have set in motion. He represents the ontological whither of evil in that he not only opposes, but removes and replaces, the limits of sin with a yoke of freedom. Augustine never characterizes the solution Christ offers as one among many others, the existential problem of evil being possibly resolved by many other means. Rather, he asks, "How will a person who has been sold into slavery and is bound by it find freedom to do good unless he is redeemed by the one who said, *If the Son makes you free, you will be free indeed* (Jn 8:36)?"[24] Christ is not *a* solution to the evil of slavery to sin but *the* solution to the evil of slavery to sin.[25]

21. Augustine, *Enchir.* 9.30; 8.27 (CCSL 46:64–66).

22. Augustine, *Enchir.* 16.61; 9.30 (CCSL 46:82, 65): *a perdition liberatus.* I have tweaked Harbert's translation here to make it a bit more literal.

23. Augustine observes that we would be eternally punished if "the one who is just were not also so merciful, showing his unmerited mercy the more clearly in choosing rather to set free the unworthy" (8.27).

24. Augustine, *Enchir.* 9.30 (CCSL 46:66): "Sed ad bene faciendum ista libertas unde erit homini addict et vendito, nisi redimat cuius illa vox est." Not simply any redeemer will do. Liberation comes from the good shepherd known by his particular message and particular voice.

25. Evans rightly observes the increasing importance of Christ in Augustine's approach to evil. Less convincing is her argument that as grace and the role of Christ become more

The *Enchiridion* contains two images for the work of Christ in putting a stop to evil that highlight the relation of his work, as the ontological endpoint of sin, to the outer limit of sin in the other direction, at its start. The whither relates to the whence. Christ's work of liberation, contends Augustine, goes beyond mere repair. It is *recreation*. Christ ends the tyranny of sin in a person's life with such decisiveness that we can speak of a new beginning being made:

> We are truly made [*efficimur*] free when God makes us [*fingit*], that is, forms [*format*] and creates [*creat*] us, not that we may be men, which he has already done, but that we may be good men: this he does now by his grace, that we may be a new creation [*nova creatura*] in Christ, according to the saying, *Create* [*crea*] *a pure heart in me, O God* [Ps 51:10]. For it could not be said that God had not already created [*creaverat*] his heart, as far as the nature of a human heart is concerned.[26]

The transformation of the evil will to a good will is so radical as to be like a creation *ex nihilo*. There are no preceding merits, no hints of good antecedent intentions that anticipate God's work in Christ to set us free from sin: "For the good will of man precedes many of God's gifts but not all of them, and it is itself one of the gifts that it does not precede."[27] Human willing is no more responsible for the change of heart God works in believers than was dust for the creation of Adam. Christ brings an end to evil as abrupt as the disjunction between nothingness and creation or—to reverse the contrast—between creation and the relapse into nothingness that followed. Evil is bracketed on either side by two glorious words of light: creation's first word, "Let there be ... " and Christ's advent. Evil is bounded by the light of the world.

---

important to Augustine he becomes increasingly persuaded of the "triviality" of evil. See Evans, *Augustine on Evil*, 149. It is true that, according to Augustine, Christ removes evil. But to diminish evil by removing it does not diminish the importance of evil. Quite the contrary. If evil were trivial, God would not become incarnate to deal with it. As is shown by larger connections between the development of his doctrines of sin and grace, Augustine's estimation of the seriousness of sin and evil is positively, rather than negatively, related to his understanding of the magnitude of the grace of Christ.

26. Augustine, *Enchir.* 9.31 (CCSL 46:66).

27. Augustine, *Enchir.* 9.32 (CCSL 46:67): "Praecedit enim bona voluntas hominis multa dei dona sed non omnia; quae autem non praecedit ipsa."

PRACTICAL IMPLICATIONS OF A
CHRISTOLOGICAL APPROACH
TO THE PROBLEM OF EVIL

Over the course of the *Enchiridion*, a number of implications of Augustine's christologically oriented approach to the problem of evil come to light. This approach has implications for how people ought to relate to God in light of the problem of evil, for the strategies necessary to diagnose the problem of evil, and for the practical response one should adopt toward those who struggle with evil.

If evil requires a new creation in Christ to be stopped, then human beings cannot address the problem of evil on their own. An act of the Creator is needed to effect a new creation; God's help is essential. This is the case not only with respect to petitioning God to intervene to address evil threatening from without but also with respect to the evil within the human heart. God must help us repent; to even get to the point of requesting forgiveness we require divine aid: "We need God's mercy not only when we do penance but also in order that we may do penance."[28] If the only thing that can limit evil is a creative act of God, then the appropriate response to evil is to pray, flinging oneself on God's mercy.

Only the one who can repair evil once and for all can deliver us from it on a daily basis. Augustine emphasizes that we repeatedly require God's aid not only to repent for evil deeds of the past but also to receive forgiveness for them: "We must daily and often pray to the Lord and say, *Forgive us our debts*."[29] In addition to needing God's aid to respond appropriately to the evil in our past, to repent and forgive, we need God to help us avoid moral evil in the future. This assistance for what lies ahead includes both guidance to recognize the right course of action and fortitude to execute what we know to be right. Psalm 27:1 is shorthand for the daily assistance Christ provides: *The Lord is my light and my salvation* (salus). Christ illumines us, so that in his light we may see the right course of action, and heals us, so that we may delight in doing good.[30]

---

28. Augustine, *Enchir.* 22.82 (CCSL 46:95).
29. Augustine, *Enchir.* 21.78 (CCSL 46:93).
30. Augustine, *Enchir.* 21.78.

All this requires more prayer: "So we should pray to God not only that he will forgive us if we have sinned, which is why we say, *Forgive us our debts as we also forgive our debtors,* but also that he will guide us so that we do not sin, which is why we say, *And do not bring us to the time of trial* [Mt 6:13]."[31] Christ's work putting a stop to evil both provides a reason to be confident that God can answer these petitions and gives us the very words to pray as we repeat the prayer he taught. By placing a limit on evil, Christ invites us to acknowledge our own limits and to turn to God in prayer.

Not only prayers of petition, but also prayers of praise are in order given what Christ has accomplished. Though it would be easy to conclude that the presence of evil in the world makes God less good rather than more so, Augustine presses the point that God's way of dealing with evil in Christ makes God's goodness even more obvious than it would have been otherwise. That God can bring good even out of evil shows just how profoundly good God is. "Making good use even of evil creatures," Augustine argues, "befits the one who is supremely good."[32] God's resourcefulness in addressing evil in Christ, his providential plan to bring good out of evil, means that God deserves our praise.

In addition to recommending petition and praise in response to evil, Augustine offers a suggestion for how to diagnose evil that follows from his theologically curbed account of it. Given that the light of Christ is required for us to distinguish good from evil, where should we turn for concrete moral guidance? Augustine points out the dangers of relying on moral intuition to determine the correct course of action. The habitual practice of evil can make even the most serious of sins seem trivial.[33] Desensitization to sin, he observes, is at work not only in the wider culture but within the walls of the church: "So in our days many evils [*multa mala*] ... have come to be openly and habitually practiced, so that we are afraid not only to excommunicate a lay person for them but even to degrade a cleric." How then, should Christians protect against the coarsening of their moral sensibilities? Here Augustine underlines God's provision of Scripture, which

---

31. Augustine, *Enchir. Ench.* 22.81 (CCSL 46:94).

32. Augustine, *Enchir.* 26.100 (CCSL 46:103).

33. "There are also some sins that might be thought very trivial were they not shown in the holy scriptures to be more serious than is thought" (*Enchir.* 21.79).

"give[s] us a standard to measure the seriousness of ... evil."[34] The light of Christ is refracted into the dimmest moral corners of our lives through the lens of holy Scripture. The Christ who puts a stop to evil in a cosmic sense reveals in the Bible the evil that needs to end in a person's everyday behavior. When it comes to dealing with evil, Augustine recommends that we turn to revelation, rather than relying merely on "natural theology that seems amenable to reason," to return to Davies's phrase.

Finally, Augustine recommends a practical response to those struggling with evil that flows from how Christ himself has dealt with it. In a word, this response is to forgive. Just as Christ's work shows us we need God's forgiveness, it also demonstrates our responsibility to forgive others. As with other implications of Christ's work to end evil, Christ points us in the direction of forgiveness both by what he does and by what he says. Augustine's highly paradoxical interpretation of Christ's teaching on the unforgivable sin against the Holy Spirit drives home the paramount importance Augustine accords to forgiveness. For Augustine the only unforgivable sin is failing to "believe that sins are forgiven in the Church."[35] It is illegitimate, he makes clear, to declare moral evil a problem too great for the divine mercy to cover, too severe to permit forgiveness in Christ's church. Christ's own response to evil, both in the form of the forgiveness he extended to humankind on the cross and in the form of his explicit teaching about forgiveness, makes clear that the way to defang moral evil is neither to condone nor to condemn but to forgive.

CONCLUSION

With Augustine's near constant stirring, the simmering pot of the problem of evil boils down to two basic questions. Where does evil come from? and, How can we be delivered from it? As we have seen, the answer to the first question is, "The cause of our evils is the will of a changeable good falling away from the unchangeable good," while the answer to the second is that the cause of redemption is Christ.[36] According to Augustine, then, evil is limited by the good on either side, flanked by creation and new creation.

---

34. Augustine, *Enchir.* 21.79–80 (CCSL 46:93–94).
35. Augustine, *Enchir.* 22.83 (CCSL 46:95).
36. Augustine, *Enchir.* 8.23 (CCSL 46:63).

In the latter part of the *Enchiridion*, as in the latter part of his career, Augustine becomes fixated on how Christ brings about deliverance from evil.[37] What are the preconditions of this work, how does Christ effect it, and what does it do to the human person? Augustine debated these questions endlessly in the Pelagian controversy—literally, as he died before he was able to complete his final tome against Julian. To say that Christ put an end to evil did not mean there was an easy resolution to human reflections about evil. To look to Christ as evil's end was to contemplate a mystery.

Yet, even as it highlights the challenges and unresolved tensions of presenting Christ as the outer limit of evil, Augustine's work reminds his readers of why a christological approach to the problem of evil is absolutely indispensable. While creation always retains a certain kind of logical and ontological priority, there is also a sense in which Christ's work in response to evil possesses a priority of its own, a kind of comprehensiveness, sufficiency, and personal force that creation does not.

In the middle of the *Enchiridion*, there is an extended description of the poetic justice of Christ's work. Whereas one sin of the one man Adam led to the condemnation of the whole human race, so "the one mediator between God and humanity, the man Christ Jesus," undoes and washes away this sin.[38] While as a result of his sin Adam was "driven by a pitiable necessity [*miseranda necessitate*]," Christ responded to the human plight out of a firm and free purpose, "by his merciful will [*miserante ... voluntate*)."[39] Parallels between the first and second Adam abound.

But Augustine is not content to reduce Christ to Adam's inverse, to portray him as the mere flip image of his predecessor. Christ's work introduces an asymmetry between the story of how evil entered the world through one man and how it was purged from the world by the other. Augustine puts it this way, "There is this difference: that one man brought one sin

---

37. Evans identifies a "turning-point" in Augustine's thinking whereby he pivots from a focus on one of these limits to focusing on the other. Early in his career, she argues, Augustine was preoccupied with the question of the origin of evil. As he became embroiled in the Pelagian controversies, his interest shifted to the question of how to escape evil so as to regain the original good. See Evans, *Augustine on Evil*, 148. Grace certainly does loom large in Augustine's later work. It is even fair to speak of a shift from focusing on an approach to evil grounded in creation to an approach grounded in Christ.

38. Augustine, *Enchir.* 14.48 (CCSL 46:75): "Unum mediatorem dei et hominum, hominem Christum Iesum."

39. Augustine, *Enchir.* 14.49 (CCSL 46:76).

into the world, but the other one took away not only that one sin but all the other sins that he found had been added to it." Adam's impact pales in comparison to Christ's since beyond wiping away the stain of original sin that inheres in each person because of Adam's original sin, Christ also "justifies a person who has committed many sins of his own in addition to that one which he has contracted from his origins in common with everybody else."[40] Christ does far more than undo the damage Adam had done; his free gift undoes the damage all of us have done, which is something no mere human being could ever do.

In that Christ's work both includes and goes beyond undoing what Adam did, to give an account of God's response to the problem of evil in Christ is to address the problem of evil more comprehensively than is possible with respect to creation alone. Like the last chapter of a mystery novel, the story of Christ's work tells us how the plot ends even while presupposing the story's beginning.

Sufficiency, as well as comprehensiveness, speaks in favor of according priority to Christ's work when addressing the problem of evil. At one point early on in the *Enchiridion*, Augustine observes,

> If we were obliged to know the causes of the movements of physical objects, there would be nothing more necessary for us to know than the causes of our own health; but since we seek out physicians in our ignorance of them, who cannot see with what great patience we should bear our ignorance of the secrets of the heavens and the earth?[41]

Augustine's point here is that if we are content to dispense with knowledge of the causes affecting our own physical health, then surely our incomplete grasp of the workings of the natural world need not concern us.

This logic applies as well to the cognate issue of spiritual and moral causes. Causes pertaining to spiritual or moral health, like causes pertaining to physical health, are of first importance to a person. Yet in this arena, too, it is possible to seek out a physician while remaining ignorant about the source of a malady. Indeed, one often consults a physician

---

40. Augustine, *Enchir.* 14.50 (CCSL 46:76).
41. Augustine, *Enchir.* 5.16.

precisely because one cannot arrive at a diagnosis without expert assistance. Moreover, a physician's prescription can work even if she keeps the details of the diagnosis under wraps.

As this logic makes clear, however helpful it might be to know the causes of the problem of evil and however "necessary" this knowledge may seem from an existential viewpoint, one need not know where evil comes from or why it exists to be made well. It is possible to be entirely ignorant of the causes of evil and yet be restored to health by the offices of a good physician. Conversely, one might know as much as there is to know about the causes of evil, yet remain fatally infected with it for the lack of a doctor's healing touch. Even the demons believe—and shudder. Christology, then, is more important than protology when it comes to evil in this sense: one is dispensable for health and wholeness while the other is not. [42] Christ's work may not provide an exhaustive explanation of why evil exists, but it does offer a salutary response to the existence of evil.

Finally, while the misfired willing of any changeable good could have resulted in the fall, according to Augustine, only God could have saved the human race from the mire of evil. Evil's origins are human, but its end is divine. When approaching the problem of evil, is not God's personal response to it to be granted a certain kind of priority? Of the two theological bookends that uphold the Christian understanding of evil, one has to do with its origins in a free human decision and the other with its decisive demise because of a free decision that was divine as well as human. The gravitas of the primary agent responsible in the latter case certainly speaks in favor of according greater weight to the latter bookend.

At this point we are in a position to return to the two questions posed at the outset. Was Davies right about Augustine when he included him in a "traditional" group that did not tend to emphasize Christology in dealing with the problem of evil? And was he right that Christology is insufficient for addressing the problem of evil?

By now it should be clear that the answer to the first question is no. Like the contemporary approaches that vexed Davies, Augustine's mature approach to the problem of evil is predominantly christological and also,

---

42. While Augustine does not connect his image of *Enchir.* 5.16 to Christology, he does refer to Christ as physician in *Enchir.* 21.79.

as we have just seen, presupposes at least two reasons why a christological approach, while never to be opposed to an approach "from creation," goes beyond what one can say about the problem of evil drawing on the doctrine of creation alone. That said, two caveats need to be registered.

The first is that Augustine's use of Christology in the *Enchiridion* to respond to the problem of evil is not equivalent to the use one finds in the contemporary approaches about which Davies is concerned. Augustine is preoccupied with moral evil, and his focus is therefore Christ's opposition to and victory over evil, rather than Christ's solidarity with the human race in suffering the evils of injustice. So while it is the case *that* Augustine gives a central role to Christology in addressing the problem of evil, *how* he does so is different from what Davies observes in more recent theology.

The second caveat is that Augustine's approach to the problem of evil is a bit of a moving target. This paper has aimed to describe the approach he takes in the *Enchiridion*, which is representative of his mature view. Treatments of the problem of evil from early in his career, however, do not have the same clarity of christological focus one finds here. Over the course of his career, as within this single work, Augustine's preoccupation switched from metaphysical to moral evil.

The second question raised by Davies's assessment is difficult to address in an absolute way. However, this paper has shown both some of the practical implications for the Christian life of Augustine's christological approach and that Christology is indispensable to addressing the problem of evil. Taking one step further, the *Enchiridion* also demonstrates that Christology deserves a kind of priority in Christian responses to the problem of evil insofar as its comprehensiveness, sufficiency, and personal force surpass what is on offer from any other angle. Given all this, it is perhaps unsurprising that at the end of the day, Augustine—both in the *Enchiridion* and in the overall trajectory of his career—is less concerned with epistemology than with soteriology, less concerned with causes of evil than with its cure, and less concerned with "justifying the ways of God to men" than with God's justification of human beings.

6

AUGUSTINE ON ANIMAL DEATH

Gavin Ortlund

One of the most contested issues in contemporary evangelical debate about the doctrine of creation concerns the prospect of animal death, predation, pain, disease, and extinction before the human fall. Indeed, some claim it is *the* issue. David Snoke, for instance, observes that in his experience, "this is the fundamental issue of Bible interpretation caught up in the debate," and that the interpretation of Genesis 1 is actually "of secondary importance."[1]

Why should animal death (and the related conditions of animal life) be so prominent? Part of the answer may be that, for many people (including me), the question has an emotional component. Part of it doubtless lies in its implication for theodicy and apologetics.[2] More deeply, I would suggest that it is here that we begin to push through the more strictly hermeneutical issues of reading Genesis 1-3 into the deeper theological *consequences* of these different readings. Our position on animal death touches on deeper intuitions about the nature of createdness and fallenness, the character of the prehuman world, and the shape of the biblical narrative. Young-earth, old-earth, and (evangelical) evolutionary creationists all conceive of the Christian story as *creation-fall-redemption*—but their differences involve more than the mere time scale involved in each phase.[3]

---

1. David Snoke, *A Biblical Case for an Old Earth* (Grand Rapids: Baker, 2006), 48.

2. Charles Darwin himself wondered, and he was not the last to do so, "What advantage can there be in the sufferings of millions of the lower animals throughout almost endless time?" Quoted in John C. Munday Jr., "Animal Pain: Beyond the Threshold?," in *Perspectives on an Evolving Creation*, ed. Keith B. Miller (Grand Rapids: Eerdmans, 2003), 450.

3. Here our focus will primarily be on differences between a young-earth creationist view of animal death, on the one hand, and old-earth/evolutionary views, on the other. For an illuminating discussion of the differences between old-earth creationist and evolutionary

It is often claimed that old-earth and evolutionary creationist views represent a capitulation to Darwinian and secular claims, in contrast to the settled consensus of pre-nineteenth-century Christianity. In other words, all Christians believed that animal death was bad until they the claims of modern science put pressure on this conviction. Thus, one prominent young-earth creationist describes his view of creation as the same as that of "Jesus, the apostles, and *virtually all orthodox Christians prior to 1800*," and claims that "the idea of millions of years of animal death, disease, violence, and extinction is utterly incompatible with the Bible's teaching *as well as orthodox Christian teaching for two thousand years.*"[4]

In this paper, however, we draw attention to greater complexity in the historical record by engaging Augustine's view of animal death. There are many other theologians who could be engaged for the same purpose.[5] But Augustine is a particularly helpful voice to consider on this topic since

---

creationist views on this topic, see Kenneth Keathley, J. B. Stump, and Joe Aguirre, *Old Earth or Evolutionary Creation? Discussing Origins with Reasons to Believe and BioLogos*, Biologos Books on Science and Christianity (Downers Grove, IL: InterVarsity, 2017), 68–84.

4. Ken Ham, "Rejoinder," in *Four Views on Creation, Evolution, and Intelligent Design*, ed. J. B. Stump, Counterpoints (Grand Rapids: Zondervan, 2017), 67–69, italics added. In the earlier (1999) book in the same series, the young-earth contributors, John Mark Reynolds and Paul Nelson, appeal to the same problem: "The problem of evil in the world is already hard enough to explain without the addition of millions of years of animal suffering to round it out. What is the justification for all that animal pain?" See Paul Nelson and John Mark Reynolds, "Young-Earth Creationism," in *Three Views on Creation and Evolution*, ed. J. P. Moreland and John Mark Reynolds, Counterpoints (Grand Rapids: Zondervan, 1999), 47.

5. Ambrose expounds God's wisdom in creating carnivorous animals such as lions and bears, and dangerous animals like elephants and poisonous serpents, in his *Hexaemeron* 6.5.30–6.6.39. See Saint Ambrose, *Hexaemeron, Paradise, and Cain and Abel*, trans. John J. Savage, Fathers of the Church 42 (Washington, DC: Catholic University of America Press, 1961), 246–53. Much of Ambrose's material is drawn from Basil, who develops an arsenal of moral lessons for humanity from the animal kingdom, including from carnivorous animals, in his *Hexaemeron* 7.3–9.6. See Basil, *Letters and Selected Works*, ed. Philip Schaff and Henry Wace, trans. Blomfield Jackson, Nicene and Post-Nicene Fathers 8 (Peabody, MA: Hendrickson, 1994), 91–107. In the context of this effort Basil explicitly defends the goodness of venomous and dangerous animals, despite their threat to human life: "Let nobody accuse the Creator of having produced venomous animals, destroyers and enemies of our life. Else let them consider it a crime in the schoolmaster when he disciplines the restlessness of youth by the use of the rod and whip to maintain order" (*Hexaemeron* 9.5). On into the medieval period, Thomas Aquinas maintained that "the nature of animals was not changed by man's sin, as if those whose nature now it is to devour the flesh of others, would then have lived on herbs, like the lion and falcon." See *Summa Theologica* I, q. 96, art. 1, trans. Fathers of the English Dominican Province (Notre Dame: Christian Classics, 1948), 486. Likewise, earlier he quotes Augustine to oppose the view that there ought to have been nothing injurious to humanity before the fall (*Summa Theologica* I, q. 72, 352). I am grateful to my friend Joel Chopp for directing me to several of these references.

he regularly faced the Manichaean criticism of the alleged evils of the animal kingdom in relation to their dualistic cosmology. It is striking that Augustine did not attribute such phenomena to the human fall, but vigorously defended the current state of the animal kingdom as a reflection of the goodness and wisdom of God. In fact, as we will see, Augustine devoted considerable energy to expounding the goodness of things such as worms, flies, ants, rats, fleas, frogs, larger predatory mammals, thorns and thistles, physical pain, and death itself.

What led Augustine to emphasize the goodness of insects and carnivores at such length, and with such conviction? Developing an overview of his thought on this point may serve not only to hamper the young-earth appeal to historical continuity, but more deeply to probe the nature of createdness, and in so doing deepen and nuance Christian hope in the face of suffering.[6]

We will probe two Augustinian principles in turn: temporal beauty (which will help us understand why Augustine thinks animal death is good) and perspectival prejudice (which will help us understand why Augustine thinks animal death *appears* bad).

TEMPORAL BEAUTY

As is well-known, Augustine holds that *human* death came into existence as a consequence of the fall of Adam and Eve. But he does not regard this event as the origin of death as such. Thus, when Augustine describes the effects of the human fall, he does not envision that Adam and Eve through their act of sin spread death and corruption to the animal kingdom, spoiling an unspotted, deathless, herbivorous environment. Just the opposite: at their fall, Adam and Eve "contract" the death that was already present around them in the animal kingdom. Referring to their eating the fruit in Genesis 3, Augustine writes:

> By this deed, in fact, they forfeited the wonderful condition, which was to be bestowed upon them through the mystical virtue in the

---

6. Obviously other considerations will be necessary to develop a full response to the challenge of natural evil theodicy. I trace out some of the literature in this vein, and provide a fourfold taxonomy of different responses to the challenge of prehuman natural evil, in my "On the Fall of Angels and the Falleness of Nature: An Evangelical Hypothesis Regarding Natural Evil," *Evangelical Quarterly* 87, no. 2 (2015): 114–36.

tree of life. In this condition it would have been impossible for them
to be tried by disease or altered by age. ... When they forfeited this
condition, then, their bodies contracted that liability to disease and
death which is present in the flesh of animals.[7]

But if human sin did not introduce death and disease to the world, why is
it a part of God's good creation?

Augustine is well aware of this problem. In *The City of God* he references
how the Manichees find fault with "fire, frost, and wild beasts" because
they threaten "this thin-blooded and frail mortality of our flesh." Augustine
faults the Manichees for failing to consider how admirable these things are
in their own natures, and how "beautifully adjusted" to the rest of creation.
Moreover, their threat to humanity often depends on their misuse—even
many poisons, Augustine points out, are "wholesome and medicinal" when
used properly. In addition, Augustine faults the Manichees for breaching
humility by passing judgment on what they do not understand. "Divine
providence admonishes us not foolishly to vituperate things, but to investigate their utility with care." When we cannot find any utility with a part
of God's creation, we should assume that there is one that lies beyond our
knowledge. In fact, he asserts that the very concealment of the use of something may be for the purpose of "a levelling of our pride."[8]

But as he proceeds, Augustine goes beyond merely cautioning judgments against the animal kingdom. He is not reluctantly at peace with
predatory animals; nor does he regard insect life as a neutral feature of
God's world. Rather, he affirms animal death as a beautiful part of the way
God has made the world, for which God should be praised. In particular, he
develops a vision of the world in which the passing into nonexistence of

---

7. Augustine, *Gen. litt.* 11.32.42 (CSEL 28:1, 365–66). Citations of Augustine's works are
generally drawn from the critical edition of Augustine's Latin text in CSEL and are listed
as follows: CSEL, volume and part, page number. Any exceptions to this practice, such as
quotations from Augustine's sermons, are indicated in the relevant footnote. I have generally
relied on the translations of Edmund Hill in *The Works of Saint Augustine: A Translation for the
21st Century*, with the following exceptions. For the *Confessiones*, I have used R. S. Pine-Coffin,
Saint Augustine, *Confessions* (New York: Penguin, 1961); for *Civitate Dei*, I have used Marcus
Dods, Saint Augustine, *The City of God* (New York: Modern Library, 2000); for *De Libero Arbitrio*,
I have used Anna S. Benjamin and L. H. Hackstaff, *On Free Choice of the Will* (Upper Saddle
River, NJ: Prentice Hall, 1964).

8. Augustine, *Civ.* 11:22 (CSEL 40:1, 542–43).

some created things, including animals, displays the beauty of successive seasons in God's creation. For instance, he maintains:

> It is ridiculous to condemn the faults of beasts and of trees, and other such mortal and mutable things as are void of intelligence, sensation, or life, even though these faults should destroy their corruptible nature; for these creatures received, at their Creator's will, an existence fitting them, by passing away and giving place to others, to secure that lowest form of beauty, the beauty of seasons, which in its own place is a requisite part of the world.[9]

What does he mean by the "lowest form of beauty" here? He is drawing on a distinction throughout his writings between the spiritual creation, which shares in God's immutability, and the lower creation, which is mutable and thus exists by the passing of one thing into another. Thus, when commenting on God's blessing to the animals to "multiply" in Genesis 1:22 in his literal commentary, Augustine explains "Because they were created weak and mortal, they might preserve their kind by giving birth."[10] Then, in the context of commenting on the assertion "and God saw that it was good" throughout Genesis 1, Augustine articulates a distinction between abiding and transient created objects: "Some things, you see, abide by soaring over the whole rolling wheel of time in the widest range of holiness under God; while other things do so according to the limits of their time, and thus is through things giving way to and taking the place of one another that the beautiful tapestry of the ages of woven."[11] Augustine sees this process of mutable creatures passing away and replacing one another as inferior kind of beauty—but beautiful nonetheless.

In his *De libero arbitrio*, Augustine develops this view:

> It is foolish for us to say that temporal objects ought not to pass away. They have been placed in the order of the universe in such a way that, unless they do pass away, future objects cannot succeed to past ones, and only thus can the whole beauty of times past, present, and future be accomplished in their own kind. They use what they

---

9. Augustine, *Civ.* 12.4 (CSEL 40.1, 571).
10. Augustine, *Gen. imp.* 15.50 (CSEL 28:1, 494).
11. Augustine, *Gen. litt.* 1.8.14 (CSEL 28:1, 11).

have received and return it to Him to whom they owe their existence and greatness. The man who grieves that these things pass away ought to listen to his own speech, to see if he thinks the complaint that he makes is just and proceeds from prudence. ... In the case of objects which pass away because they have been granted only a limited existence in order that everything may be accomplished in its time, no one is right to blame this deficiency.[12]

Here Augustine reasons that God has the right to withdraw the existence of temporal objects, since he was the one who gave it in the first place. He also observes that temporal objects must pass away in order to make space for new ones (for instance, if no animal species ever went extinct, far fewer kinds of animals would be created, and if no individual animals ever died, far fewer actual animals would be created). All this entails, for Augustine, that we are wrong to sit in judgment on the passing away of created objects as though this were a blameworthy aspect of God's creation. On the contrary, this seasonal progression in God's creation contains a kind of beauty ("the beautiful tapestry of the ages").

This language of seasonal beauty suggests as a possible analogy for Augustine's idea the four seasons of the year: winter, spring, summer, fall. There is a kind of beauty in each of these seasons, considered in isolation: white snow is beautiful, for instance, as are colorful autumn leaves. But there is also a different and deeper kind a kind of beauty in the larger whole of which they are all a part, and each particular season would be less beautiful if it were extracted from this gradual larger pattern. For instance, we appreciate autumn leaves precisely because they follow and replace green summer leaves, and every child knows that "always winter and never Christmas" in *The Lion, the Witch, and the Wardrobe* is no fun. But this larger beauty (seasonal beauty) can only be accomplished by the changing of one season into another—that is, by the cessation of the lesser beauty of each part. Unless the leaves fall off, they cannot grow back again; unless the snow melts, we have no spring greenery.

Augustine applies this language of transient/temporal/seasonal beauty not only to the animal kingdom wholesale, but to various particular

---

12. Augustine, *Lib.* 3.15 (CSEL 74, 125–26).

creatures, including the ones we often find unpleasant. At one point in his
De vera religione he refers to the smaller creatures such as insects as "break-
able beauties" (*pulchritudines corruptibiliores*), claiming, "Let us not be surprised at my stilling calling them beauties," citing Romans 13:1 ("all order
is from God") to establish that beauty is inherent in all order. Augustine
continues: "We are bound to admit that a weeping man is better than a
rejoicing worm, and yet I am not lying when I say that I can say volumes
in praise of the worm." Specifically, Augustine praises the worm's "bright
color, the smooth round shape of its body, the first sections fitting into the
middle ones, the middles ones fitting into those at the end, all observing
the aim of unity according to the lowliness of their nature, nothing being
formed from one part which does not correspond in parallel dimensions
with another." Augustine also marvels at its ability to move rhythmically,
aim toward what suits it, and avoid danger. Perhaps anticipating that not all
of his readers will share his intuition that worms are beautiful, Augustine
then goes even further, asserting that "many have spoken most truly and
eloquently in praise of ashes and dung."[13]

In his sermons as well, Augustine praises the orderly nature of "the
tiniest and least of living mites ... the seeds, roots, trunks, branches, leaves,
flowers, fruits of countless trees and herbs, from nature's secret stores."[14]
He sees all of these parts of God's creation as evidences of the magnificent and "omnificent" (Latin: *omnifica*; he apparently develops this word
as a superlative of magnificent) wisdom of God. He proceeds to warn his
listeners:

> It is surely the last word in absurdity to deny in great matters that
> divine provision and forethought which we admire in small ones.
> ... Let us therefore please have no hesitation believing that was
> seems to be messy and disordered in human affairs is governed,
> not by no plan at all, but rather by an altogether loftier one, and
> by a more all-embracing divine order that can be grasped by our
> human littleness.[15]

---

13. Augustine, *Ver. rel.* 41.77 (CSEL 77, 56).

14. Augustine, *Sermon* 29.7, in *Sermons III.11*, ed. John E. Rotelle, trans. Edmund Hill, *Works
of Saint Augustine: A Translation for the 21st Century* (Hyde Park, NY: New City, 1997), 58.

15. Augustine, *Sermon* 29.7, in *Sermons III.11*, 58.

Evidently it is not just post-Darwinian Christians who can be dis-
turbed by the apparent *messiness* and *disorder* of the natural world—and
the impression of purposelessness it engenders. The differences between
Augustine's time and ours therefore need not render less relevant his warning that God may have "loftier" and "more all-embracing" purposes that lie
beyond the comprehension of "human littleness." On this point Augustine
represents a different set of instincts than those modern skeptics who
wield the quip of J. B. S. Haldane to undermine the plausibility of theism:
"God must have an inordinate fondness of beetles."[16]

In finished literal commentary, Augustine poses the question of
whether "the minutest animals" were created in the original establishment of things, or whether they are the result of the "putrefaction conse-
quent upon material things being perishable." Augustine notes that such
animals are typically bred from sores of living bodies, or from garbage,
rotting corpses, or some other rotting material. Augustine affirms, "We
cannot possibly say that there are any of them of which God is not the creator."[17] Augustine then establishes this claim by arguing that all creatures,
however small, reflect the wisdom of the Creator. Far from being outside
the scope of God's goodness and wisdom, the activity of insects gives us
all more reason to praise him:

> All things, after all, have in them a certain worth or grace of nature,
> each of its own kind, so that in these minute creatures there is even
> more for us to wonder at as we observe them, and so to praise the
> almighty craftsman for them more rapturously than ever. ... If we
> pay close attention we are more amazed at the agile flight of a fly
> than at the stamina of a sturdy mule on the march; and the coop-
> erative labors of tiny ants strike us as far more wonderful than the
> colossal loads that can be carried by camels.[18]

Augustine proceeds to argue that some insects were created at the original creation, while those that are generated from the body of animals
were not, unless they were somehow "seeded" into the animals to arise

16. The quotation is disputed; see the discussion in K. N. Ganeshaiah, "Haldane's God and
the Honoured Beetles: The Cost of a Quip," *Current Science* 74, no. 8 (1998): 656–60.

17. Augustine, *Gen. litt.* 3.14.22 (CSEL 28:1, 79).

18. Augustine, *Gen. litt.* 3.14.22 (CSEL 28:1, 79–80).

later.[19] Augustine does not develop this ambiguous suggestion or pose an alternative possibility.

Augustine's instinct to praise God for insects is also evident in the *Confessions*, where he bemoans that worship is not his first instinct while he is sitting at home watching flies getting eaten by lizards and spiders:

> What excuse can I make for myself when often, as I sit at home, I cannot turn my eyes from the sight of a lizard catching flies or a spider entangling them as they fly into her web? Does it make any difference that these are only small animals? It is true that the sight of them inspires me to praise you for the wonders of your creation and the order in which you have disposed all things, but I am not intent upon your praises when I first begin to watch.[20]

Elsewhere Augustine extends his defense of the goodness of insects to larger predatory animals as well, and applies his conception of temporal beauty not only to animal death, but to animal pain and predation as well. Thus, Augustine maintains that animal predation should not be regarded as bad, since it plays a larger role in God's good and wise government of the world. For instance, in his literal commentary on Genesis, Augustine tackles the "commonly asked" question of whether poisonous and dangerous animals were created after human sin as a punishment, or had already been created as harmless and simply began to do sinners harm after the fall. He argues that if they existed before the fall, they would not have harmed human beings—but he sees the peaceful coexistence of unfallen humans and predatory animals as entirely possible, citing the examples of Daniel in the lions' den in Daniel 6 and Paul being unharmed by the deadly viper in Acts 28. Later he envisions the possibility of Adam in his prefallen state guarding Eden against wild beasts—he finds it implausible that in this scenario the beasts could be a threat to him, but does not rule it out. But then Augustine anticipates this question: "Someone is going to say: 'then why do the beasts injure each other, though they neither have any sins, so that this kind of thing could be called punishment, nor by such trials do they gain at all in virtue?' "[21]

---

19. Augustine, *Gen. litt.* 3.14.23 (CSEL 28:1, 80).

20. Augustine, *Conf.* 10.35 (CSEL 33, 269–70).

21. Augustine, *Gen. litt.* 3.15.24; 8.10.21; 3.16.25 (CSEL 28:1, 80–81, 246).

Here Augustine has stated the classic theological problem of "natural evil" as applied to the animal kingdom as clearly as C. S. Lewis puts it in his *The Problem of Pain*.[22] Augustine's response to this question involves an appeal to principle of temporal beauty that we explored above:

> For the simple reason, of course, that some are the proper diet of others. Nor can we have any right to say, "There shouldn't be some on which others feed." All things, you see, as long as they continue to be, have their own proper measures, numbers, and destinies. So all things, properly considered, are worthy of acclaim; nor is it without some contribution in its own way to the temporal beauty of the world that they undergo change by passing from one thing into another. This may escape fools; those making progress have some glimmering of it; to the perfect it is as clear as daylight.[23]

The forcefulness of Augustine's conviction here is striking. He not only defends animal predation, but he rebukes the tendency to sit in judgment on it as an illegitimate and even foolish impulse.

Ultimately, Augustine divides the entire animal kingdom into three categories in their relation to humanity: some are beneficial, some are pernicious, and some are superfluous. He argues that pernicious animals serve a spiritual purpose in relation to humanity, helping us to long for heaven. They are here either to punish or frighten us, "so that instead of loving and desiring this life, subject to so many dangers and trials, we should set our hearts on another better one, where there is total freedom from all worries and anxieties." As for the superfluous ones, we should not call them into question, for "they contribute to the completion of this universe, which is not only much bigger than our homes, but much better as well; God manages it after all, much better than any of us can manage

---

22. C. S. Lewis, *The Problem of Pain*, in *The Complete C. S. Lewis Signature Classics* (New York: HarperOne, 2002), 628: "The problem of animal suffering is appalling; not because the animals are so numerous (for, as we have seen, no more pain is felt when a million suffer than when one suffers) but because the Christian explanation of human pain cannot be extended to animal pain. So far as we know beasts are incapable either of sin or virtue: therefore they can neither deserve pain nor be improved by it."

23. Augustine, *Gen. litt.* 3.16.25 (CSEL 28:1, 81–82). The reference to "measures, numbers, and weights" here likely draws from Wisdom 11:20: "You have arranged all things in measure, number, and weight."

our homes."[24] The introduction of this comparison between the universe and a human home, though serving the rhetorical effect of cautioning human judgments against creation, also reflects Augustine's vision of the universe as a place of order and intrinsic value that God "manages" wisely. Augustine concludes by emphasizing that although different creatures call for a different response from human beings, they should all cause us to praise the Creator:

> So then, make use of the useful ones, be careful with the pernicious ones, let the superfluous ones be. In all of them, though, when you observe their measure and numbers and order, look for the crafts-man. ... In this way you will perhaps find more genuine satisfaction when you praise God in the tiny little ant down on the ground, than when you are crossing a river high up, let us say, on an elephant.[25]

Augustine admits his own personal uncertainty about why God made certain animals. But he also maintains that this does not inhibit his ability to find them beautiful: "I, however, must confess that I have not the slightest idea why mice and frogs were created, and flies and worms; yet I can still see that they are all beautiful in their own specific kind." He emphasizes that there is a beauty in the organization of all living creatures, even the tiniest ones: "There is not a single living creature, after all, in whose body I will not find, when I reflect upon it, that its measures and numbers and order are geared to a harmonious unity." The language of *measure and number and order* is drawn from Wisdom of Solomon 11:20, though here Augustine has substituted "order" for "weight," in line with his emphasis. If the Manichees were to observe this orderliness in even the tiniest creatures, Augustine argues, "they wouldn't go on boring us to death, but by reflecting themselves on all such beauties from the highest to the lowest would in all cases praise God the craftsman." Augustine acknowledges that the lower animals cause a certain kind of offense to humanity, but he introduces a distinction between that which is offensive to reason versus that which is

---

24. Augustine, *Gen. Man.* 1.16.26 (CSEL 91, 93).
25. Augustine, *Gen. Man.* 1.16.26 (CSEL 91, 93–94).

merely offensive to our "carnal senses."[26] The lower animals, such as mice and frogs, or insects, are only offensive to our carnal senses, not to reason.

This distinction between carnal senses and reason relates to a common theme in Augustine's treatment of animal death: the danger of making self-referential judgment. In *The City of God*, Augustine warns against reducing the value of animals to their utility for humanity, and in particular with denigrating those creatures we would foolishly want to abolish from existence altogether: "Who, e.g., would not rather have bread in his house than mice, gold than fleas?" For Augustine, finding fault with such creatures is not a judgment resulting from wisdom, but rather a judgment resulting from pleasure, need, or desire. Thus, Augustine maintains, if we desire to get rid of those animals that annoy us (such as mice or fleas), we may be motivated impulsively, failing to taking into account their role in the larger created order.[27]

Augustine also emphasizes that animal death provides humanity with many "salutary admonitions" that may contribute to our understanding of salvation. Specifically, he argues that by observing the struggle of animals to secure their bodily, temporal welfare, we might learn what trouble we should take in pursuing our everlasting spiritual welfare. We can learn such lessons from the entire animal kingdom, "from the biggest elephants down to the smallest little worms." Augustine emphasizes in particular the salutary value of bodily pain in animals, which he regards as a "great and wonderful power of the soul."[28]

Elsewhere Augustine pushes back further against the Manichaean intuition that pain is necessarily evil. In his *De natura boni*, he argues that pain exists precisely because our natures are good: "Even pain, however, which some persons consider especially evil, whether it is in the mind or in the body, cannot exist except in good natures." Augustine observes that pain results from resisting that which is destructive—when the will resists a greater power, it produces mental pain, and when the senses resist a more powerful body, it produces bodily pain. Augustine therefore distinguishes between different results from pain: "When it is forced to something better,

---

26. Augustine, *Gen. Man.* 1.16.26 (CSEL 91–93).

27. Augustine, *Civ.* 11.16 (CSEL 40.1, 535).

28. Augustine, *Gen. litt.* 3.16.25 (CSEL 28:1, 82).

pain is beneficial; when it is forced to something worse, it is harmful." Nonetheless, Augustine emphasizes that there are many worse evils that occur without pain.[29] In his allegorical commentary on Genesis, similarly, Augustine speculates that pain in child-bearing is not itself a consequence of sin, but rather a function of being mortal, since female animals also give birth in pain.[30]

When Augustine turns in his literal commentary to address whether thorns, thistles, and trees that produce no fruit existed before the fall, he again urges caution. Quoting the reference to "fruit-bearing trees" in Genesis 1:11, Augustine stipulates that the word "fruit" refers to the things' use for those who enjoy, and emphasizes that there are many different kinds of uses that the things of the earth have. He distinguishes between obvious uses that people can observe for themselves and the hidden ones we must learn the experts. We must therefore be careful in our judgment of what a "fruitless" tree is. When it comes to thorns and thistles, Augustine quotes the curse of Genesis 3:18: "Thorns and thistles shall it bring forth for you."[31] But Augustine cautions that this verse does not give anyone warrant to conclude that thorns and thistles began with the fall. Augustine had articulated this view in his earlier allegorical work, in response to Manichaean objections.[32] But here he reasons, "Many uses can be found for seeds of this kind too, and so they could have had their place without any penal inconvenience to the man." Augustine sees several ways to under-stand this possibility. For instance, thorns and thistles could have been produced specifically in the field that man was given to cultivate. Or they could have been produced in all places, but simply become noxious *to the man* after the fall.[33] In all this, Augustine displays caution about exaggerat-ing the effects of the fall as producing an absolute contrast. He sees the fall not as originating human pain and labor, but rather as aggravating them.

Augustine's emphasis here was different from the approach of other fathers, such as Basil (329–379) and Ambrose (ca. 340–397), who interpreted the threat of "thorns and thistles" in Genesis 3:18 as a metaphor for the

---

29. Augustine, *De Natura Boni* 20 (CSEL 25.2, 863).

30. Augustine, *Gen. Man.* 2.19.29 (CSEL 91, 150).

31. Augustine, *Gen. litt.* 3.18.27–28 (CSEL 28:1, 83).

32. Augustine, *Gen. Man.* 1.13.19 (CSEL 91, 85–86).

33. Augustine, *Gen. litt.* 3.18.28 (CSEL 28:1, 84).

deterioration of postlapsarian life.[34] Yet Augustine's view became more common in his wake of influence—it is picked up, for instance, in the fifth century by Claudius Marius Victorius and the Roman emperor Avitus, and persisted into the medieval era (e.g., in Peter Lombard's [1096–1160] *Sentences*) despite Augustine's earlier opposing view (from his *De Genesi contra Manichaeos*) being mistakenly attributed to Augustine's literal commentary in Bede's (ca. 673–735) writings.[35]

PERSPECTIVAL PREJUDICE

But all this raises a question: If animal death contributes to the beauty of the world, why does it trouble us so much? If it is beautiful, why do we often find it ugly? To answer this, we must consider a broader principle of Augustine's theodicy, which we will call, following William Mann's terminology, "perspectival prejudice." Mann does not spend much time developing this idea, but defines it as "failing to see how local privations, especially the ones that affect us, contribute to the good of the whole."[36] The challenge of perspectival prejudice is a huge part of Augustine's thought on this topic, and comes up again and again in his writings.

That this idea is present in Augustine's mind following his rejection of Manicheism is evidenced by his claim in *De ordine*, the first book written after his conversion:

Whoever narrow-mindedly considers this life by itself alone is repelled by its enormous foulness, and turns away in sheer disgust. But, if he raises the eyes of the mind and broadens his field of vision and surveys all things as a whole, then he will find nothing unarranged, unclassed, or unassigned to its own place.[37]

---

34. See Karla Pollmann, " 'And without Thorn the Rose'? Augustine's Interpretation of Genesis 3:18 and the Intellectual Tradition," in *Genesis and Christian Theology*, ed. Nathan MacDonald, Mark W. Elliott, and Grant Macaskill (Grand Rapids: Eerdmans, 2012), 217–18.

35. Pollmann, " 'And without Thorn,' " 222–25. In Bede's commentary on Genesis 3:17–18, a quotation from Augustine's *De Genesi contra Manichaeos* is apparently falsely attributed to Augustine's *De Genesi ad litteram*.

36. William E. Mann, "Augustine on Evil and Original Sin," in *The Cambridge Companion to Augustine*, ed. David Vincent Meconi and Eleonore Stump, 2nd ed. (Cambridge: Cambridge University Press, 2014), 103.

37. Augustine, *De ordine* 2.4.11 (CSEL 63, 154). Translation from N. Joseph Torchia, *Creatio Ex Nihilo and the Theology of Augustine: The Anti-Manichaean Polemic and Beyond*, American University Studies 205 (New York: Peter Lang, 1999), 172.

Here Augustine emphasizes the *organization* of creation as an answer to its unpleasantness—what undercuts the reaction of "disgust" at the "foulness" of the world is specifically the recognition that there is nothing that is "unarranged, unclassed, or unassigned to its own place." The acuteness of Augustine's sensitivity to this challenge is reflected in his language here ("enormous foulness ... sheer disgust")—whatever else we might say, we cannot dismiss Augustine as failing to take seriously the weight of the problem.

As he develops this notion throughout his subsequent writings, Augustine draws together his rebuke against narrowness of vision with a rebuke against self-referential judgment. In other words, the problem of perspectival prejudice involves not merely people failing to interpret local phenomena in relation to the whole, but people failing to take their own location and involvement in what they are judging into account. Thus, after describing animal and plant death as constituting the "lowest form of beauty" in *The City of God*, Augustine observes that "of this order the beauty does not strike us, because by our mortal frailty we are so involved in a part of it, that we cannot perceive the whole, in which these fragments that offend us are harmonized with the most accurate fitness and beauty."[38] Here the problem of not seeing the whole is drawn out of the problem of our own self-involvement in the situation we are seeking to judge: it is because our own "mortal frailty" involves us in this form of beauty that we cannot see the bigger picture. Augustine proceeds by rebuking the rashness of the Manichees, who judge animals self-referentially by their utility rather than by their nature:

> But in this way of estimating, they may find fault with the sun itself; for certain criminals or debtors are sentenced by the judges to be set in the sun. Therefore, it is not with respect to our convenience or comfort, but with respect to their own nature, that the creatures are glorifying to their Artificer. ... We must not listen, then, to those who praise the light of fire but find fault with its heat, judging it not by its nature, but by their comfort or convenience. For they wish to see, but not to be burnt.

---

38. Augustine, *Civ.* 12.4 (CSEL 40.1, 571).

Augustine proceeds to argue that God is to be praised for every nature he has made, rather than blamed for their faults.[39]

In his allegorical commentary on Genesis, Augustine develops a metaphor to emphasize this same point. In context, Augustine is dealing with the Manichaean objection that God has made so many animals that are not necessary for human beings and that many of them are "pernicious and to be feared."[40] His response is worth quoting at length:

> But when they say things like that, they are failing to understand how all these things are beautiful to their maker and craftsman, who has a use for them all in his management of the whole universe which is under the control of his sovereign law. After all, if a layman enters a mechanic's workshop, he will see many instruments there whose purpose he is ignorant of, and which, if he is more than usually silly, he thinks are superfluous. What's more, if he carelessly tumbles into the furnace, or cuts himself on a sharp steel implement when he handles it wrongly, then he reckons that there are many pernicious and harmful things there too. The mechanic, however, who knows the use of everything there, has a good laugh at his silliness, takes no notice of his inept remarks, and just presses on with the work in hand. And yet people are so astonishingly foolish, that with a human craftsman they won't dream of objecting to things whose function they are ignorant of, but will assume when they notice them that they are necessary, and put there for various uses, and yet will have the audacity, looking round this world of which God is the acknowledged founder and administrator to find fault with many things which they cannot see the point of.[41]

Here Augustine goes beyond merely rebuking self-referential judgments about things such as predatory animals, inviting as an alternative the consideration of God's judgments—some parts of the natural order might seem superfluous or even dangerous to us, and yet appear "beautiful to their maker and craftsman." In the metaphor Augustine employs to

39. Augustine, *Civ.* 12.5 (CSEL 40.1, 572–73).
40. Augustine, *Gen. Man.* 1.16.25 (CSEL 91, 91).
41. Augustine, *Gen. Man.* 1.16.25 (CSEL 91, 91–92).

make this point, God is the mechanic, we are the layman, and the world is God's workshop. What is emphasized here is the limitation of human knowledge, and the qualitative difference between God's relation to the natural world and our relation to it. To put it simply, God knows how the world works, and we do not. He is the mechanic; we are the layman. Sitting in judgment on the world is therefore a very grave error, which Augustine here depicts with strong language as the result of carelessness, resulting from audacity and silliness, and inviting laughter as "astonishingly foolish."

Throughout his writings, Augustine utilizes a number of other metaphors to develop his conception of perspectival prejudice. In his allegorical commentary on Genesis, for example, Augustine observes that individual created works are called "good," while the entire creation is called "very good." From this Augustine develops the principle that the beauty of the whole world is greater than that of the individual parts, comparing this to a human body, in which individual parts (like eyes, nose, cheeks, etc.) are beautiful, but the beauty of the entire body working together is greater. Augustine then applies this image to the created world: "Such is the force and power of completeness and unity, that many things, all good in themselves, are only found satisfying when they come together and fit into one universal whole. The universal, the universe, of course, takes its name from unity." Augustine then introduces the further metaphor of a speech, in which the individual parts are meaningless unless they are heard in relation to the whole. This inability to interpret the parts in relation to the whole is at the root of the Manichaean error: "if the Manichees would only consider this truth, they would praise God the author and founder of the whole universe, and they would fit any particular part that distresses them because of our mortal condition into the beauty of the universal whole, and thus would see how God made all things not only good, but very good."[42]

This speech metaphor recurs in *The City of God*, where Augustine compares evil in creation to verbal antitheses (which he also calls oppositions or contrapositions), which he regards as "among the most elegant of the ornaments of speech." After quoting from 2 Corinthians 6:7-10 as an example of this literary phenomenon, he concludes: "As, then, these oppositions of contraries lend beauty to the language, so the beauty of the course of

---

42. Augustine, *Gen. Man.* 1.21.32 (CSEL 91, 100–101).

this world is achieved by the opposition of contraries, arranged, as it were, by an eloquence not of words, but of things."[43]

In his *De musica*, written around 391, Augustine combines the metaphors of a statue, a solder, and a poem to convey the temporal beauty and "harmonious succession" of God's creation:

> Terrestrial things are subject to celestial, and their time circuits join together in harmonious succession for a poem of the universe. And so many of these things seem to us disordered and perturbed, because we have been sewn into their order according to our merits, not knowing what a beautiful thing divine providence purposes for us. For, if someone should be put as a statue in an angle of the most spacious and beautiful building, he could not perceive the beauty of the building he himself is a part of. Nor can the solder in the front line of battle get the order of the whole army. And in a poem, if syllables should live and perceive only so long as they sound, the harmony and beauty of the connected work would in no way please them. For they could not see or approve the whole, since it would be fashioned and perfected by the very passing away of these singulars.[44]

These images once again signal the danger of self-referential judgment: it is the *location* of the statue in an "angle" of the building, and of the solider in the "front line of battle," that makes a detached, comprehensive view impossible. Similarly, we are a part of the universe ("sewn" into it) and thus do not see it as God (who is not a part of it) sees it. This is why "things seem to us disordered and perturbed"—it would not appear this way to us if we did not suffer from this limited perspective, but instead could see "knowing what a beautiful thing divine providence purposes for us."

If the statue and building metaphors here draw attention to our spatial limitations, the poetry metaphor draws attention to our temporal limitations. This metaphor recurs in Augustine's *De vera religione*, which was written around the same time as *De musica*. Here Augustine contrasts the resurrection body, which will not be subject to decay, with our current

---

43. Augustine, *Civ.* 11.18 (CSEL 40.1, 537–38).

44. Augustine, *De Musica* 6.11; translation from Torchia, *Creatio Ex Nihilo*, 171.

bodily condition, which belongs to "the least and lowest beauty of bodies." This is that form of beauty that is "carried along in a successive order … because it cannot have everything at once and all together; but, while some things give way and others take their place, they fill up the number of time-bound forms and shapes into a single beauty."[45] Then Augustine uses an illustration to argue that this lower form of beauty, although much inferior to our resurrection status, is not on that account bad:

> The fact that all this is transitory does not make it evil. For this is the way in which a line of poetry is beautiful, even though two syllables of it cannot possibly in any way be spoken simultaneously. I mean that the second one cannot be profound unless the first one has passed away, and so in due course you reach the end, so that the last syllable is heard, without the previous ones being heard simultaneously, it still completes the form and beauty of the meter by being woven in with the previous ones.[46]

What is particularly emphasized by Augustine's poetry metaphor is the *successive* nature of God's purposes and activity in his creation. A few chapters later Augustine refers to "a certain time-bound method of healing" of the human race, and how God gradually brings about his purposes for humanity over the course of many different ages. Thus, Augustine conceives of God's purposes for the natural order as a kind of poem, proceeding verse by verse toward its end. To object to particular instances of pain or discord in the world as evil is therefore comparable to criticizing the literary quality of a poem before you have heard how it ends. Augustine even goes so far as to assert that those who have no appreciation for this aspect of divine providence are "behaving as absurdly as if someone in the recitation of some well-known poem wanted to listen to just one single syllable all the time."[47]

Augustine does not share the intuition occasionally found in contemporary views that if creation is good, it must be perfect. Nor does he understand the goodness of creation in static terms. Rather, there is a

---

45. Augustine, *Ver. rel.* 21.41 (CSEL 77, 29).
46. Augustine, *Ver. rel.* 22.42 (CSEL 77, 29–30).
47. Augustine, *Ver. rel.* 22.45, 43 (CSEL 77, 30, 32); see also *Ver. rel.* 26.48–49 (CSEL 77, 34–35).

developmental component to Augustine's conception of the goodness of creation. At one point in his finished commentary, for instance, in connection to his conception of *seminales rationales*, he asks, "If God were to make anything imperfect, which he would then himself bring to perfection, what would be reprehensible about such an idea?"[48] The logic here involves the assumption that the ultimate end of God's purposes must be considered in order to make judgment about the process leading to that end. This is not exactly tantamount to the claim that the ends justify the means—for one thing, Augustine does seem to think of the means as "bad" and in need of *justification* so much as "imperfect" and in need of *development*, and this is an important distinction. Nonetheless, his comment does seem to envision a developmental model of creation and the necessity of considering its ultimate end to determine and understand its goodness.

Later in *De vera religione* he returns to spatial imagery. Again here Augustine casts various unpleasant phenomena in nature as a lower form of beauty—indeed, at the very edge of what may be called beautiful: "Divine providence is at hand to show us both that this lowest kind of beauty is not bad ... and yet to make it clear that it is at the outermost edge of beauty by mixing in with it pains and diseases and distortion of limbs and dark coloring and rivalries and quarrels of spirits."[49] But God uses these unpleasant elements to provide warnings and training to the good, so that "in this way all are directed by their functions, their duties and their ends toward the beauty of the whole universe, so that if what shocks us in the part is considered together with the whole, it gives us entire satisfaction." Augustine then introduces new illustrations to advance this point:

> After all, in making a judgment on a building we ought not to consider just one single corner; or in assessing the beauty of human beings just their hair; or with good public speakers just the movements of their fingers; or with the course of the moon just its changes during three days. These things, you see, which are at the lowest level precisely because, while complete in themselves, as

---

48. Augustine, *Gen. litt.* 2.15.30 (CSEL 28:1, 210).
49. Augustine, *Ver. rel.* 40.75 (CSEL 77, 54).

parts they are incomplete, are to be considered with the wholes they are part of, if we wish to make a right judgment.[50]

In his following commentary Augustine adds the further image of how "the color black in a picture becomes beautiful within the whole," using this to describe God's providential oversight over good and evil. These metaphors emphasize the utter foolishness of passing judgment on God's creation, even those aspects that are at the "outermost edge of beauty." To judge the beauty of a human being only by looking at their hair, or to judge a speech by only looking at the speaker's fingers—these are not only imperfect judgements, but utterly absurd ones. So Augustine urges with our judgments when we are shocked by particular aspects of God's creation.

Augustine's conception of evil as essentially a privation plays an important role in his appeal to the principal of perspectival prejudice, particularly as this appeal plays out in metaphor. In his unfinished literal commentary, Augustine refers to those "lacks and absences" that "have their due place in the total pattern of things designed and controlled by God." He uses various metaphors to develop how such privations contribute to the good of God's creation, comparing them to silences in singing that "contribute to the overall sweetness of the whole song," and shadows in pictures that "mark out the more striking features, and satisfy by the rightness not form but of order and arrangement." Augustine develops a distinction as a consequence of these images: "So then, there are some things that God both makes and controls or regulates, while there are some that he only regulates." This distinction allows Augustine to attribute the organization of the entire universe to God without thereby making him the author of evil. As an example, Augustine appeals not only to just human beings (whom God both makes and regulates) and unjust human beings (whom God only regulates), but also the broader realm of nature: "So it is that he both makes and regulates the forms and natures of different species, while as for the shortcomings of forms and the defects of natures, he does not make them but only regulates them." He appeals to the existence of darkness as opposite light as another example, concluding that "thus there is beauty in every

---

50. Augustine, Ver. rel. 40.76 (CSEL 77, 55).

single thing, with him making it; and with him arranging them in regular order there is beauty in all things together."[51]

Another component of Augustine's principle of perspectival prejudice is his emphasis on the hierarchical structuring of creatures. Not only does Augustine lack the assumption that a good creation must be a perfect one; he also lacks the assumption that if God makes all things good, he must make them all *equally* good. Rather, Augustine maintains that it is perfectly appropriate for God to make some natures better than others. After all, Augustine reasons, a world with varying kinds of goods is, *in the whole*, better than one in which all is equally good. Thus, in the *Confessions*, Augustine contrasts the lower beauty of earth with the higher beauty of the spiritual creation, insisting that while beauty has been distributed to all of God's creation, it is "not uniformly throughout."[52] In fact, these different kinds of beauty are so different from each other that one (heaven) is "close to yourself" while the other (the earth) is "little more than nothing."[53] Augustine ridicules the insistence that God should have made all things equally good as a failure of perspectival prejudice, comparing this claim to those who reason, "since the sense of sight is better than that of hearing, it would have been better to have four eyes and no ears."[54]

At the conclusion of his allegorical commentary on Genesis, Augustine draws together his principles of evil as privation, the hierarchy of creatures, and the superiority of the whole over the parts:

> We say that there is no natural evil, but that all natures are good, and God himself is the supreme nature and all other natures come from him; and all are good insofar as they exist, since God made all things very good (Gen. 1:31), but ranged them in an order of graded distinctions, so that one is better than another; and in this way the whole universe is completed out of every kind of good thing, and with some of them being perfect, others imperfect, is itself a perfect whole.[55]

51. Augustine, *Gen. imp.* 5.25 (CSEL 28:1, 475–76).
52. Augustine, *Conf.* 11.2 (CSEL 33, 311).
53. Augustine, *Conf.* 11.7 (CSEL 33, 314).
54. Augustine, *Gen. litt.* 11.8.10 (CSEL 28:1, 341).
55. Augustine, *Gen. Man.* 2.29.43 (CSEL 91, 171).

Here again, for Augustine, that some objects in the world are perfect and others are imperfect is *itself* part of what constitutes the perfection of the whole. Similarly, as we hinted at earlier, in the *Confessions* Augustine emphasizes this point by drawing on the distinction between the "good" of each thing and the "very good" of the entire creation in Genesis 1, speaking of how God's individual works have both "progress and decline, beauty and defect," all of which serve to contribute more greatly to the beauty of the whole.[56]

But Augustine goes even further than this. Not only are some creatures not as good as others, but some creatures have defects in themselves, but are still good in relation to the entire creation. In his literal commentary, Augustine asserts that sin corrupts, but nonetheless those things corrupted by sin are still good in relation to the rest of creation: "Those things, however, which lose their comeliness by sinning, do not in the least for all that bring it about that they too are not good when rightly coordinated with the whole, with the universe." Augustine even goes so far as to correlate God's ability to create good things with his ability to providentially rule over bad things: "God, after all, while being the best creator of natural things, is also the most just co-ordinator of sinners; so that even if things individually become deformed by transgressing, nonetheless the totality together with them in it remains beautiful."[57] Similarly, in *The City of God* he writes, "As the beauty of a picture is increased by well-managed shadows, so, to the eye that has skill to discern it, the universe is beautified by sinners, though, considered by themselves, their deformity is a sad blemish."[58] In his *Enchiridion*, Augustine claims, "in this universe even that which is called evil, well ordered and kept in its place, sets the good in higher relief, so that good things are more pleasing and praiseworthy than evil ones."[59] Elsewhere he makes this point with yet another metaphor: "No loser enjoys the wrestling matches in the games, and yet his defeat contributes to their success. And this, after all, is a kind of copy of the Truth.

---

56. Augustine, *Conf.* 13.32–33 (CSEL 33, 385).

57. Augustine, *Gen. litt.* 3.24.37 (CSEL 28:1, 92).

58. Augustine, *Civ.* 11:23 (CSEL 40:1, 545).

59. Augustine, *Enchir.* 3.11, in Boniface Ramsey, ed., Michael Fiedrowicz, trans., *Enchiridion, Works of Saint Augustine: A Translation for the 21st Century* (Hyde Park, NY: New City, 2005), 278.

... In the same kind of way it is only godless and condemned souls who take no pleasure in the state and organization of this universe."[60] It is striking that Augustine not only can claim, contrary to some modern perspectives, that "the universe is beautified by sinners," but that only the godless fail to appreciate this point!

It is clear from the sharpness of various rebukes that Augustine regards judging the parts rather than the whole as not merely an error of judgment, but a moral error. In his *Confessions* he even associates this preference for the parts over the whole with pride and abandonment of God: "This is what happens, O Fountain of life, when we abandon you, who are the one true Creator of all that ever was or is, and each of us proudly sets his heart on some one part of your creation instead of on the whole." Elsewhere he rebukes his soul for delighting in the senses of the flesh, telling his soul that this delight "is only a part and you have no knowledge of the whole."[61] In these passages and some others, Augustine seems to associate the "whole" with God himself, since he is the fount of all being. This emphasis on the *completeness* of the whole is as important as his emphasis on its organization and beauty. To make this point, Augustine compares the organization of the universe as a complete entity to particular objects within the universe that bear a similar organizational unity: "Every nature, whether it is perceived by merely sentient or fully rational observers, preserves, in its parts, being like one another, the effigy of the whole universe."[62]

Now, it must be clearly stated that Augustine's emphasis on the harmonization of evil in relation to the whole is not the *complete* answer to the problem of evil, but rather works in conjunction with his broader theodicy effort. For instance, Augustine is famous for his freewill defense against the problem of evil. In the *Enchiridion,* he stipulates that "the cause of our evils is the will of a changeable good falling away from the unchangeable good, first the will of an angel, then the will of a human being."[63] Moreover, Augustine explicitly opposes the appeal to the "beauty of the whole" as a way to displace the notion of *fallenness*. For instance, in

60. Augustine, *Ver. rel.* 22.43 (CSEL 77, 30–31).
61. Augustine, *Conf.* 3.8; 4.11 (CSEL 33, 58, 77).
62. Augustine, *Gen. imp.* 15.59 (CSEL 28:1, 499).
63. Augustine, *Enchir.* 8.23, in *On Christian Belief,* 288.

a lengthy intermezzo on the nature of pride in book 11 of his literal commentary, Augustine deals with the view that God made the devil bad from the beginning, drawing from a misusage of Job 40:19. Those who advanced this argument, in order to account for the goodness of creation affirmed in Genesis 1:31, appealed to something like the problem of perspectival prejudice: those who are bad "do not succeed with their badness in disfiguring or upsetting at any point the beauty and order of the whole." They also emphasized that their "deserts are weighed up," such that justice and the beauty of the world are maintained.[64] Augustine forcefully rejects this view, claiming that it is "manifestly contrary to justice" for God to condemn any creature for what he himself had created in them. Thus, it is evident that Augustine does not appear to conceive of the appeal to the "beauty of the whole" and the appeal to a freewill theodicy as mutually exclusive. In fact, an appeal to perspectival prejudice would appear problematic if isolated from a corollary emphasis on the misuse of free will by rational creatures.

A "greater goods" theodicy also functions, in general terms, as a part of Augustine's resolution to the problem of evil. "God judged it better to bring good out of evil than not to allow evil to exist," he writes in the *Enchiridion*.[65] In a sermon expounding the Apostles' Creed, Augustine emphasizes God's ability to use evil for good, providing the crucifixion of Christ as an example, which God used for great good but only came about through the malice of the devil, the Jews, and Judas. Augustine then declares: "So too in the hidden and secret recesses of the whole of creation, which neither our eyes nor our minds are sharp enough to penetrate, God knows how he makes good use of the bad, so that in everything that comes to be and is accomplished in the world the will of the Almighty may be fulfilled."[66] Augustine does not specify what he means here by "the hidden and secret recesses of the whole of creation," but the terms "secret" and "hidden" make it clear that he has some conception of God using evil for good throughout creation in ways that surpass human understanding.

---

64. Augustine, *Gen. litt.* 11.21.28 (CSEL 28:1, 353–54).

65. Augustine, *Enchir.* 8.27, in *On Christian Belief*, 290.

66. Augustine, *Sermon* 214.3, in *Sermons* III.6:184–229Z, 152.

CONCLUSION

Reference to these broader theodicy considerations allows us to conclude with one more limited point of application to contemporary creation debate, and one broader consideration in relation to the problem of natural evil. First, with reference to contemporary debate, we must appreciate that Augustine's treatment of this problem predates many of the scientific and philosophical challenges that mark the contemporary discussion. Augustine had no conception of a thirteen-billion-year-old universe or hundreds of millions of years of evolutionary struggle and competition. In fact, we have no reason to think that Augustine was particularly interested in the challenge of *prehuman* animal death, as opposed to animal death as such. For this reason, it is all the more striking that Augustine, under the enormous pressure of Manichaean criticisms, does not respond, "Yes, animal death is bad, but this is only because Adam and Eve sinned." To be sure, the misuse of free will is a huge part of his broader theodicy (though here he puts more emphasis on the angelic fall than many contemporary views).[67] But animal death itself is, for Augustine, not a problem to be solved so much as a beauty to be admired—a cause for praising God more than blaming him.

Now, of course, we might not agree with Augustine. For my own part, I consider Augustine's approach to the challenge of animal death most helpful when used in conjunction with other considerations in natural-evil theodicy, and not an exhaustive and sufficient answer in itself. Nonetheless, many of his insights may be instructive at various points within the contemporary discussion. And at the very least, unless we are willing to question Augustine's orthodoxy, his views on this topic will certainly discourage us from tolerating the claims of those who think it obvious that any acceptance of animal death prior to the human fall "undermines the very foundation of the gospel."[68]

Beyond this, and more basically, the developmental nature of Augustine's vision of created reality may enrich the nature of Christian

---

67. I have not included a treatment of this aspect of his thought but hope to write further in this area in the future.

68. Avery Foley, "Did Adam Step on an Ant before the Fall?," Answers in Genesis, https://answersingenesis.org/death-before-sin/did-adam-step-on-an-ant-before-fall/, accessed March 5, 2018.

hope in the face of the suffering and disorder we see in natural history, directing our attention forward rather than backward for the ultimate answer. Think of Augustine's claim that dying creatures "fill up the number of time-bound forms and shapes into a single beauty," or his metaphor of the universe as a successive poem, or his references to the world's "beauty of seasons" and God's "time-bound method of healing." This language, together with Augustine's reference to God's "loftier" and "all-embracing" purposes beyond human knowledge, may function not only to caution our judgment, but to invite our imagination. "Good but imperfect" need not be the whole story: perfection may be the goal rather than the starting point; God might be accomplishing something through the passage of time that is not yet visible. Indeed, Augustine's language hints that the current state of the world may simply be one step—one line in a long poem—toward something far better. Something of this hope can be captured with reference to a final quote in the *Confessions*:

> It is always the case that the greater the joy, the greater is the pain which precedes it. ... Why is it that in this part of your creation which we know there is this ebb and flow of progress and retreat, of hurt and reconciliation? Is this the rhythm of our world? Is this what you prescribed when from the heights of heaven to the depths of earth, from the first beginnings to the end of time, from the angel to the worm, from the first movement to the last, you allotted a proper place and a proper time to good things of every kind and to all your just works?[69]

---

69. Augustine, *Conf.* 8.3 (CSEL 33, 176).

Part 2

—

CONTEMPORARY EXPLORATIONS

7

—

THE EVIL WE BURY,
THE DEAD WE CARRY

Michel René Barnes

Yet the fact that some things really do matter, matter desperately, is what provides local worlds with their immense power to absorb attention, orient interest, and direct action. Moreover, it is these local worlds that have the power to transform the transpersonal and subjective poles of experience.

Arthur Kleinman, "'Everything That Really Matters'"

Someone who is perennially surprised that depravity exists, who continues to feel disillusioned (even incredulous) when confronted with evidence of what humans are capable of inflicting in the way of gruesome, hands-on cruelties upon other humans, has not reached moral or psychological adulthood.

Susan Sontag, *Regarding the Pain of Others*

Among Christians, the word "evil" and the expression "the experience of evil" can mean a variety of aspects or events in human life. For some, the terrain of evil is mapped according to the limits of our autonomy, whatever one takes those limits to our action to be. Modern theodicies, such as those of Gottfried Wilhelm Leibnitz, Immanuel Kant, or Karl Marx, are usually employed with this understanding of power that enables or restrains.

Modern political theologies, such as those of Jürgen Moltmann, work with such a map. For still others, evil is a force so powerful and ungoverned that it must be accorded a life if not a mind of its own. This form of radical dualism is more at home in modern thought than is generally admitted, not only in popular comics and video games, but also in the neo-mythological, postmetaphysical theologies of biblical scholars such as Catherine Keller.[1] Finally, there is what I mean in this paper: evil denotes that open-ended set of events that cause us injury, pain, and enduring trauma, typically both physical and emotional pain, but often only the latter. The paradigmatic cases of this kind of evil are events that occur beyond our control—"beyond our control" not only in the physical sense but in the emotional sense as well.[2] My emphasis is on what "happens" to us—those traumas intrinsic to being alive. I want to make those things legitimate subjects of theological reflection. Some modern philosophies insist with great vigor on the difference between what happens to us through human instrumentality (including, e.g., human social history) and what happens through the material causality of physics (what, ironically, used to be called acts of God). I am interested in what we experience whatever the cause: our "local world."

I am by no means writing any kind of consolation. I am writing to insist on the reality of personal catastrophe and loss; to insist that the devastation that haunts human life not be explained away or ignored; that pain, suffering, and death be recognized and experienced first as trauma—before the trauma is recognized as a problem to be solved. My intention is to engage these experiences before they are subsumed into some ideological narrative in which the "problems" are "solved." Many theological reflections on

---

1. Catherine Keller, *Face of the Deep: A Theology of Becoming* (London: Routledge, 2003).

2. For this paper Gregory of Nyssa will be one of principal sources for paradigmatic examples of "beyond our control" evil. Some modern theologians identify "trauma from events beyond our control" with "limits of autonomy" or "political theology" through the use of the conceptual device "consciousness" [*Bewusstein*]—particularly *species consciousness* as opposed to *individual consciousness*. One sees this most in liberation or postcolonial theologies. I reject such co-opting. What I am saying here could be understood as falling within the rubrics of a kind of theology of lament—a narrative which makes possible the expression of grief for grief's own ends. See Arthur Kleinman, " 'Everything That Really Matters': Social Suffering, Subjectivity, and the Remaking of Human Experience in a Disordering World," *Harvard Theological Review* 90, no. 3 (1997): 315–35. Moreover, the reader will notice that I nowhere engage in any kind of historical judgment about whether the passing of decades has produced in our modern culture (or any industrialized nation) a greater awareness of suffering or an eroding desensitization.

evil proceed—to offer one metaphor—as though the Christian response to evil should be like that of a person *arriving at the scene of a serious car accident, and the first words out of the Christian's mouth ought be, "Who's responsible for this?"* Justice may require knowing "Who is responsible?"—but it cannot require that this question becomes the content of first responders—and Christians must reject any notion of evil that displaces the faithful from the role of being first responders to what evil causes. Christians cannot leave mercy to be someone else's primary responsibility rather than our own. I want to write about evil in a way that gives pain the integrity that those who suffer deserve.

BIBLICAL AND CLASSICAL PARADIGMS

It is chiefly from the mental state of passion that we experience evil— either as the agent of that passion or the object of that passion's energy. Someone who is swept away by a passion experiences evil—say, the evil of anger—acts through assent to that impulse, and transforms that experience into the cause of someone else experiencing evil—say, the evil of violence.[3] The exemplary Scripture case of the experience of evil outside act is Job. The exemplary classical case of evil outside sin is Oedipus. The case of Job I assume is still relatively familiar in our culture; the case of Oedipus as an exemplar of the experience of evil outside action is not quite so familiar, and to the degree that it is known it is known as someone inflicting violence on others and suffering punishment. This is Sigmund Freud's Oedipus: a man who unknowingly killed his biological father and with equal unknowing married his biological mother. This is the story that survives in Sophocles' play *Oedipus the King*. Much less known, but of greater moral interest, is the middle play of the Oedipus trilogy—the play Sophocles wrote last of the three. In *Oedipus at Colonus*, the old, blind, homeless, and defiled Oedipus wanders into Athens led by his oldest daughter, Antigone. When Oedipus' identity becomes known and the citizens

---

3. See Cicero, *Tusculan Disputations* 3–4, or Seneca, *On Anger*; Clement of Alexandria, *The Miscellanies* 2.11–17, or Augustine, *On the Free Will* 17.47–21.60; Martha C. Nussbaum, *The Therapy of Desire: Theory and Practice in Hellenistic Ethics* (Princeton, NJ: Princeton University Press, 1994); or Ernst Tugendhat, *Self-Consciousness and Self-Determination* (Cambridge, MA: MIT Press, 1986). A helpful modern vocabulary for emotions (in general, but of suffering in particular) may be found in Hunter Lewis, *The Beguiling Serpent: A Re-evaluation of Emotions and Values* (Mount Jackson, VA: Axios, 2000).

would turn him out, he argues that while it is true that he killed his father and married his mother—breaking two powerful taboos that leave him impure and profane—he is not guilty of any crime. Oedipus struck in anger at the older man in self-defense, not knowing who the man was since he had never seen his biological parents. Similarly, Oedipus married Queen Persephone with no knowledge of who she truly was: she invited him to take the throne beside her after he killed the sphinx. None of the horrible things that he did were done intentionally and with full knowledge—and therefore, Oedipus argues, he is innocent.[4] Like the book of Job, *Oedipus at Colonus* ends with an ambiguous theophany that communicates the gods' judgment in his favor. Paul Ricoeur, among others, argues that the book of Job represents the moment in Israelite religion when suffering ceased to be explained as divine punishment, and the way was opened up for the categories of intention and guilt.[5] The play *Oedipus at Colonus* represents the same kind of crisis as captured in a different language-tradition: without disallowing the reality of Oedipus' need to be purified, Sophocles raises up a new perspective on suffering in life; the evil that Oedipus suffered is not a punishment for his own guilt. The horrible acts that Oedipus committed were without choice, and the evil he suffered could no longer be construed as divine punishment. Why then do we suffer evil?[6]

EVIL, NOT SIN

Before proceeding any further, register an important caveat: I am not interested in the category of *sin*, by which I mean an intention act of evil. The point I made earlier is that I want to avoid being in a theological and philosophical analogy with *arriving at the scene of a serious car accident, and the first words out of one's mouth being, "All right, who's responsible for this?"* That question immediately arises not out of anyone's callous inhumanity, but

---

4. We can think of the situation as the Attic Greek predecessor to the question of whether Bucky Barnes, the Winter Soldier, is guilty of all those murders, or is he innocent even though "he did it"?

5. Paul Ricoeur, *The Symbolism of Evil*, trans. Emerson Buchanan (Boston: Beacon Press, 1986) 23–46.

6. It could be expected that I would go straight to original sin, but I do not—I do not refer to original sin at all except to reinterpret it with a secular, existential lens (as in "broken before we were born"). See either Thomas Aquinas, *Summa Theologica*, 1.2.1a2 81–85, or James Alison, *The Joy of Being Wrong: Original Sin Through Easter Eyes* (New York: Crossroad, 1998).

THE EVIL WE BURY, THE DEAD WE CARRY

due to a strong belief that in every case of evil the most important thing to determine is *who is responsible—who or what is the causal agent?* The origin of theodicy is the need to decide "Is God responsible for evil? Is God guilty?"[7] However, the pressing obligation to determine a specific evil's causal agent has limited fruition for a Christian. Augustine made this point long ago; Dietrich Bonhoeffer reaffirmed this point not so long ago.[8] When the apostles ask, "Tell us, Rabbi, is this man blind because of his own sins, or the sins of his parents?" they reveal that they are deeply off track with Christ's revelation and redemption. (A truly modern restatement of the disciples' question would be, "Tell us, [first] citizen, is that man blind because of his faults, the faults of his parents, or reactionary *Bewusstein?*") In short, I find the sin-oriented account of evil in our lives dangerously open to the risk of not only the cliche of legalism, but the greater and more destructive risk of the prideful confidence and self-indulgence of Romanticism. Working only with the grammar of right and wrong, of innocence or guilt, is too often a project of overwriting experience with a new narrative: turning the tragic into the romantic, or into the scientific, or into the postcolonial.[9]

---

7. See, of course, G. W. Leibniz, *Theodicy* (1710). Contemporary forms of radicalism—e.g., many political theologies—might argue that it is the only way to convert critical theory into decisive practice, and revolutionary transformation requires nothing less than the postponement of the rights of the citizen (I am paraphrasing Robespierre) or the bracketing off of Christian mercy until justice "wins." Secular or Christian, the point is that the real urgency presented by contemporary human suffering is the here and now need for immediate judgment. Somehow, the present historical circumstances require the immediate justice of "Who is guilty here?" But all such arguments avoid the fact that modernity's accommodation with the apparently act-less God has been, since Leibnitz, theodicy, which is a concept of judgment and justice—and thus the urgent policing of suffering required by a state has been perceived to have this radical urgency since the time Leibnitz offered the theological existential called "Theodicy" (i.e., 1). Today policing actions for guilt is justified by those with a claim that they commit these actions "as if" they were Christ himself—Christ, who has already accomplished them perfectly. However, such arguments and radical self-justification fail because our larger moment in history is in fact one in which the tragic collapse of the perfect transcendental into the savage empirical is evident and the history we live with (or deny). See Paul Connerton, *The Tragedy of Enlightenment: An Essay on the Frankfurt School* (1980), 116–21. Any claims on moral authority have to be made in the shadow of the fact that the transcendental "as if" Perfect Man has been seen and heard, and the body count from that visitation has not ended.

8. See my article, "Ebion at the Barricades: Moral Narratives and Post-Christian Catholic Theology," *Modern Theology* 26 (2010): 511–48.

9. For a critique of this project, see Bernard Yack, *The Longing for Total Revolution: Philosophical Sources of Social Discontent from Rousseau to Nietzsche* (Princeton, NJ: Princeton University Press, 1992). For a positive alternative, see Lourens Minnema, *Tragic Views of the Human Condition: Cross-Cultural Comparisons Between Views of Human Nature in Greek and Shakespearean Tragedy and the Mahabharata and Bhagavadgita* (London: Bloomsbury, 2013).

Modern Christian theology has never come clean about its hot and heavy romance with German Romanticism. In Romanticism, when we reflect on life as we experience it we feel a "rush"—induced by the genre itself—to get to "the good parts": the triumphs, the restorations, the long-postponed unity consummated.[10] However, if Augustine is correct, then the good parts of our lives—the best parts, in which grace is received—are recognizable truly only in recollection. In reality, the experience of good parts often turns out to be barely distinguishable from the bad parts, except in recollection. *Some experiences are so emotionally explosive that morally all they leave behind are the shadows of where our sense of right and wrong were when it happened.* It would be only slight hyperbole for me to say that what I'm offering here is the preamble to *a preferential option for the mortal* or *for the tragic*—but that is, for a certain pool of language, what I'm doing. (For a different pool of language, what I am going to talk about is the "all our griefs he had to bear" part, rather than the "all our sins.")

DIFFICULTIES

One difficulty in talking about the individual's experience is deciding, What kind of expressions are representational and in what way? All forms of first-person writing and works of art communicate to some degree, but no one can claim that our strongest experiences can be communicated using any kind of symbolic means. That personal experience lies beyond our perceptual or deductive horizons—and this is true for our greatest joys as well as our greatest sorrows—is a jarring, frustrating, and occasionally despair-inducing fact of life that each of us must come to grips with as we live through more and more of the mystery of our lives.[11] Although what I am about to say is childish, I know, I'm saying it anyway: sometimes I am feel a kind of wistfulness about the fact that God gets to be perfectly expressed perfectly in his incarnate Word. I do not think it a minor thing to be promised the beatitude of knowing as we are known. I

---

10. See Friedrich Nietzsche's Introduction to his *The Birth of Tragedy* for his famous list of what constitutes "Romanticism."

11. James Agee speaks directly to this point in *Let Us Now Praise Famous Men* (Boston: Houghton Mifflin, 1941), and I bring the question up both to insist on the very limited goals I have in this paper and to acknowledge the limitations all speech-acts (texts) bring to the project of recognizing the suffering of others. Agee remarks, "A piece of the body torn out by the roots might be more to the point" (10). Susan Sontag would probably agree.

place a great deal of hope in the fact that—because we do not how to pray properly—the Spirit supplies our prayers: the Spirit groans for us (*stenagmos*; besides Rom 8:26, the word occurs in only one place in the Bible, in Acts 7:34, in the account of God appearing to Moses and saying that he had heard the Israelites groaning in Egypt). The Spirit "groans" for us—he does not supply for us the words of Euclid's *Elements*, a grocery list, or even any Scripture. He groans.

THREE THESES ON EVIL

I offer here three theses on evil in God's creation: that evil is an experience, that the experience of evil is unavoidably fundamental to our lives, and that evil ought to be understood to encompass experiences outside the conventional moral category of sin or injustice.[12]

1. EVIL IS AN EXPERIENCE

Evil exists for us primarily in the realm of our personal experience. An experience is an event—it can be active as well as passive. By saying that evil is a personal experience I do not in any way mean to suggest any kind of relativism, as if I were saying, "Evil is a matter of *individual* judgment." When I say that *evil exists for us primarily in the realm of our personal experience*, I mean that there is a difference between—to use a Shakespearean trope—the truth that if pricked all humans will bleed and the truth that only some specific individual is, at any given moment, bleeding out from a wound. The individual bleeding out leads us to the understanding that all humans—because they are indeed human—bleed; more significantly for understanding our experience of evil is that in our lives we will encounter ("meet"?) human individuals bleeding. Whatever later exegetical use may be made of Jesus' bleeding out,[13] in the gospel story of Jesus' death, he bleeds out because that is what human bodies do under those conditions. There are many ways we can bleed to death: traumatic limb amputation, a punctured

---

12. My emphasis is on the *experience*, not theodicy or definition. Dietrich Bonhoeffer, among others, articulated accounts of "evil as privation," but his experience of evil was in the sadness he felt over his country, the complexity of moral decisions (e.g., assassination), his grief over the murder of friends and family, and the brutalization he felt each day in the camps until he lost his life on the gallows by suffocation or a broken neck.

13. That is, for example, antidocetist interpretations of Ignatius of Antioch, or the "full humanity" interpretations typical of Gregory of Nazianzen.

organ, or a weakened artery. A specific human being suffers trauma and pain ("On a scale of one to ten ... ?"). We may empathize, we may find analogies to our own experiences, but any person who suffers here and now suffers in their own individual, unique mystery (or horizon) of evil.[14]

We are, and always will be, spectators to the injuries each human suffers, and, more to the point, no other human can share in any individual's experience of evil.[15] The radical singularity of the experience of evil is undeniable when we consider that the more traumatic or painful experience of an evil occurs in the individual's memory rather than in the event itself. There is nothing more singularly distinct to each of us than our memory: there is no more intimate experience of individual existence than our memories. The memory of a loss, the later discovery of the trauma only through recollection, or reflection on the injury, brings forth lament. (There are a number of traumas and pains that we will experience in our lives that we are able to survive emotionally or spiritually only because we could not imagine beforehand just how horrific the event was going to be—just how much it was going to hurt or reduce us.)

2. EVIL IS INELUCTABLE FOR HUMAN BEINGS

We live lives of radical contingency: the instruments or agents of suffering and death are functionally infinite and radically outside our control. Our actual experience of evil—"I have this horrible feeling inside me because ... "—is unavoidable—or, as Augustine puts it in his critique of Stoicsm, the only way to free ourselves from monstrous experiences would be to become a monster ourselves. The very fact of being biologically alive is by itself the guarantee that we will suffer some evil from, for example, the effects of a faulty biophysics that leaves a weak-walled blood vessel in the brain which one day will simply burst like a bad plumbing job, or an intimately placed IED of a genetically triggered disease such as cancer. Whether or not one believes that our liability to evil lies wholly

---

14. See Tomasz R. Okon, " 'Nobody Understands': On a Cardinal Phenomenon of Palliative Care," *Journal of Medicine and Philosophy* 90, no. 3 (1997): 13–46.

15. James Wetzel, "Scenes of Inner Devastation: Confessional Improvisation," *Kilikya Felsefe Dergisi* [*The Cilicia Journal of Philosophy*] 3 (2015): 37–50. Wetzel's essay approaches similar questions to Wittgenstein and Cavell, working the technical character and content of their expressions to open up the "inner scenes of devastation."

in our materiality,[16] or in our contingency or thrown-ness (*Geworfenheit*), the fact that we are embodied creatures does indeed set us in a realm in which great emotional and spiritual trauma can be visited on us through our body. If indeed it is true, as was once popularly said, that "our bodies [are] our selves," then no matter how just our claims for autonomy may be, the fact is that a corrupted gene or a car accident can reduce our world to a bed, a toilet, and a room more completely and irrevocably than any police state could. Despite what Marxist science might promise us, we know that the war against material contingency is lost from the get-go—which is why the sense of evil is gathered up into the political or economic: realms we can, in theory, affect. But I am not talking here about the intellectual borders (i.e., consciousness or *Bewusstsein*) theoreticians postulate; I am talking about the sense of damage, loss, or trauma that individuals feel.[17] To repeat myself, in this essay I am telling the story of the evil we all carry and lamenting the invasion and loss delivered to the mortal as we all live in this world, the "good creation" of God elaborated on by so many Christian commentaries on Genesis 1 and the "six days," that is, the *Hexaemerons*.

3. THE FIRST EVIL, WHICH WE CANNOT ESCAPE, IS THE IMMEDIATE EVIL OF OUR PERSONAL EXPERIENCE

The third thesis is one that I have already begun to advance: if we regard evil as a kind of experience, then what qualifies as evil is much more than what many theologians regard as evil. It includes any sort of traumatic physical suffering, all forms of physical or emotional violation, and every occasion of loss that results in grief. By thinking of what is to be called evil in this way, I can align myself with premodern sensibilities—especially those responsibilities of the biblical and classical worlds. The one way in which my sensibility is not premodern is that I have no tendency that I am aware of regarding the experience of evil as a consequence of divine judgment—punishment—of an individual. However, in one important regard my sensibilities are premodern, at least if we take Paul Ricoeur at

---

16. Here I am not thinking of radical dualism so much as Marxism.

17. In *Harvest of Sorrow* (Oxford: Oxford University Press, 1986), 285–86, Robert Conquest tells the story of a woman who after the Ukraine famine of 1932 was complemented for keeping her three children alive, and her response was that originally she had six children, but she gave their limited rations to the ones she thought the strongest and most likely to survive.

his word: I very intentionally include the experiences of defilement, violation, and stain as meaningful cases of evil. To quote the character Shane at the end of the eponymous film, "killing leaves a mark on a person." Shane's explanation of his fate is repeated in full at the end of the very recent film *Logan*, so such a judgment still makes sense to a good number of people.

By now it is clear that I regard the experience of evil as tragedy—that life itself is fundamentally tragic.

HOME, IT'S WHERE THE HURT IS

I began my undergraduate class on good and evil with the students—sophomores mostly—reading Euripides' *Medea*.[18] The story of Medea—the mother who killed her own children out of anger—was, for more than a thousand years, the go-to text to illustrate the dangers and enduring trauma of unchecked passions. There are other issues that the play illuminates, but what causes an instant hush in the classroom is when I say, "*Medea* reveals the truth that the first place that one experiences evil usually is in the family." In that sentence I have, as it were, *hit too close to home*.

I don't make the observation that we usually experience evil first in the family as a sociological statement or as a political statement (it has often been made either of those two ways). I make it first as an existential statement about a deep structure of our lives—for *How can we not talk about family when family's all that we got?* I make the observation that the first place anyone experiences evil is in the family in order to identify just how radical our openness to the experience of evil is, how inescapable such experiences are, and to emphasize that there is a recognized if largely unacknowledged historical consensus that to talk substantially about the experience of evil, we turn to the family as the mechanism or setting.[19] In fact, all I can claim to be offering here is to be bringing to our attention what we already know. What I'm going to say is that when we

---

18. The title of this section comes from a U2 song written by Bono, "Walk On," *All That You Can't Leave Behind* (2000).

19. Alexander Elchaninov said, "Man enters deeply into the texture of the world through his family alone." See *The Diary of a Russian Priest* (London: Faber, 1967), 46. The texture or the world—the experience of life—that Elchaninov spoke of was limited neither to the great joy he experienced as a husband and father but included the deep chasm of potential loss that he felt ought not, as a Christian, be avoided or shrunk from. Compare his sentiment with that of Gregory of Nyssa as it appears later in this chapter.

really want to reflect on the experience of evil, we turn to the family as its setting. (We all know that everything has gotten so much worse when we hear the words, "Luke, I am your *father*.")

The ancient Greeks recognized the deep ambiguity of the power of the family to affect. In the ancient Greek legends *family was the "tragedy,"* and vice versa. Everyone who mattered was someone's father or son, someone's mother or daughter. The oldest Greek mythology depicts Kronos devouring his own children, and Zeus becomes all-ruler by killing his father. For the Greeks, the change of seasons was a dynamic within a family—in 2006 poet Louise Gluck published a magnificent piece on the abduction of Persephone by Hades and the response of her mother, Demeter, which was to withhold from the earth sunshine, warmth, fertility. I have already referred to the Oedipus legend and to the much older legend of Medea. Anything else I could say about the Greeks' need to talk out the powers of the family can be exemplified by referring to the Orestrian trilogy of plays by Aeschylus, in which King Agammenon sacrifices his daughter Iphengenia to appease the gods; Clytemnestra, Agammenon's wife and Iphengenia's mother, murders Agammenon; and finally the son, Orestes, kills his mother in retribution for her killing his father. Everyone in the family (except Iphengenia) has done something evil, has experienced something evil—but the last play in Aeschylus' trilogy is about who in that family is to be judged as "guilty." Who can measure a father's pain—his self-destruction, really—for sacrificing a child because "the gods required it"? Who can measure a mother's pain for the loss of a child because some larger community needed that life? Who can measure a child's pain when one parent turns against the other and plots their destruction?

It then came as a surprise to me to recognize that—excepting the creation and fall material (Gen 1 3) the book of Genesis is a collection of stories that reveal the varieties of evil that a human encounters in their own family. The Genesis account of human life outside Eden begins with the story of one brother murdering another brother and ends with the story of eleven brothers selling one other brother into slavery. Genesis 6 reports, in an abbreviated way, the existence of a parallel and depraved species of family—the union of angel and human woman producing offspring—and this notion of an unnatural family receives development in the Enochian tradition and further development in gnostic myths of the origin of the

aeons and the three genetic types of humans, all identified by their gene-
alogies: those descended from Adam and Eve, those from Adam and Lilith,
and those from Lilith and the Archons.[20] The story of the naked, drunken
Noah being seen inadvertently by his son Ham alerts us to the minefield of
taboos existing within the family, which are later defined by Deuteronomy
and Leviticus. (In *Life of Macrina*, the Noah-Ham story becomes a synecdoche for the "mechanism" of evil.)[21] The story of Abraham and Isaac is so
familiar that I need not repeat it here, but only acknowledge its existence
and enduring significance.[22] Personally, I do not know whether the full
resonance of the Epistle to the Hebrews can be heard without knowing
the story of Abraham and Isaac.

I want to follow this thread in the Pentateuch just a little bit further: in
the book of Exodus the story of Moses begins with his mother and sister
leaving him to the kindness of strangers. Moses is taken in by an Egyptian
princess who raises him as her own. In a religion and nation such as the
Israelites', so dependent on genealogy for its community (*Gemeinschaft*)
and faith, Moses' own family history is, at best, troublesome. Small wonder
then that when Moses returns to Egypt from Midian that

> At a lodging place on the way the LORD met him and sought to kill
> him. Then Zippo'rah took a flint and cut off[23] her son's foreskin, and
> touched Moses' feet with it, and said, "Surely you are a bridegroom
> of blood to me!" So he [the LORD] let him [Moses] alone. Then it was
> that she said [to Moses], "You are a bridegroom of blood," because
> of the circumcision. (Exod 4:24–26 RSV)[24]

---

20. See the gnostic retelling of Genesis and "family origins" in *The Hypostasis of the Archons* (NHL 2.4).

21. See my article, "Snowden's Secret: Gregory of Nyssa on Passion and Death," in *A Man of the Church* (Eugene, OR: Wipf & Stock, 2012), 107–22.

22. The most widely regarded modern example of the enduring significance of the story of Abraham and Isaac is undoubtedly Soren Kierkegaard's treatment in his book *Fear and Trembling*, trans. Alastair Hannay (London: Penguin, 1986).

23. The verb *karath* is a strong action word, with significant overtones of violence. We and the redactor may "know" that Zipporah is circumcising (*mullah*) her son, but the pericope is, in Hebrew, ambiguous.

24. Tikvah Frymer-Kensky writes, " 'The Lord met him [Moses] and tried to kill him' (Exod 4:24). No reason is given, just as no reason is given for the angel's attack on Jacob as he came back from Mesopotamia (Gen 32:24). Jacob was alone and wrestled with the angel all night; Moses is with his wife, who comes to his rescue. She takes a flint and cuts off her son's foreskin. She then flings the foreskin at 'his' feet, declaring that he is *hatan damim* to

Until Moses became a bridegroom of the blood (his son's blood, at that) the Lord was going to treat him as an Egyptian. In that little room, containing two parents, their child (son), and the presence of God, a mystery of danger, violence, and family is acted out. We recognize the actors' different roles—mother, wife, father, husband, and so on—and understand that something weird and powerful happened, but—then we hit a wall or limit.

DEATH, GRIEF, AND FAMILY
GLIMPSED: GREGORY OF NYSSA

To help elaborate my observation on the experience of evil within the family, it will be instructive to turn to an author already mentioned, Gregory of Nyssa. The family as the site of inevitable personal suffering, pain, and grief is a strong *topos* in Gregory's theology. The problem of parental anguish, in particular, is a theme that remains with Gregory throughout his literary career. It is present in *Life of Macrina* when he gives his account of his mother's crushed response to the death of her son Naucratius. More importantly, in *On the Death of Infants*, likely the very last work Gregory wrote, he feels the necessity to explain why it is that God allows the death of newborns and infants.[25]

Gregory argues that marriage is an extremely painful experience that virginity allows one to avoid or escape.[26] Gregory gives an honest, if one-sided, description of married life. A man falls in love and marries, and eventually his wife becomes pregnant. This occasion for joy contains sadness, however, for it is all too possible that the wife will die in childbirth.

---

her (Exod 4:26). Zipporah's enigmatic statement has two possible explanations: she flings the foreskin at *Moses's* feet, saying, 'You are a bridegroom of blood to me' (NRSV), or she flings it at *God's* feet, saying, 'You are a blood father-in-law to me.' (*Damim* means 'blood,' and *hatan* can mean either 'bridegroom' or 'father-in-law.') Either way, her deed and words stop the attack. The story is already difficult for the narrator, who adds a comment that *hatan damim* refers to circumcision. [*mullah—mrb*] The situation remains unclear to us. Zipporah, however, understood it and acted decisively to rescue Moses. Zipporah's name, meaning 'bird,' combined with her protection of Moses, is reminiscent of the fierce loyalty to her husband Osiris of the Egyptian goddess Isis, who is often portrayed as a bird of prey." Frymer-Kensky, "Zipporah: Bible," Jewish Women's Archive, February 27, 2009, https://jwa.org/encyclopedia/article/zipporah-bible. "Bird" does not remind me of Isis but of Gen 1:2.

25. This is not the most credible or appealing argument that Gregory ever offered, but it does illustrate just how fundamental Gregory took the dynamic of parental pain to be, even for God's providence.

26. The pain-free state of virginity has an eschatological character, in which humans attain to the life of the angels, an accomplishment familiar to any reader of the *Life of Macrina*.

Perhaps she doesn't die, but the child may. Even if the mother and child survive childbirth, then it is all too possible that the child will die in infancy and that the next pregnancy (or the one after that) will end in death for the woman. Gregory goes on: sometimes it is the woman whose bridal joy is swept away by the death of her husband, and "suddenly she has to take the name of a poor lonely widow. ... Death comes in an instant and changes that bright creature in her white and rich attire into a black-robed mourner."[27]

Occasionally throughout the book, Gregory uses terms and phrasings borrowed from tragic literature, all justified by recognizing marriage as a "tragedy";[28] Gregory's verbal echoes of tragedy are meant to intimate this insight: there is tragedy when great potential is the source of pitiable self-destruction, and because marriage carries such hopes for comfort and joy, its painful reality is all the more of a dramatic overturning. The reality of marriage is that it is all the more tragic because the expectation for comfort and joy is so great. At this point Gregory turns the Stoic description into a revelation: the human point of contact with the human hope for love is in fact the entryway into deep pain, an entryway into separation, not union. Looking at marriage, Gregory says: "You would see there, if only you could do it without danger, many contraries uniting; smiles melting into tears, pain mingled with pleasure, death always hanging over the children that are born, and putting a finger upon each of the sweetest joys."[29] As anyone who has read Gregory's On Perfection or his Fifth Sermon on the Beatitudes knows, such dissolving opposition is at the heart of our conception, which means that it is the guarantee of our death.[30] As Gregory

---

27. Gregory of Nyssa, On Virginity, trans. Henry Wace, in Gregory of Nyssa: Dogmatic Treatises, Etc., Nicene and Post-Nicene Fathers, ed. Philip Schaff and Henry Wace, vol. 5 (Peabody, MA: Hendrickson, 1995), 343–71, at 347.

28. Michel Aubineau, Grégoire de Nysse: Traité de la Virginité, Sources Chretiens 119 (Paris: Éditions du Cerf, 1966), especially 87–94.

29. Gregory, On Virginity, 346.

30. It is this resemblance between On Virginity and the two works, On Perfection and Fifth Sermon on the Beatitudes, that causes May to date On Virginity as approximately 380, or contemporary to the two later writings. I remind the reader of my earlier quotation of Alexander Elchaninov on entering the fulness of life only through marriage. I emphasize the contemporary Eastern Orthodox theologian lest the reader imagine some kind of East-West divide, in which European Christianity draws the family to the center of human experience while east Asian (Asia Minor) Christianity such as Russian Orthodoxy brackets family off from the moral or spiritual life. One need only think of the great literary works of Russian Orthodoxy, such as Dostoevsky's The Brothers Karamazov to recognize how superficial a judgment that would be.

says in his early work *On Virginity*, "The very sweetness which surrounds the lives of lovers is the spark which kindles pain."[31]

DEATH, GRIEF, AND FAMILY AS OUR STORY:
RUSSELL BANKS AND THE SWEET HEREAFTER

What I have offered here as a theological description of the experience of evil.[32] The elaboration of that experience as the role and rule of death in our lives, and as the localization of that experience in the family, is given a rich existential recapitulation in a work from 1991: Russell Banks's novel *The Sweet Hereafter*—a contemporary articulation of the experience of evil in modern, ordinary life.[33] The novel tells the story (or stories) of the aftermath of a schoolbus accident in which all the children of a small New England village die. Each chapter is written as a first-person description of the trauma by different townspeople. The chapter I am interested in is the account given by Billy Ansell (chap. 2), a man who lost his wife to cancer four years earlier and who loses their two children in the bus accident. As Billy speaks of his trauma, he explains the events by connecting them to his experience as a soldier in the war in Vietnam. In Vietnam, dying was everywhere, every moment of each day. When as a nineteen-year-old he left the war, he returned to "normal life" with the confidence that he had left "dying everywhere, all the time" behind. Approaching the dead bodies of his children for the first time, he realized, "There was death, and it was everywhere on the planet and it was natural and forever; not just dying, perversely here and merely now" (67). "What had been an exception was now ... the rule" (53). This is what Ansell calls the "Vietnamization of [his] life" (53). Vietnam was a place—for Billy, a kind of zone—where people died, usually unexpectedly and often violently.[34] Billy thought of life as a world

---

31. Gregory, *On Virginity*, 346 (trans. altered). The first time I visited Oxford I found scrawled on the wall of a pub's restroom the graffiti, "Life: sexually transmitted, 100% fatal." I was amazed to see that Gregory had traveled so far north ...

32. See, in particular, the theses on evil. Death, unlike confirmation or a rite of worship, is not an experience or object of reflection only for the churched, much less one only for the professional theologian. There are no borders to the genre "secondary sources on the experience of death" or "on evil." Suffering and death are, like evil, well-documented phenomena.

33. Russell Banks, *The Sweet Hereafter* (New York: HarperCollins, 1991).

34. A more contemporary idiom would be to speak of a "Fallujah-ization" or the "Kandahar-ization" of life—or the original experience of 9/11.

without threat; more to the point—my point—is that Billy made sense of his life by separating "evil" (as I've used it here) off into a distinct place and time.[35] What follows in this essay is my theological elaboration of the experience of evil in life as described by Russell in his novel.[36] I am glossing the novel as Gregory glossed the classical tragedies that represented life to and for him. To be alive is intrinsically to be subject to unexpected, heartbreaking loss and pain of all varieties. In *The Sweet Hereafter* Billy Ansel becomes aware that there is almost a kind of invisible force that affects everything that is alive: that force might be called the economy of tragedy.

As we try to speak about the general experience of evil, an analogy occurs to me: We all know that gravity exists, that there is an invisible force that affects everything that exists, even something as small as a photon or as large as a planet. The force has laws: some of these laws are complicated, and some of them are simple. Our knowledge and recognition of this pervasive force is part of every dynamic decision we make: if a glass slips from our fingers, we expect it fall down, to impact, and to break. We know, without seeing it for ourselves, that such a glass will follow a trajectory through the strongest gravitational field; we do not expect that field, or force, to cease; we do not need signs reminding us "Gravity Zone." This force can be captioned as death—which is a simplification, just as gravity is a simplification. The killing field or force that affects every living thing

---

35. In my opinion, much of modern Christian theology tends to *locate and separate* evil *out* in order to localize it: this institution, that economy, those people. The moral space theologians themselves occupy is a "safe zone" (ironically, a kind of "green zone").

36. War gives over the immersed participant to the absolute rule of physics, to a chaos of kinetic death. The war in Vietnam was experienced by Americans as an especially chaotic field of death compared to other modern wars. Banks—or Billy—uses that distinct experience of combat violence as a synecdoche for the fatal chaos Billy perceives all of life to be. The violence of the war that was "contained" as in a sphere ("Vietnam") is now seen to be the sphere that contains us. Among all the forms of combat that constitutes our existential state, the most fatal to the human spirit is the loss a child. The especially appalling character of an image of a dead child—e.g., the body of a Syrian child washed up on the resort beach in France—has become such a cliché successfully to manipulate the viewer that we can fail to stop and recognize why this should be so, why it is in fact the case. (What is it that makes Medea's acts so horrible?) In Dudley Randal's 1969 poem, "Ballad of Birmingham," the depth of violence in racism is revealed in the murder of four children in a bombed church: Randall constructs, as it were, a hermeneutical circle in which the murder of the child reveals the violence of racism, and the violence then recognized in racism opens further our experience of the "total war" that swallows even children. Randal says of the mother, "For when she heard the explosion,/Her eyes grew wet and wild./She raced through the streets of Birmingham/Calling for her child."

Billy calls Vietnamization:[37] it is the fact of loss, of the field of loss, of the fact of being able to be lost, that is as intrinsic to being alive as mass is intrinsic to being a thing.[38]

In the nature of things now, there is no peace, there is no certainty: we are fragile creatures subject to unpredictable, uncontrollable, forces[39] that are not completely or adequately described as *inertia*—for example, the tendency of a bus full of children to slide down a hill until the resistance of the friction of ice and water dissipates that energy—but have to be described as *heartbreaking*, as destructive to our consciousness as a bayonet is to abdomen. Death is normal and natural and near. I think here of a popular kind of picture that has two images: the one you see immediately and the one you eventually see. Once you see or recognize the second image, you can't stop seeing it. For the character Billy there is a moment, or series of moments, in which he discovers the presence of an invisible force that affects everything that is alive. After he sees it in life, he can't stop seeing it. This force is called death; the field or force that affects every living thing is—given the character Billy—Vietnamization. "Death" is not just one person dying: it is the *fact* of loss, of the field of loss, of the fact of being able to be lost.[40]

---

37. "Of course, I thought of Vietnam, but nothing I had seen or felt in Vietnam prepared me for this... there was death, and it was everywhere on the planet and it was natural and forever." *Sweet Hereafter*, 67.

38. Gregory of Nyssa, *On Virginity*, 346: "I affirm that this very thing, this sweetness that surrounds their lives, is the spark which kindles pain. They are human all the time, things weak and perishing; they have to look upon the tombs of their progenitors; and so pain is inseparably bound up with their existence, if they have the least power of reflection. This continued expectancy of death, realized by no sure tokens, but hanging over them the terrible uncertainty of the future, disturbs their present joy, clouding it over with the fear of what is coming."

39. The fragility of the human body—its weakness before the kinetic forces that invade its world—is revealed in a scene from the novel *Catch-22* by Joseph Heller: "Snowden *was* wounded inside his flak suit. Yossarian ripped open the snaps of Snowden's flak suit and heard himself scream wildly as Snowden's insides slithered down to the floor in a soggy pile and just kept dripping out. ... He forced himself to look again. Here was God's plenty, all right, he thought bitterly as he stared—liver, lungs, kidneys, ribs, stomach and bits of the stewed tomatoes Snowden had eaten that day for lunch. Yossarian hated stewed tomatoes and turned away dizzily and began to vomit, clutching his burning throat." (Heller, *Catch-22*, [New York: Dell, 1963] 449). See the very beginning of my article "Snowden's Secret."

40. "The only way I could go on living was to believe that I was not living. I can't explain it; I can only tell you how it felt. ... Death permanently entered our lives with that accident" (*Sweet Hereafter*, 72).

For every action there is an equal and opposite reaction. For every injury there is a deadening. For the injury of living tissue, there is scar tissue. For an injury to emotional attachment or consciousness, there is grief.[41] The binding we call a scar is healing—but it can also be the border of live versus dead. Grief can be the border between life versus death. It can be a border that fails: that breaks, that allows death to invade life—our consciousness of life.[42] There is a grief that Banks illustrates for us in the character Billy that precedes all experienced loss; it is a grief that makes grief possible,[43] like the sin that makes sin possible. Original grief.[44] Gregory of Nyssa, Augustine of Hippo, and Dietrich Bonhoeffer would all agree.

CONCLUSION

I conclude by returning to the quotation from Susan Sontag I used, along with Arthur Kleinman, as a preamble to this essay. "Someone who is perennially surprised that depravity exists," Sontag says, "has not yet reached moral or psychological adulthood." From this we gather that our task regarding suffering and evil is to reach adulthood. To mature.

To mature is to be able to experience or "absorb" evils that previously would have injured us radically, that would have wounded us, left us traumatized, crippled emotionally. Indeed, one sign of growing in maturity is an expanded capacity to experience suffering and evil and to still be present—to survive as ourselves. Anyone who has experienced serious loss—physical or emotional—knows that there are pains out there that can and will change who you are. This maturity is necessary for us to be able to love properly, for how else could we wager ourselves to the risks that loving places on us? Not knowing the risks, how could we be said to be loving without limit and with consent?[45] To mature is to experience and endure

---

41. As Billy puts it, reflecting on the course of his grief: "There began the secret hardening of my heart, a process that today, as I guess is obvious, is nearly complete" (*Sweet Hereafter*, 53–54).

42. See Augustine, *Confessions* 4.

43. "He has suffered an irretrievable loss, has discovered that he is inconsolable" (*Sweet Hereafter*, 77).

44. Original grief, like original sin, is a state or condition from which no human can remove us. It is a given. Billy says of himself, "The truth is that I'm beyond help: most people are" (*Sweet Hereafter*, 76).

45. Gregory of Nyssa's point is that love's experience of loss is an inevitable suffering, an evil that we experience, and through memory experience again and again. See also Augustine's

more pain than we could before; to mature as a human means to be able to recognize and feel pains not previously felt, pains previously outside our range of sensibility.[46] But enduring such loss comes at a price: we change, we develop defenses, we take precautions, we toughen, and we may even have "exfiltration" plans. We keep our senses when before we would have been knocked senseless, but what was once living issue is now scar tissue.[47]

In one conspicuous way, this kind of maturing is clearly a "good" thing: a parent should be able to absorb more damage than a child, so that under the same trauma the adult continues while a child could not. Maturity is measured by the amount of emotional violence one can absorb. That's a tough, mean thought, but it is true.[48] If there is nothing else about human nature that is tragic, there is still this sad, sad reality (and there are in fact other candidates for the tragic in human nature). How much must

Confessions 4, and, strongly recommended, James Wetzel's commentary on it: "Book Four: The Trappings of Woe and Confession of Grief," in A Reader's Companion to Augustine's Confessions, ed. Kim Paffenroth and Robert Peter Kennedy (Louisville, KY: Westminster John Knox, 2003), 53–69.

46. In A Farewell to Arms (New York: Scribner, 1929), Ernest Hemingway tells the story of young man so shallow that he treats the war around him (Italy, World War I) as a spectacle—even as an ambulance driver on the front he remains unaffected. He takes a woman, a nurse, for his comfort—but to his own amazement he begins to love her. Through his growing love for her, the discovery of her pregnancy, he remains both baffled by and radically invested in his love for her. The novel ends by both her and their child dying during childbirth. Her last words to him, "Don't worry. ... It's just a dirty trick," appeal to the laws of romance—the close call, the survival, the happy ending—but life is not a romance (342). Gregory of Nyssa's account of the devastation that the loss of a spouse inflicts could not be better portrayed than by Hemingway. The limits of an immature, selfish love are revealed as well. He could not comfort her; he cannot endure himself; he has nowhere to go in this world. He and Billy (Sweet Hereafter) would have a lot of silence to share if they could have met.

47. A powerful and paradigmatic portrait of "surviving at the cost of one's humanity" may be found in Elie Wiesel's Night (New York: Hill and Wang, 2006), in which the main character, a young teenage boy (the book is a fictionalized autobiography of Wiesel's own experiences), survives the horror of the concentration camps only to find that he has lost his humanity: on the last page we are told that he looks in the mirror and sees a corpse. This loss of humanity is distinct from the bestialization that the Nazis inflicted on the prisoners; this loss of humanity is measured by the author's own standard of being human—to feel inside himself emotional ties and obligations for his father (also a prisoner). After the young Elie abandons his sick father, his story of being a prisoner ends: the book is over. The next two years of imprisonment and then his liberation are treated in hardly more than a paragraph. The living corpse has no story.

48. "Maturity" does not mean no longer feeling suffering or evil—that would be to become the "monster" that Augustine warned us against becoming, the monster he saw in Stoicism, and the monster to which Christianity was diametrically opposed.

Job or Oedipus suffer in order to obtain the wisdom (and theophany) they finally arrive at?

There is a strong and widespread sense in the patristic church that God can and does make good out of evil. From a religious point of view, the task is then to understand that God must be making use of our (fallen) need to "toughen up." We can look at this making use in two ways: anthropologically and christologically. First, anthropologically, God takes this harshness of our existence and accepts it as a kind of virtue: for example, it is, in a way (as I have already suggested) at the basis of the parent-child relationship. It is also behind the "laying down one's life" practice, which depends on the insight that *I can accept or absorb death and not lose myself in the face of that*. We give up tenderness in exchange for growth. Christ is recognizably in this tradition of practicing the laying down of one's life; Christ accepted—absorbed!—death and did not lose himself in the face of that.[49] However, the incarnation leaves its own unique and revealing mark on the fact of this theological anthropology. This mark is the christological aspect of God making use of our fallen need to toughen up if we are to mature.

Jesus seems to be someone who matures without hardening, who is continuously vulnerable. This is a dangerous thing to judge, since there are few personal disasters that can compare with imagining maturity where there is little or none. But Christ certainly *seems* not to have been bound by the rule that the cost of maturity is hardness or a kind of absorbability (of pain). This freedom is not a divine thing in the sense of a miracle, but it may be a *perfectly* human thing in the sense of how we once were, should have remained, and may yet be again. The freedom from growth at an expense is certainly a divine thing in the sense of "This is what God's love is like."[50] This is a new kind of love, an unearthly love, because *on earth true love is mature love*, and maturity is "absorbability" (that is, the ability

---

49. What makes Christ's acceptance of death unique is that he accepted death freely—nothing could bring about his death unless he consented. This fact is forcefully stated in the Gospels and is taken up energetically by the church fathers. Athanasius insists on the total freedom of Christ's death, as does Augustine (see *On the Incarnation* 20–24 and *On the Trinity* 13.13–18, respectively).

50. In the last few decades the divine freedom has been explored under the rubric of "God as Gift-Giver": God as uniquely the only true Gift-Giver. A modern (late nineteenth century into the twentieth) criticism of this notion of God—a rejection of this claim for God—is articulated from a Marxist perspective (however diluted): the notion of "God" is the strong case of a hidden means of production (as announced by God himself in Job 38).

to absorb pain and still to continue), and absorbability has the end of inno-cence built into it as a zero-sum dynamic. Christ loves with a *truly* mature love—without having his absorbability limited by the kind of hardness or shielding that maturity requires in other humans.

It is a perfect christological paradox to say that the impassible Son loves without any self-protection, without any personal safeguards, and without defense, absorbing all suffering.

8
—

CREATION AND THE
PROBLEM OF EVIL AFTER
THE APOCALYPTIC TURN

R. David Nelson

One of the most significant and alluring trends in the recent history of Christian thought is the rediscovery of the apocalyptic imagination at the origins of the New Testament and Christian theology.[1] "Apocalyptic was the mother of all Christian theology," Ernst Käsemann famously remarks, going on in a programmatic essay from 1960 on "The Beginnings of Christian Theology" to demonstrate how, as he puts it, "apocalyptic after Easter" gave shape to the New Testament texts and, in turn, inaugurated the historical trajectory of Christian theology.[2] In the essay, Käsemann explores the rise of early Christian apocalypticism against the backdrop of its intellectual and religious roots in antecedent Jewish apocalyptic thought during the late Second Temple period. Significantly, though, for Käsemann it is *Easter* that marks the decisive turning point in the course of the world and necessitates a new mode of thought, exhibited first in the New Testament and continuing on in the theological discourse of incipient Christianity.

---

1. I am grateful to Philip Ziegler, who read a draft of this chapter and offered invaluable feedback and several suggestions for improvement.

2. Ernst Käsemann, "The Beginnings of Christian Theology," in *New Testament Questions of Today* (Philadelphia: Fortress, 1969), 102. On Käsemann's significance for contemporary apocalyptic theology, see Ry O. Siggelkow, "Ernst Käsemann and the Specter of Apocalyptic," *Theology Today* 75, no. 1 (2018): 37–50.

The last century of critical biblical scholarship and theology has witnessed an ongoing and often acrimonious debate over the extent to which apocalyptic played the formative role in the Christian tradition that Käsemann and others before and after him have claimed for it.[3] In my opening sentence, I called the apocalyptic turn in modern theology significant for precisely this reason. It has become a genuine interpretive option in biblical studies and systematic theology; for some, it is a skeleton key for opening up the New Testament (the origins, meanings, and repercussions of the canonical documents) and for establishing an apocalyptic posture in theology that seeks to correspond to the biblical texts. For others, the apocalyptic turn is decisively a *wrong* turn, leading to an all-too-narrow and thus confounding style of engagement with biblical material that yields disastrous consequences for the theology following in tow. The apocalyptic turn is significant, then, as a polarizing point of debate—convincing to some, resolutely unconvincing to others.

Additionally, it is no small thing that today's revival of apocalyptic is one of the very few trends in contemporary religious thought that has managed to bring to the debate chamber both biblical scholars and systematic theologians and ethicists. Far from simply being a cause of neuralgia among the guild of Pauline scholars, this recent resurgence of interest in early Christian apocalyptic has brought together critical exegetes and constructive theologians for some surprising exchanges of ideas. It also has exacerbated ongoing conflicts between the disciplines, as efforts to sort out the implications of early Christian apocalyptic for critical exegesis and constructive theology have highlighted the conceptual and methodological differences between the guilds. All of this suggests that the apocalyptic turn has had and should continue to have a profound impact on contemporary Christian thought.

---

3. On the history of the reception of and critical engagement with apocalypticism in modern NT studies and systematic theology, see Joshua B. Davis's excellent, even if perhaps too sympathetic, essay, "Introduction: The Challenge of Apocalyptic to Modern Theology," in *Apocalyptic and the Future of Theology: With and beyond J. Louis Martyn*, ed. Joshua B. Davis and Douglas Harink (Eugene, OR: Cascade, 2012), 1–48. See also Ben C. Blackwell, John K. Goodrich, and Jason Matson, "Paul and the Apocalyptic Imagination—an Introduction," in *Paul and the Apocalyptic Imagination*, ed. Ben C. Blackwell, John K. Goodrich, and Jason Matson (Minneapolis: Fortress, 2016), 3–21.

In my initial sentence I also described the apocalyptic turn in modern theology as alluring. In strands of contemporary theology animated by the apocalyptic imagination, the accent marks are placed over those aspects of the Christian message that stress the radical newness, unearthliness, mysteriousness, and disruptiveness of Good Friday and Easter Sunday. In the context of modern religious thought, wherein theology so easily can become crusty, bureaucratic, banal, bourgeois, and even blasphemous, theological work done in an apocalyptic key blows like a breath of fresh air, restoring to the center of Christian discourse the christological mystery at the heart of the gospel. Moreover, the contemporary emphasis on apocalypticism has engendered new ways of understanding historic Christianity's (and Christian theology's) entanglements with structures of power. By underscoring the Pauline notion that the gospel of Jesus Christ cuts against the "rulers ... authorities ... and cosmic powers of this present darkness" (Eph 6:12), apocalyptic theology is inspiring new and creative ways for addressing issues such as racism, misogyny, xenophobia, disenfranchisement, poverty, and so on as genuine theological problems. Indeed, it is demonstrable that some of the most provocative and profitable work being done at the intersection of theology and areas of inquiry such as politics, economics, and sociology is drawing its inspiration from contemporary theology's engagement with apocalyptic themes.[4] For those interested in theological interventions into systemic and institutionalized structures of injustice and oppression, apocalyptic theology appears to offer great promise as a resource and stimulus.

This chapter considers what happens to the themes of creation and the problem of evil in theology after the apocalyptic turn. I argue that apocalyptic theology is generating some fascinating insights into these themes.

---

4. To mention but a few key texts that exhibit the application of apocalyptic discourse to the discipline and concerns of practical theology: Nancy J. Duff, "Pauline Apocalyptic and Theological Ethics," in *Apocalyptic and the New Testament: Essays in Honor of J. Louis Martyn*, ed. Joel Marcus and Marion L. Soards (Sheffield: Sheffield Academic, 1989), 279–96; Nathan R. Kerr, *Christ, History and Apocalyptic: The Politics of Christian Mission*, Theopolitical Visions 4 (Eugene, OR: Cascade, 2009); Travis Kroeker, *Messianic Political Theology and Diaspora Ethics: Essays in Exile*, Theopolitical Visions 23 (Eugene, OR: Cascade, 2017); Paul L. Lehmann, *Ethics in a Christian Context* (New York: Harper & Row, 1963). See also the essays composing the third unit (titled "Part 3: Living Faithfully at the Turn of the Ages") in Philip G. Ziegler, *Militant Grace: The Apocalyptic Turn and the Future of Christian Theology* (Grand Rapids: Baker Academic, 2018), 113–200.

At the same time, these insights reveal some of the methodological and material shortfalls and unfinished tasks of theology that locates itself at the turn of the ages.

THE APOCALYPTIC TURN IN MODERN THEOLOGY: A SYLLABUS

A few general remarks on apocalyptic theology are in order before we concentrate on the themes of creation and evil. It is beyond the scope of the present chapter to attempt anything more than a cursory overview of the apocalyptic turn. Instead, here we will briefly consider the major emphases, key texts, and prominent interlocutors marking apocalyptic theology, and along the way will encounter several notable foils to the apocalyptic imagination.

In a programmatic essay on the "background, tone, and tasks" of apocalyptic theology, Philip Ziegler drafts six theses summarizing the contribution of apocalypticism to contemporary theology:[5]

1. A Christian theology funded by a fresh hearing of New Testament apocalyptic will discern in that distinctive and difficult idiom a discourse uniquely adequate both to announce the full scope, depth, and radicality of the gospel of God, and to bespeak the actual and manifest contradiction of that gospel by the actuality of the times in which we live.

2. A Christian theology funded by a fresh hearing of New Testament apocalyptic will turn on a vigorous account of divine revelation in Jesus Christ as the unsurpassable eschatological act of redemption; its talk of God and treatment of all other doctrines will thus be marked by an intense christological concentration.

3. A Christian theology funded by a fresh hearing of New Testament apocalyptic will stress the unexpected, new, and disjunctive character of the divine work of salvation that

---

5. The essay is available as chap. 2, "Apocalyptic Theology: Background, Tone, and Tasks," in Ziegler, *Militant Grace*, 17–31.

comes on the world of sin in and through Christ. As a consequence, in its account of the Christian life, faith, and hope, it
will make much of the ensuing evangelical "dualisms."

4. A Christian theology funded by a fresh hearing of New
    Testament apocalyptic will provide an account of salvation as
    a "three-agent drama" of divine redemption in which human
    beings are rescued from captivity to the anti-God powers of
    sin, death, and the devil. In addition to looking to honor the
    biblical witness, this is also, it is wagered, an astute and real-
    istic gesture of notable explanatory power.

5. A Christian theology funded by a fresh hearing of New
    Testament apocalyptic will acknowledge that it is the world
    and not the church that is the ultimate object of divine salva-
    tion. It will thus conceive of the church as a creation of the
    Word, a provisional and pilgrim community gathered, upheld,
    and sent to testify in word and deed to the gospel for the sake
    of the world. Both individually and corporately, the Christian
    life is chiefly to be understood as militant discipleship in evan-
    gelical freedom.

6. A Christian theology funded by a fresh hearing of New
    Testament apocalyptic will adopt a posture of prayerful expec-
    tation of an imminent future in which God will act decisively
    and publicly to vindicate the victory of Life and Love over Sin
    and Death. The ordering of its tasks and concentration of its
    energies will befit the critical self-reflection of a community
    that prays, "Let grace come and let this world pass away."[6]

Zeigler's theses helpfully encapsulate the mood of apocalyptic theology and also pinpoint a number of the issues that crop up in the literature
of the movement. For our purposes here, let me highlight three aspects
of contemporary apocalyptic theology that emerge in Ziegler's sketch.
First, we do well to note that all six of these theses commence with the
phrase "a Christian theology funded by a fresh hearing of New Testament

---

6. Ziegler, *Militant Grace*, 26–30. The citation in thesis 6 is from Didache 10.6.

apocalyptic ... " This construction alerts us to a significant methodological feature of apocalyptic theology, namely, that it builds on a particular
variety of *New Testament exegesis*—specifically, an apocalyptic approach to
the interpretation of *Paul's letters*. Second, as Ziegler's theses 1 and 3 make
especially clear, apocalyptic theology advertises the *radical, new,* and *dis-*
ruptive elements of evangelical discourse, and in doing so frequently positions itself over against the familiar, traditional, and continuous. Third, as
far as apocalyptic theology's systematicity is concerned, *Christology*—to
be precise, a staurocentric, eschatological translation of the person and
work of Jesus Christ—plays, as it were, a *criteriological* role in relation to
other regions of Christian teaching. As Ziegler puts it in thesis 2, the "talk
of God and treatment of all other doctrines will ... be marked by an intense
christological concentration." He tips his hand to how this christological
concentration governs ecclesiology in thesis 5. We will encounter a similar
pattern below in regard to the "first article" issues of creation and theodicy.

As a distinct development in the history of modern Christian thought,
apocalyptic theology is a relatively recent phenomenon residing at the
intersection of dogmatics and critical biblical scholarship. To be sure, the
story of Christian theology includes a few episodes during which the apocalyptic imagination materialized. However, as D. Stephen Long observes,
"apocalyptic has often been marginalized in theology."[7] Cyril O'Regan
elaborates:

> Throughout its long history, theology has developed largely in
> non-apocalyptic directions that variously featured doctrine, insti-
> tutions, spiritual and moral disciplines and practices. Even with
> those inclined to a dose of nostalgia for the early church, there is
> a general recognition that the emergence of catholic Christianity
> debilitated, even if it did not sign the death warrant of, biblical apoc-
> alyptic, already riven by disappointment regarding the parousia.[8]

Such remarks help us to locate the major periods of the history of
Christian thought during which apocalyptic has been in ascendancy;

---

7. D. Stephen Long, *Hebrews*, Belief: A Theological Commentary on the Bible, ed. Amy
Plantinga Pauw and William C. Placher (Louisville: Westminster John Knox, 2011), 208.

8. Cyril O'Regan, *Theology and the Spaces of Apocalyptic* (Milwaukee: Marquette University
Press, 2009), 12, cited in Long, *Hebrews*, 208–9.

namely, it retreated into the catacombs following the apostolic period, only to reemerge in the late nineteenth century when certain New Testament scholars challenged the prevailing historical-critical consensus on the origins of Christianity and the significance of Jesus and his teachings. But even then it took some time for the apocalyptic imagination to inspire a new direction in Christian *theology*. It is demonstrable that the movement of apocalyptic theology is just now reaching its zenith, with a number of today's theologians working on the constellation of issues epitomized in Ziegler's theses.

At the vanguard of efforts today to resurrect apocalyptic themes for use in Christian theology is the Explorations in Theology and Apocalyptic working group, organized in 2009 as an additional meeting of the American Academic of Religion and convening each November since (with the exception of 2017). This working group, which is chaired by Ziegler and Douglas Harink, brings together scholars from across the theological disciplines to discuss the apocalyptic turn and its entailments. The group has devoted two meetings to considering the work of J. Louis Martyn, whose exegetical studies of Paul and John continue to inspire the cause of apocalyptic theology.[9] Other sessions have explored the apocalyptic aspects of the incarnation and crucifixion, the biblical motif of divine judgment, the significance of Pauline apocalyptic for Christian dogmatics, the figure of Satan, and ecclesiology. The library of contemporary apocalyptic theology is emerging from scholars associated with this network, and several key books and articles were first tested at the annual meetings.

The past two decades or so have witnessed the publication of a number of books giving voice to theology after the apocalyptic turn. In the field of biblical studies, monographs and commentaries by Beverly Gaventa, Douglas Campbell, Susan Eastman, and Martinus de Boer have suggested new approaches for reading the texts of the New Testament against the backdrop of late Second Temple Jewish and early Christian apocalyptic.[10]

---

9. The key texts are J. Louis Martyn, *Galatians*, AB 33A (New York: Doubleday, 1997); Martyn, *History and Theology in the Fourth Gospel*, 3rd ed., rev. and exp., New Testament Library (Louisville: Westminster John Knox, 2003); Martyn, *Theological Issues in the Letters of Paul* (Nashville: Abingdon, 1997).

10. Beverly Roberts Gaventa, *Our Mother Saint Paul* (Louisville: Westminster John Knox, 2007); Gaventa, *When in Romans: An Invitation to Linger with the Gospel according to Paul*, Theological Explorations for the Church Catholic (Grand Rapids: Baker Academic, 2016);

In theology and religious studies, Douglas Harink's book *Paul among the Postliberals* investigates the reception of Paul's thought in dogmatics, philosophy, and ethics.[11] Nathan Kerr's 2009 book *Christ, History and Apocalyptic*, which addresses themes at the intersection of Christology, ecclesiology, and the problem of history, continues to generate attention and discussion. In a monograph and several short pieces, Nancy Duff, dialoguing chiefly with Princeton ethicist Paul Lehmann, endeavors to work out an agenda for Christian ethics at the turn of the ages.[12] Two collections bring together scholars from across the disciplines—some on board with the contemporary revival of interest in apocalyptic, others not—to discuss the future of apocalyptic theology.[13] We have already encountered Ziegler's book *Militant Grace*, a primer on apocalyptic theology that draws on some of his previous publications in the area.

Reading this flock of recent texts, the ancestry of contemporary apocalyptic theology immediately becomes self-evident. Several prominent New Testament scholars from the second half of the twentieth century frequently are featured in lists of recommended reading, most notably Martyn (whose commentary on Galatians is perhaps the quintessential text on Pauline apocalyptic), J. Christiaan Beker, Leander Keck, Roy Harrisville, and, a bit earlier and exerting great influence, Ernst Käsemann.[14] Käsemann

---

Douglas A. Campbell, *The Quest for Paul's Gospel: A Suggested Strategy*, Journal for the Study of the New Testament Supplement Series 274 (New York: T&T Clark, 2005); Campbell, *The Deliverance of God: An Apocalyptic Rereading of Justification in Paul* (Grand Rapids: Eerdmans, 2013); Susan Grove Eastman, *Recovering Paul's Mother Tongue: Language and Theology in Galatians* (Grand Rapids: Eerdmans, 2007); Eastman, *Paul and the Person: Reframing Paul's Anthropology* (Grand Rapids: Eerdmans, 2017); Martinus C. de Boer, *The Defeat of Death: Apocalyptic Eschatology in 1 Corinthians 15 and Romans 5*, Journal for the Study of the New Testament Supplement Series 22 (Sheffield: Sheffield Academic, 1988); de Boer, *Galatians: A Commentary*, New Testament Library (Louisville: Westminster John Knox, 2011). For critical engagements with Campbell's work, see Chris Tilling, ed., *Beyond Old and New Perspectives on Paul: Reflections on the Work of Douglas Campbell* (Eugene, OR: Cascade, 2014).

11. Douglas Harink, *Paul among the Postliberals: Pauline Theology beyond Christendom and Modernity* (Grand Rapids: Brazos, 2003).

12. In addition to the essay cited above: Nancy J. Duff, *Humanization and the Politics of God: The Koinonia Ethics of Paul Lehmann* (Grand Rapids: Eerdmans, 1992).

13. Davis and Harink, *Apocalyptic and the Future*; Blackwell, Goodrich, and Matson, *Paul and the Apocalyptic Imagination*.

14. For J. Christiaan Beker, the two key texts are *Paul's Apocalyptic Gospel: The Coming Triumph of God* (Philadelphia: Fortress, 1982); Beker, *Paul the Apostle: The Triumph of God in Life and Thought* (Philadelphia: Fortress, 1984). For Leander Keck, see especially the essays collected in *Christ's First Theologian: The Shape of Paul's Thought* (Waco, TX: Baylor University Press,

is significant not only for reading New Testament literature in light of Jewish and early Christian apocalyptic, but also for his programmatic 1953 essay "The Problem of the Historical Jesus," which inspired the "new" or second quest for the historical Jesus.[15] Key theologians of the second quest—especially Gerhard Ebeling, Ernst Fuchs, Eberhard Jüngel, and James Robinson—are invoked as interlocutors in the literature of contemporary apocalyptic theology. Moving back in time a generation, the theological concerns of neo-orthodoxy and dialectical theology (problems such as religion, natural theology, subjectivity and objectivity, historical consciousness, and so on), are foregrounded in the contemporary literature. For this reason, signature texts by Karl Barth, Rudolf Bultmann, and Dietrich Bonhoeffer, and even by Emil Brunner and Friedrich Gogarten, find shelf space in the library of apocalyptic theology. From the long nineteenth century, Søren Kierkegaard's theological existentialism and Christoph and Johann Blumhardt's theology of the immanent kingdom of God continue to inspire today's proponents of theology in an apocalyptic key. Johannes Weiss, Franz Overbeck, and Albert Schweitzer also stand out in this period for initiating the modern quest for apocalyptic at the origins of the New Testament and of Christian theology.[16] Revealingly, from the history of Christian thought from the close of the New Testament up to the turn of the eighteenth century, only a handful of figures regularly are cited as resources for contemporary apocalyptic theology: Augustine,

---

2015). For Roy A. Harrisville, two works stand out, both on the cross: "Christian Life in Light of the Cross," *Lutheran Quarterly* 23 (2009): 218–32; Harrisville, *Fracture: The Cross as Irreconcilable in the Language and Thought of the Biblical Writers* (Grand Rapids: Eerdmans, 2006). Two collections of Käsemann's essays deserve special mention here: Ernst Käsemann, *New Testament Questions of Today*, trans. W. J. Montague (Philadelphia: Fortress, 1969); Käsemann , *On Being a Disciple of the Crucified Nazarene*, trans. Roy A. Harrisville (Grand Rapids: Eerdmans, 2010). An English translation of Käsemann's *Kirchliche Konflikte*, vol. 1 (Göttingen: Vandenhoeck & Ruprecht, 1982), which contains several key essays on apocalyptic themes, is currently underway.

15. Ernst Käsemann, "The Problem of the Historical Jesus," in *Essays on New Testament Themes*, trans. W. J. Montague (London: SCM, 1964), 15–47. An excellent summary of the second quest for the historical Jesus is found in the chapter titled "Hermeneutic since Barth," in James M. Robinson, *Language, Hermeneutic, and History: Theology after Barth and Bultmann* (Eugene, OR: Cascade, 2008), 69–146.

16. Three key sources are worth mentioning: Johannes Weiss, *Jesus' Proclamation of the Kingdom of God*, trans. Richard H. Hiers and D. Larrimore Holland (Philadelphia: Fortress, 1971); Franz Overbeck, *On the Christianity of Theology*, ed. and trans. John Elbert Wilson (Eugene, OR: 2002); Albert Schweitzer, *The Quest of the Historical Jesus: The First Complete Edition*, ed. and trans. John Bowden (Minneapolis: Fortress, 2001).

John Calvin, and Martin Luther more than anyone else from these many centuries.

Apocalyptic theology tends to take militant postures vis-à-vis contemporaneous trends in biblical studies and theology perceived as having neutralized the apocalyptic essence of the New Testament and early Christian theology. Today's iteration of the movement often sights the new perspective on Paul (and particularly the exegetical work of N. T. Wright), postliberal theology, and vestiges of scholasticism in contemporary Protestant thought.[17] Earlier generations of apocalyptic exegetes of the New Testament from Käsemann to Martyn and Beker demonstrably did not possess the habit of, as it were, naming names when distinguishing their own programs from those of their predecessors and peers. However, taken as a whole, the body of literature produced by such exegetes runs against mainstream trends of modern historical-critical scholarship into the biblical and contemporaneous Jewish and early Christian texts.[18] Predecessor

---

17. The most penetrating and nuanced critique of Wright's work approached from the perspective of apocalyptic theology is Samuel V. Adams, *The Reality of God and Historical Method: Apocalyptic Theology in Conversation with N. T. Wright*, New Explorations in Theology (Downers Grove, IL: IVP Academic, 2015). See also Harink's critical interactions with Wright in *Paul among the Postliberals*. Of late, the discussion of postliberalism among apocalyptic theologians centers on the role of "practices" in theological discourse on the nature of the church. This discussion is at the heart of Kerr's argument in *Christ, History and Apocalyptic*. See also Siggelkow's succinct engagement with the issue in "Ernst Käsemann and the Specter." For my own truncated and rather clumsy attempt to formulate a position on this issue, see R. David Nelson, "No Room for the Church?," in *Syndicate Theology* 3, no. 5 (September–October 2016): 103–8. David W. Congdon offers a clear, if somewhat overstated, rebuttal—"No!"—in the same journal on pages 109–12. Concerning vestiges of scholasticism in contemporary Protestant thought, Ziegler, for instance, comments, "Apocalyptic theology will be a nonspeculative, concrete, and practical form of knowing, committed to the work of discerning the signs of the times by Scripture and Spirit. It will itself be a militant discourse, always on the verge of tipping over into proclamation, offering at most a kind of urgent and sufficient traveling instruction for pilgrims, and as such will be lovingly impatient with more contemplative theological postures" (*Militant Grace*, 30). The tension between apocalyptic theology and "more contemplative theological postures" is an undercurrent that runs across the essays that compose the book. For a very different approach to framing and resolving this tension, see Anselm K. Min, *Paths to the Triune God: An Encounter between Aquinas and Recent Theologies* (Notre Dame: University of Notre Dame Press, 2005), 307–37. My own attempt, such as it is, to address the tension between apocalyptic and "curricular" modes of theological reasoning is found in R. David Nelson, "The Word of the Cross and Christian Theology: Paul's Theological Temperament Today," *Theology Today* 75, no. 1 (2018): 64–76.

18. Perhaps the quintessential example of this bucking of trends is Martyn's *Galatians*, which consists of so many path-breaking exegetical moves that one reviewer, remarking on the commentary's abundance of "reconstructions"—which, in the reviewer's eyes, are "always challenging and interesting, (and) sometimes imaginative and perhaps too confident"—voices

movements in the vicinity of apocalyptic theology also reveal a similar company of foils. For instance, the second quest for the historical Jesus was, by and large, an intramural conversation among Bultmann's former students.[19] But the issues cropping up in the literature reveal the positions against which the second questers aligned themselves: on one hand, the utterly naturalistic reading of Scripture put on display in professional historical-critical exegesis, which, in their reading, neutralizes the mystery of the gospel; on the other hand, extreme versions of demythologization that so sharply distinguish between God and history that they lead inevitably to the death of God.[20] Earlier still, the dialectical theologians waged war against all expressions of naturalism, bourgeois religion, and historicism in Christian theology. Barth and others regarded the entire sweep of Protestant thought from at least Friedrich Schleiermacher to the Great War as indicative of an immanentist framework for the theological topics—an immanentism emboldened by confidence in human scientific and industrial progress, which had reached its climax at the end of the nineteenth century and collapsed at the sound of the "guns of August" in 1914. Most famous among the books written to protest against the god of liberal Protestant theology is Barth's *Der Römerbrief*, a key volume from

---

the caveat that "when a commentary is based on extensive reconstruction it is either awfully right or awfully wrong." See Frank J. Matera, review of J. Louis Martyn, *Galatians*, *Catholic Biblical Quarterly* 61, no. 2 (1999): 368.

19. As mentioned, Käsemann, the pioneer of the second quest, made a number of signal contributions to the modern recovery of apocalypticism's formative role in early Christianity, and for this reason deserves a prominent place within the ranks of apocalyptic theologians. The extent to which other pursuers of the second quest also count as apocalyptic theologians is difficult to determine and, besides, largely transcends the scope of the present chapter. However, even a superficial reading of key texts by Ebeling, Fuchs, Jüngel, Robinson, and others uncovers themes common in the literature of today's apocalyptic theology. I have argued elsewhere, for instance, that Jüngel's thought orbits around, among a few other things, the three issues with which I summarized Ziegler's theses above: namely, an engagement with Scripture circumscribed to select NT (mainly Pauline) passages, an emphasis on the disruptive character of divine agency, and a categorical use of the doctrine of the crucified and resurrected Christ in relation to other regions of theology. See the entirety of my analysis in R. David Nelson, *The Interruptive Word: Eberhard Jüngel on the Sacramental Structure of God's Relation to the World*, T&T Clark Studies in Systematic Theology (London: Bloomsbury T&T Clark, 2013).

20. For examples, see the essays contained in the anthologies by "new hermeneutic" theologians Gerhard Ebeling and Ernst Fuchs: Ebeling, *Theology and Proclamation: A Discussion with Rudolf Bultmann*, trans. John Riches (London: Collins, 1966); Fuchs, *Studies of the Historical Jesus*, trans. Andrew Scobie, Studies in Biblical Theology 42 (London: SCM, 1960).

the modern period that continues to find its way into the footnotes in the literature of contemporary apocalyptic theology.[21]

While there is much more to be said about the key themes, sources, interlocutors, and foils of apocalyptic theology, this brief tour along the *grandes lignes* will suffice for our purposes in the present chapter. A number of the features we have turned up here will remain with us as we examine contemporary apocalyptic interventions into the doctrine of creation and the perennial theological problem of evil.

THE DOCTRINE OF CREATION AT
THE TURN OF THE AGES

A sustained engagement with the doctrine of creation undertaken from the vantage point of apocalyptic theology has yet to be attempted.[22] However, the theme of creation—specifically, the Pauline motif of new creation— is, in the words of Martyn, "at home in apocalyptic."[23] The locution "new creation" has become part of the vernacular of theology done in an apocalyptic key, deployed with some frequency in the literature to express the fundamental change that occurs at the turn of the ages. At the same time, we do not find much discussion in this literature of primal, or originary creation; that is, the beginning of creation and creatures, of the universe, of all that exists, of time and motion, and so on, as the yield of God's creative design. Bultmann famously contended that the biblical accounts of primal creation are ingredient to an ancient worldview rendered obsolete by the discoveries of modern science.[24] As such, the narratives of primal creation must be demythologized in order to uncover their abiding theological content.

---

21. Karl Barth, *The Epistle to the Romans*, trans. Edwyn C. Hoskins (New York: Oxford University Press, 1968).

22. My exposition of these two topics—first on creation and then on the problem of evil—follows the ordering of the conference theme. I could just as easily begin with evil, as it is demonstrable that apocalyptic theology's understanding of evil serves as the basis for the circumscription of talk of creation to the idea of new creation.

23. J. Louis Martyn, "Apocalyptic Antinomies," in *Theological Issues in the Letters of Paul*, 114n11.

24. For an especially clear statement of this argument, see Rudolf Bultmann, "The Meaning of Christian Faith in Creation," in *Existence and Faith: Shorter Writings of Rudolf Bultmann*, trans. Schubert M. Ogden (Cleveland: Living Age Books, 1960), 206–25.

Whether we might identify demythologization as the quintessential hermeneutical program for apocalyptic theology is a question that transcends the scope of the present chapter. At any rate, the conspicuous absence of discussion of primal creation in the contemporary literature of apocalyptic theology suggests an abiding commitment to a mythological conception of biblical and traditional theological accounts of creation's first beginnings. Furthermore, it is worth noting that we do not find much mention in the canon of apocalyptic theology of continuous creation, or of God's providential maintenance of the created order. Rather, and once again, commentary on creation is largely circumscribed to the soteriological category of new creation. The insight of apocalyptic theology is that we are able to access the doctrine of creation, and, indeed, the entire range of doctrinal material located beneath the heading of the first creedal article, only through the lens of the second article.

To illustrate what happens to the doctrine of creation in apocalyptic theology, let me briefly take us into a paradigmatic text—Martyn's oft-cited essay "Epistemology at the Turn of the Ages."[25] The piece is an exercise in Pauline exegesis, and, as the title suggests, Martyn is concerned to test Paul's understanding of how we know God in light of the message of the crucifixion and resurrection of Jesus. In the essay he argues that, for Paul,

> There are two ways of knowing, and ... what separates the two is the turn of the ages, the apocalyptic event of Christ's death/resurrection. There is a way of knowing which is characteristic of the old age. ... There must be a new way of knowing that is proper either to the new age or to that point at which the ages meet.[26]

For Martyn's Paul, that is, the crucifixion and resurrection of Jesus signify the invasion of the new age into the fabric of the old, and this intervention ushers in a new mode of epistemology. Furthermore, in Martyn's reading, for Paul the "two ways of knowing," which diverge at the fulcrum of the gospel, correspond to "two kinds of knowers." The knowledge proper to the old age is knowledge *kata sarka*, knowledge according to the

---

25. J. Louis Martyn, "Epistemology at the Turn of the Ages," in *Theological Issues in the Letters of Paul*, 89–110.

26. Martyn, "Epistemology at the Turn," 95.

flesh. Apart from the gospel, every one of us knows according to the flesh, and knowledge *of God* according to the flesh avails us nothing, for God is known only according to the Spirit. Martyn thus notes that, although the basic idea encapsulated in knowledge *kata sarka* is knowledge on the basis of sensory perception, what Paul actually has in mind goes beyond mere empirical judgment. Rather, the one who knows and thinks *kata sarka* is, for Paul, "the *psychikos anthrōpos* ('the unspiritual person')." Unanimated by the Spirit, the unspiritual person is incapable of knowing that the new age has arrived in the crucified Christ. Hence, "it is clear that the implied opposite of knowing by the norm of the flesh is not knowing by the norm of the Spirit, but rather knowing *kata stauron* ('by the cross')." In Martyn's reading, then, Paul understood the cross as "the absolute epistemological watershed," a dividing line between knowledge *kata sarka* and knowledge *kata stauron*. In the present epoch stretching from the crucifixion to the parousia, the foolishness of the cross is set against the wisdom of the world—that is: knowledge is *either* according to the flesh *or* according the "the Spirit of the crucified Christ."[27]

What is critical for our purposes here is to see how, for Martyn, the idea of new creation fits into the apocalyptic structure of the epistemological watershed occurring in the crucifixion and the word of the cross. Martyn begins the paper with an epigraph from 2 Corinthians 5:16–17, the second verse of which is Paul's well-known assertion that "if anyone is in Christ, there is a new creation; everything old has passed away; see, everything has become new." Throughout the essay, Martyn seizes on the distinction Paul draws in this verse between, on one hand, "the old," and, on the other, new creation, as a way of depicting, in dramatic fashion, the turn of the ages occurring in the gospel and the epistemological before and after marked by the encounter with the Christ of the gospel. Ingredient to Martyn's reading of Paul is the notion that, for the apostle, *both* the actual event of the resurrection of the crucified Christ *and* the preaching of the word of the cross mark the fulcrum of the ages, signifying, both for the world and for the one who receives the message of the cross, a "turning point of earth shattering proportions." In this pivot between the times, the new creation invades the old, bearing with it the promise that all has been renewed in

---

27. Martyn, "Epistemology at the Turn," 99, 108.

Christ. Further, Martyn argues here that the church is "the new-creation community," in the life of which the power of the cross is enacted through sacrificial love for neighbor.[28]

This use of Paul's locution "new creation" to encapsulate the crisis in the world that occurred in the original Good Friday and Easter Sunday and that continues to occur in the preaching of the gospel is found throughout Martyn's highly influential essays on Paul's theology. In his paper "Apocalyptic Antinomies," he argues that the apostle envisages the gospel as the meeting point of "two different worlds … an old word, from which he has been painfully separated, by Christ's death, by the death of the world, and by his own death … [and] a new world, which he grasps under the arresting expression, 'new creation.'"[29] Elsewhere, in an essay in which he places Paul and Flannery O'Connor in a dialogue across the centuries, he summarizes the sheer contrast between the old age and the new creation in the following way:

In Paul's apocalyptic, as in war, there are two opposing sides, the Old Age and the new creation.

Old Age	New Creation
orb of evil and sin	orb of grace
sphere under the power of Satan	sphere under the power of God
the ruler of this age	the Spirit of Christ
slavery	freedom
death	life
the oppressive status quo	the genuinely new

Here the imagery of apocalyptic war presupposes a provisional eschatological dualism. As in war, so in apocalypse, two sides are dynamically interrelated. It would be a serious mistake to link them

---

28. Martyn, "Epistemology at the Turn," 89, 94, 107–9.
29. Martyn, "Apocalyptic Antinomies," in *Theological Issues in the Letters of Paul*, 114.

simply with heaven and earth as though the New Creation were statically existent *up there*, and the Old Age statically existent *down here*. Apocalyptic is not a matter of metaphysical transcendentalism, or of static polarization. On the apocalyptic landscape there is always movement, and for this reason the English word "revelation" is an inadequate translation of the Greek term "apocalypse."[30]

Here we see the sheer distinction between the ages described as a *war* between two sides engaged in fierce skirmish with each other.[31] The new creation violently interrupts and invades the old, exposing it for what it is, namely, a downward slide toward the abyss of death and nothingness. But the old is a sturdy foe of the new creation, resisting at all costs the light shed abroad in the gospel against the world's darkness.[32]

At several points along the way here, I have suggested that, in Martyn's apocalyptic reading of Paul, the new creative agency of God that invades the world in the cross is set at odds with the idea of original creation. We can take this suggestion a step further by briefly considering a key passage from *Galatians*. Martyn observes that Paul's depiction *of creation* in the epistle is "not altogether dissimilar to the one later proposed by Marcion and the second-century gnostics." Martyn goes as far as to wonder aloud whether Paul in fact "denies the divine origin both of creation and the Law." He proposes, however, that an acknowledgment of the apocalyptic structure of God's creative agency in the world helps to resolve these tensions. Accordingly,

What is fundamentally wrong with both creation and the Law is that both have fallen into the company of anti-God powers. ... *God's* creation has fallen prey to anti-God powers that have turned it into "the present evil age," and that is the reason for God's having to act

---

30. Martyn, "From Paul to Flannery O'Connor with the Power of Grace," in *Theological Issues in the Letters of Paul*, 281–82.

31. Further to the usage of warfare imagery in early Christian apocalyptic, see Martyn's comments in *Galatians*, 100–102, 530–34.

32. Jüngel is especially insightful on this point. See Eberhard Jüngel, "The Emergence of the New," trans. Arnold Neufeldt-Fast, in *Theological Essays II*, ed. John B. Webster (Edinburgh: T&T Clark, 1995), 35–58; Jüngel, "New—Old—New: Theological Aphorisms," trans. R. David Nelson, in *Theological Theology: Essays in Honour of John Webster*, ed. R. David Nelson, Darren Sarisky, and Justin Stratis (New York: Bloomsbury T&T Clark, 2015), 131–35.

in Christ to terminate the elemental pairs of opposites that are anything but his servants.[33]

Not only does this astonishing passage clarify the connection between
new creation and the present evil age in Martyn's apocalyptic exegesis of
Paul; it also evinces some of the challenges for Christian theology posed
by his approach to the apostle's thought. In particular, having observed
Martyn labor to hedge a proper Pauline gloss on "new creation," it is not
altogether clear whether and how an apocalyptic theology bearing the
marks of his exegesis can say anything positive about God's relation to
creation's beginnings, and, likewise, to creatures. At best, the doctrine and
confession of original creation simply is little or no use to us theologically,
since it draws our attention to what may or may not have occurred prior
to the invasion of the world by "anti-God powers." Data from prelapsarian
times is not available to us; all we know, rather, is the present evil age from
which God has rescued us on the cross.

Taking the same concern in another direction, it is worth noting that,
in *Galatians*, Martyn resists the charge of Marcionism by asserting that an
appreciation of the apocalyptic two-age structure of worldly time broadens "the gulf that separates the apostle from Marcion and the gnostics."[34]
Furthermore, nowhere in his writings does Martyn draw an utter distinction between the God of Paul's apocalyptic gospel and the Creator of the
primeval history of Genesis 1–11. Still, the oppositional tension we find in
his work between old and new, between creation as dominated by forces
hostile to God and the new creation enacted on the cross, and so on, raises
questions concerning traditionally first-article issues such as *creatio ex
nihilo*, attribution, divine providence, and the doctrine of heaven, to name
but a few. If nothing else, such questions suggest that one of apocalyptic
theology's unfinished tasks is to clarify how an apocalyptic reading of Paul
affects the Christian confession of the first article.

---

33. Martyn, *Galatians*, 417.
34. Martyn, *Galatians*, 417.

"CHRIST, WHO GAVE HIMSELF FOR OUR SINS TO SET US FREE FROM THIS PRESENT EVIL AGE" (GALATIANS 1:3-4): THE PROBLEM OF EVIL IN AN APOCALYPTIC KEY

As we have observed, for Martyn and others who endeavor to resurrect early Christian apocalyptic themes for use in contemporary theology, the essence of the gospel, as Donald MacKinnon succinctly puts it, is "God's own protest against the world He has made, by which at the same time that world is renewed and reborn."[35] The "apocalyptic antinomies" (to borrow Martyn's idiom) between the old age and the new creation, between darkness and light, between flesh and Spirit, between knowledge *kata sarka* and knowledge *kata stauron*, and so on, form, as it were, a basic cosmological structure for understanding the New Testament's talk of the crucifixion and resurrection of Jesus and of salvation for the ungodly. In the apocalyptic reading of the New Testament, these events—on one hand, Good Friday and Easter Sunday; on the other, the encounter with the proclamation of the resurrected Crucified One, the essence of which preaching is the gospel of justification—mark a decisive turn between old and new. The old age, having been invaded and overthrown by God's cruciform, kerygmatic action, is decisively occupied by and complicit in *evil*.

To further illustrate what happens to the theological account of evil in apocalyptic cosmology, we turn to a fairly recent, though by no means insignificant, contribution to the literature of contemporary apocalypticism—de Boer's *Galatians*.[36] To his commentary on the epistolary introduction to Galatians, de Boer fastens a long excursus, "Galatians and Apocalyptic Eschatology," in which he neatly articulates an apocalyptic reading of Paul's notion of "this present evil age" (1:4).[37] De Boer begins

---

35. Donald M. MacKinnon, "Prayer, Worship, and Life," in *Christian Faith and Communist Faith*, ed. Donald M. MacKinnon (London: Macmillan, 1953), 247–48.

36. That we are exploring here yet another major commentary on Galatians should further notify us of the importance of the authentic Pauline Epistles for contemporary apocalyptic exegesis and theology.

37. De Boer, *Galatians*, 31–36. This excurses is strikingly similar to "Comment #3—Apocalyptic Theology in Galatians," in Martyn, *Galatians*, 97–105. But both commentators draw heavily from de Boer's earlier piece, "Paul and Jewish Apocalyptic Eschatology," in *Apocalyptic and the New Testament*, 169–90. For this reason I will concentrate here on de Boer's contribution to apocalyptic theology, examining his summary of the backgrounds of Paul's thought in Jewish apocalypticism in this excurses from the commentary.

the excursus by summarizing "two distinct patterns (or 'tracks')" of apocalyptic dualism exhibited in late Second Temple Jewish apocalyptic texts. Building on his previous work in Jewish apocalyptic literature, he dubs these two approaches cosmological and forensic.[38] De Boer's explanation of the cosmological pattern is worth citing in full:

> According to the cosmological pattern, the created world has come under the dominion of evil, angelic powers in some primeval time, namely, in the time of Noah. ... God's sovereign rights have been usurped, and the world, including God's own people, has been led astray into forms of idolatry. But there is a righteous remnant of people, chosen by God, who by their acknowledgment of and submission to the Creator, the God of Israel, bear witness to the fact that these evil cosmological powers are doomed to pass away. This remnant, the elect of God, awaits God's deliverance. God will invade the world, now under the dominion of the evil powers, and defeat them in a cosmic war. Only God has the power to defeat and to overthrow the demonic and diabolical powers that have subjugated and perverted the earth. God will establish his sovereignty very soon, delivering the righteous and bringing about a new age in which he will reign unopposed. God will have put right what has gone wrong in and with the world.[39]

De Boer frames the forensic pattern as "a modified form of the first." Here, the focus is on the individual's freewill decision in the "now" to reject sin and embrace God. "In this pattern," he writes, "the notion of evil, cosmological forces is absent, recedes into the background, or is even explicitly rejected."[40] The two patterns are hardly irreconcilable; each, rather, underscores certain themes at the expense of others. According to de Boer, what is most significant is to note that *both* of these patterns exhibit themselves in the apostle's letters. For de Boer's Paul (and also for Martyn's, as we encountered above), evil powers and principalities have hijacked the

---

38. In addition to the essay just cited, see also de Boer, "Paul and Apocalyptic Eschatology," in *The Encyclopedia of Apocalypticism*, vol. 1, *The Origins of Apocalypticism in Judaism and Christianity*, ed. John J. Collins (New York: Continuum, 1998), 345–83.

39. De Boer, *Galatians*, 31.

40. De Boer, *Galatians*, 32.

world from divine control and authority, in doing so enslaving human beings to the forces of sin and death. God invades the world on Good Friday and Easter Sunday, signifying the imminent end of the rule of evil and the arrival of the kingdom of God. The preaching of the message of Good Friday and Easter Sunday confronts hearers with their complicity in the world's evil, demanding a decision for or against the righteousness of God.

With this conception of Pauline apocalyptic in mind, de Boer argues that the point encapsulated in Paul's idea of a present, evil age is that "the human condition for everyone (apart from God's deed in Christ) is a form of slavery or subjugation to evil powers." Moreover, "for Paul, the problem that needs to be addressed ... is not so much 'sins,' transgressions of divinely given commandments, as Sin, a malevolent enslaving and god-like power under which all human beings are held captive."[41] In de Boer's reading of Galatians, then, evil is a malignant force that totally permeates and dominates the present age. The only hope is a new *creatio ex nihilo*, the creation of life unto God and neighbor from out of the nothingness of evil, sin, and death.

In the context of the present analysis we can leave aside the question of whether de Boer's reading of the apostle as an early Christian apocalyptic thinker is historically and exegetically warranted. Whatever the case, de Boer's Paul presents some significant challenges for systematic theologians who are wrestling with the exposition of the doctrine of creation and the problem of evil. As with Martyn's sharp differentiation between "the old" and new creation, here it remains unclear how God's salvific actions in the cross and resurrection relate to the original act of creation and to other first-article topics. As we observe in the extended citation from *Galatians* above, de Boer acknowledges that Jewish apocalyptic literature conceived God as creation's original artisan. But the Creator's control and authority over creation were usurped by God's enemies.[42] Implicitly, the fall becomes not simply the emergence of sin in the world, but the narrative of God's loss of creative fiat over creatures. In any event, the cosmological apocalyptic approach to the coordination of primal creation and the original invasion

---

41. De Boer, *Galatians*, 35.

42. For further reflection on this point, see Gaventa, "God Handed Them Over," in *Our Mother Saint Paul*, 111–23.

of evil into the world raises questions about both of these theological issues, and also about the fall and the doctrine of divine providence.

One additional note: de Boer's Paul understands evil as a force that permeates the world and enslaves all creatures. Among the many questions we might legitimately raise at this point, perhaps the most significant is how this apocalyptic understanding of evil squares with the idea of *goodness*, a motif found throughout the canonical witnesses and frequently explored in the theological tradition. To allude to one well-known counterexample to de Boer's reading of the problem of evil, in his "Treatise on Creation," Thomas Aquinas (1225–74) draws a distinction between goods that are wholly corrupted by evil, goods that are neither wholly destroyed nor diminished by evil, and essential aptitudes of a subject, which likewise cannot be utterly ruined by evil.[43] Without advocating or even explicating Thomas's solution to the problem of evil in light of the idea of the good, I enlist it here to point to but one instance of theology reaching for a nuanced philosophical account of Scripture's teachings on these difficult issues. De Boer's exegesis of Paul takes us in a different direction, namely, to evil as a material first principle of sorts for understanding anything on this side of the impending apocalypse.[44]

---

43. Thomas Aquinas, *Summa Theologica* 1, q. 48, a. 1. As Gilson points out, the basis of Thomas's distinctions is a theodicy according to which the good is acknowledged as the material cause of evil. See Gilson's discussion in *The Philosophy of St. Thomas Aquinas*, ed. G. A. Elrington, trans. Edward Bullough (New York: Dorset, 1987), 159–62; also the entirety of Thomas's argument in question 48. I am less interested here in Thomas's differentiated causality than I am with his principle that evil cannot fully overwhelm the good.

44. It remains to be seen whether an approach to theodicy by way of a "three-agent drama," as we observed in Ziegler's fourth thesis, sufficiently resolves the problems emerging here. That is, does the personification of evil agency in the demonic or the figure of the devil allow for a more complex and concrete dramatic depiction of reality as a conflict between opposing combatants? In spite of Martyn's and de Boer's frequent reminders of the significance of warfare imagery for Paul's cosmology, the description of evil remains at an abstract level; that is, evil is the principalities and powers described in Eph 6:12. Hence my claim that de Boer deploys the concept of evil as a material first principle of sorts: since evil, so it seems, permeates and governs all things apart from the invasive agency of God, it must condition our understanding of the cosmos. To put all this in another vein, if for Thomas the goodness of creation conditions theology's understanding of evil, for Martyn and de Boer (so it appears), evil is the given of the cosmos that the good action of God must overcome. I am open to the prospect that a theological account of Satan and/or demonology might take this discussion down another path.

CREATION AND THE PROBLEM OF
EVIL AFTER THE APOCALYPTIC TURN:
PROSPECTS AND UNFINISHED TASKS

While there is much more that can be said about what we have explored here, this chapter has at least succeeded in summarizing the contributions of apocalyptic theology to the perennial discussion of creation and evil. As I have presented it, apocalyptic theology makes an interesting and important contribution to this discussion by retrieving for Christian language biblical expressions concerning God's disruptive, newly creative, salvific actions. At the same time, and as we have encountered along the way, some significant methodological and material questions emerge in apocalyptic discourse on these topics. I draw attention to such questions here not to disparage theology done in an apocalyptic key, but as an invitation to further reflection and discussion about tasks which remain unfulfilled. Let me conclude by outlining my commendations and concerns, such as they are, in three movements, the points of which broadly correspond to my summary above of Ziegler's theses.

1. In the foregoing comments I selected for examination two recent commentaries on Paul's Epistle to the Galatians. As unusual a strategy as this might initially appear, it is demonstrable that the contemporary revival of apocalyptic *theology* owes more to the modern apocalyptic *exegesis of Paul* than it does to any other source or influence, ancient or modern. As such, to determine what apocalyptic theology has to say on any given theological topic, it is necessary to consider how Paul is being discussed among his apocalyptic interpreters. Just here, some of the possibilities and unfinished business of apocalyptic theology rise to the surface. On one hand, and to paraphrase Keck, apocalyptic theology endeavors to show us how we can think *with* Paul today so that we can learn to think *like* him.[45] Certainly contemporary theology has much to gain from paying heed to Paul's gritty and provocative thought.[46] On the other hand, it remains to be seen what can become of a theological movement that takes its exegetical cues primarily from a handful of Paul's letters, sometimes from the entirety of the

---

45. See Leander Keck, "Paul as Thinker," in *Christ's First Theologian: The Shape of Paul's Thought* (Waco, TX: Baylor University Press, 2015), 101.

46. Further to this, see the entirety of my essay "Word of the Cross."

Pauline corpus, occasionally from John's Gospel, from time to time from
various apocalyptic texts from the Second Temple period (particularly
Daniel and 1 Enoch), every once in a while from John's Apocalypse, and
less frequently from the other New Testament documents—the Synoptics,
Acts, and the non-Pauline epistles. It is not altogether self-evident how
exegetes and theologians wishing to capitalize on apocalyptic conceive the
entire witness of Christian Scripture.[47] Instead, often enough the literature of contemporary apocalyptic theology reads as if it is assumed that
apocalyptic texts from the Second Temple period (Pauline and otherwise)
alone stand out as sources of genuine theological insight. What has yet to
be undertaken convincingly is the apologetic task of defending the special
status of late Second Temple Jewish and early Christian apocalyptic texts
vis-à-vis other portions of canonical literature.[48]

Along these lines, we do well to observe that defenders of Pauline apocalyptic hardly can claim to have cornered the market on the interpretation
of Paul's letters and theology. In fact, at present the apocalyptic school
remains outside the majority in the guild of Pauline scholarship. This suggests, I think, that those who endeavor to capitalize on the apocalyptic
interpretation of Paul must remain alert to the fact that this is but one
of several options for how to open the apostle's letters. The ongoing conflict of interpretations is especially pertinent to the study of our topics,
since each Paul in the debates—the Augustinian-Reformation Paul, the
new-perspective Paul, the apocalyptic Paul, and so on—is conceived as
having some particular approach to the problem of how God is related
to creation and to this present, evil age. Whichever tack we take into the
exegesis of Paul's epistles determines how we perceive his contribution to
these theological themes. And the scientific study of Paul is hardly static.
Rather, as the guild of scientific exegesis continues to investigate and dis-
pute the New Testament epistolary tradition, our knowledge of the origins

---

47. To register a couple of notable exceptions to this tendency to focus on the Pauline
canon: Martyn, *History and Theology*; Dale C. Allison, *The End of the Ages Has Come: An Early
Interpretation of the Passion and Resurrection of Jesus*, Studies in the New Testament and Its
World (Edinburgh: T&T Clark, 1985); Joel Marcus, *Mark*, Anchor Bible 27 (New York: Doubleday,
2000; New Haven: Yale University Press, 2009).

48. Or perhaps a case convincingly can be made that we are able to read Scripture canon-
ically *and* apocalyptically from Genesis to Revelation. My point here, again, is that more work
needs to be done to show how apocalyptic themes pertain to other segments of the canon.

CREATION AND THE PROBLEM OF EVIL AFTER THE APOCALYPTIC TURN   157

and nature of Paul's thought both advances and continues to become more complicated. This being the case, theology of any persuasion, apocalyptic or otherwise, should be wary of, as it were, putting all of its exegetical eggs into one basket.

2. Apocalyptic readings of Paul and theologies that draw from them tend to stress the disruptive or interruptive character of God's actions in the economy of creation, redemption, and consummation. As we have seen in the literature of contemporary apocalyptic theology, this invasive, alien conception of divine agency and righteousness corresponds to an emphasis on the *new* creation at the expense of any attention to primal creation. The world is evil, its course determined by the principalities and powers that rule the present age. The creatively redemptive actions of God, "who gives life to the dead and calls into existence things which do not exist" (Rom 4:17), occur perpendicularly in the world. New creation is *entirely* new. As Fleming Rutledge puts it, summarizing Martyn, God's creatively redemptive actions mark "a genuine *novum*, a first-order reversal of all previous arrangements, an altogether new creation *ex nihilo*, out of nothing."[49] In Ziegler's idiom, apocalyptic expressions in the New Testament "are not images of mere repair, development, or incremental improvement within a broadly stable situation," but rather suggest "a radical break with what has gone before, its overturning, its revolution, its displacement."[50] Certainly this way of describing God's actions bears significant explanatory potential, as it encapsulates, in language derived largely from Paul's potent evangelical rhetoric, theology's witness against the oppressive and hegemonic forces that appear to dominate the world.

However, and as we have observed throughout this chapter, apocalyptic theology's emphasis on the interventive and interruptive aspects of divine agency raises a number of questions that call for further reflection. Exegetically, this way of structuring God's relation to the world folds back on the question of whether justice is here being done to other canonical witnesses. Demonstrably so, Scripture speaks of primal creation as good, of God doing things in the world that take time, of sequences of events

---

49. Fleming Rutledge, *The Crucifixion: Understanding the Death of Jesus Christ* (Grand Rapids: Eerdmans, 2015), 355.

50. Ziegler, *Militant Grace*, 28.

corresponding to a divine plan, and so on. Likewise, a comprehensive theological exposition of God's creative, redemptive, and consummative actions will endeavor to account for the many and various ways God relates to creatures, in doing so resisting unnuanced, contrastive cosmologies according to which God relates to the world only as the world's crisis. Robert Jenson, commenting on these options for theological cosmology, observes that "the late modern discourse of tangents and perpendiculars and incommensurabilities in general [is] just Platonism stripped to its geometry."[51] An overstatement, perhaps, but still effective for encapsulating the concern: enclosed within the world is evil and decay unto death; divine righteousness and goodness break into the world from beyond, but in no way inhabit it, like a line perpendicularly puncturing or tangentially touching a sphere at only one point. Such geometry for conceiving God's relation to the world renders it difficult to identify genuine goodness in the world or to connect the world and all it contains to God's creative agency.

3. A final comment for now takes us to the question of the systematicity of apocalyptic theology. If there is a leitmotif to what we have considered in this chapter, it is that modern expressions of apocalyptic theology trade on supposed discontinuities between certain binaries—old and new, law and gospel, Israel and the community of the faith, and so on. At the heart of the matter is a particular reading of a Pauline account of the sheer newness of the cross and resurrection of Jesus Christ. "Hearing the apocalyptic gospel," Ziegler explains, "rivets our attention to the events of incarnation, crucifixion, and resurrection as the hinge on which the 'ages turn.'" Consequently, and in terms of theology's systematic order and structure, "apocalyptic theology ... has its center of gravity firmly in the second, christological article of the ancient creeds of the church."[52]

While there is much to be admired in a Christian theology so conceived, it is not difficult to detect here the hallmarks of modern Protestantism's intellectual routine of reading the first and third creedal articles only in light of the second, of siphoning all statements about God through the confession of God's actions in the economy, and, in particular, the cross

---

51. Robert W. Jenson, "On Dogmatic/Systematic Appropriation of Paul-according-to-Martyn," in Davis and Harink, *Apocalyptic and the Future of Theology*, 160.
52. Ziegler, *Militant Grace*, 27.

and resurrection of Jesus Christ. In terms of systematic theology, the overwhelming stress on Christology folds back on the expositions of doctrines such as theology proper, creation, providence, ecclesiology, pneumatology, and sacramental theology. In the literature of apocalyptic theology, these lateral connections between regions of Christian teaching are not always drawn transparently and coherently. Hence, if there is a remaining *systematic* task for theology after the apocalyptic turn, it is to show how, to borrow a classical metaphor, the entire body of divinity holds together if the entryway into doctrine is the crucified and resurrected Christ.

While I remain open to the possibilities for theology that might be uncovered as this task is undertaken, I worry that a relentless stress on the cross and resurrection is too much for a systematic account of Christian teaching to bear. As I have suggested in this chapter, accentuating an apocalyptically invasive account of Christology may distort material arranged beneath the heading of the first article. The order of the exposition of the articles seems to run in reverse in apocalyptic theology, and, by consequence, first-article themes threaten to take on unbecoming shapes. John Webster summarizes the insight behind the alternative approach to the order of theological exposition: "The extensive material in the second domain of Christian teaching will arise naturally from and make appropriate backward reference to the material on the first domain; economy is most fully seen when illuminated by theology, which it in turn illuminates."[53] On the other hand, when theology initiates every statement from within the second domain, it becomes difficult for faith to speak clearly and concretely about "God the Father Almighty, creator of heaven and earth." Our topics—creation, the problem of evil, and (tacitly) providence—are among the themes of the first domain that tend to wane when economy is conceived as the starting point of every theological discussion.

---

53. John Webster, "Christology, Theology, Economy: The Place of Christology in Systematic Theology," in *God without Measure: Working Papers in Christian Theology*, vol. 1, *God and the Works of God* (London: Bloomsbury T&T Clark, 2015), 53.

9
—

CREATION WITHOUT COVENANT, PROVIDENCE WITHOUT WISDOM

The Example of Cormac McCarthy's The Crossing

Kenneth Oakes

INTRODUCTION

The doctrine of creation forms an integral part of Christian confession and teaching. Theology is permitted and commanded to speak of creation inasmuch as the prophetic and apostolic witness draws our attention to the God who created all things, visible and invisible; to the setting in which we live (creation); to the nature of humanity as created to the image of God (anthropology); to the universal fallenness of our world and ourselves, and our voluntary and involuntary participation in this corruption (sin); to God's continuing patient and wise work on behalf of providing for his creatures (providence); and to the ends for which creatures exist (reconciliation, eschatology).[1] As part of the prophetic and apostolic witness, the doctrine of creation and its various parts form an article of faith no less than that of the election of Israel, the incarnation of the eternal Son and the outpouring of the Spirit, the resurrection and glorification of Jesus Christ, and the just and glorious end of all things. In the words of Hebrews 11:3:

---

1. As John Webster succinctly remarks, "The Christian doctrine of creation treats four topics: the Holy Trinity as creator, the act of creation, the nature of created things, and the relation of God and creatures." John Webster, *God without Measure: Working Papers in Christian Theology*, vol. 1, *God and the Works of God* (London: Bloomsbury T&T Clark, 2015), 119.

"By faith we understand that the worlds were prepared by the word of God, so that which is seen was made from things that are not seen" (NRSV).

Not only is the doctrine of creation actually composed of a range of doctrines, but it intertwines with, abuts, and depends on other doctrines. The doctrine of creation stretches backward into the doctrine of the Trinity, the character of the divine essence, and the divine perfections; it stretches forwards into the doctrine of reconciliation as the reestablishment and elevation of the creature; and it reaches into eschatology as well, as the final judgment and glorification of all things. Similarly, one could reverse the direction of these metaphors and note that the doctrines of God, reconciliation, and redemption all affect and shape the doctrine of creation.

While each aspect of the doctrine of creation is connected to a host of other doctrines, they are not all connected in the same way. Perhaps the most significant aspect of the doctrine of creation is the infinite difference between Creator and creation. The difference between Creator and creation is primarily established by two interrelated claims: (1) by the perfection and aseity of the triune God, and (2) by the doctrine of *creatio ex nihilo*. These two claims are in fact two sides of the same coin: that the triune God has infinite life in and of himself, and that creation only has life from another. Together they deny that there are two (or more) ultimate principles and insist that there is one God who has created all things. Together they also deny that there is a larger temporal, moral, physical, or metaphysical context that God shares with his creatures. There is no overarching context or genus that the Creator shares with his creatures. These are irreducible aspects of the doctrine of God and of creation that are never sublated throughout the range of Christian doctrines.

Some aspects of the doctrine of creation only gain their full force in the light of other doctrines, such as covenant, election, reconciliation, and eschatology. The creature is not simply posited and then left to its own devices, but from the outset the creature is irreducibly and continually related to its Creator in an ongoing history. Equally, the Creator does not simply posit the creature, leave it to its own devices, and then attend to the more interesting parts of the universe. From the outset of creation, the Creator is graciously and lovingly involved with the creature in an ongoing history. The Creator has pledged himself in steadfast love and faithfulness to creation and expects creation to be faithful in turn. Another way of expressing these ideas is to repeat Karl Barth's insight that "creation is the external basis of the covenant" and that "the covenant is the internal basis of creation."[2]

Equally, the doctrine of providence, which is perhaps one of the most difficult doctrines to prevent from falling into misuse and overuse, depends on a host of other theological resources. It depends on the identity and perfection of God, and in particular God's omnipotent wisdom and patience; it depends on an understanding of evil and sin as that which God does not desire for his creatures and yet that are permitted to exercise their rage and cunning in our current age; and it depends on reconciliation and glorification as divine actions that move beyond God's caring continuance and preservation of the creature.

It is only after a good number of claims and a great deal of doctrinal content is in place and has been secured that Christian theology can turn to consider evil. Indeed, there is an interesting asymmetry to the topic of creation and evil. For, unlike creation, evil is not a mystery of the faith, it does not exist alongside the other mysteries of the faith as an equal member, and it is not worthy of our contemplative adoration. While the power and triumphal march of evil, its seeming ineradicability, and its host of subtle and less visible forms seem far more certain and enduring than these paltry confessions of faith, it remains the case that theology can speak best and most honestly about evil, its multifaceted character, and its sway only when it is confident regarding its own positive claims regarding the Creator and creation.

In what follows I consider the constellation of God, creation, providence, and evil in Cormac McCarthy's 1994 novel *The Crossing*. This exercise seems warranted given that this set of theological themes and resonances is noticeably present in McCarthy's work,[3] while other doctrines that Christians often employ when making sense of creation and evil, such as covenant, reconciliation, and eschatology, are absent. The aim of this

---

2. See Karl Barth, *Church Dogmatics* III/1, *The Doctrine of Creation*, ed. G. W. Bromiley and T. F. Torrance, trans. J. W. Edwards, O. Bussey, and H. Knight (Edinburgh: T&T Clark, 1958), 94–329.

3. For one example, see J. Douglas Cranfield, "The Border of Becoming: Theodicy in *Blood Meridian*," in *Mavericks on the Border: The Early Southwest in Historical Fiction and Film* (Lexington: University Press of Kentucky, 2001), 37–48.

exercise is thus twofold: (1) to identify some of the prominent theological themes in *The Crossing*, and (2) to consider whether these themes can be helpfully illuminated from the perspective of doctrines of God, creation, and providence disconnected from the rest of Christian doctrine.

AN INTRODUCTION TO *THE CROSSING*

The Crossing (1994) is the second book of McCarthy's border trilogy, which is preceded by *All the Pretty Horses* (1992) and followed by *Cities of the Plain* (1998). The novel takes place before and during World War II and details the misadventures and misfortunes of Billy Parham. While the title of the novel is *The Crossing* in the singular, the plot is structured by three crossings between New Mexico and Mexico, with each crossing bringing its own form of tragedy and woe. The first begins when Billy returns a female grey wolf he had trapped to Mexico (91) and ends with the merciful death of the she-wolf at Billy's own hands after she had been taken from him and used in a pit fight (122).[4] The second begins after Billy comes home to discover that his parents have been brutally murdered and reunites with his younger brother Boyd, and both of them set out to recover their stolen family horses (170). This second crossing ends after Boyd has been shot, recovers, and then disappears with a young girl. Billy returns home to find that World War II has begun, and he unsuccessfully tries to enlist in the army several times but is turned down on account of a congenital condition of having an enlarged heart. The third crossing begins as Billy sets out to discover Boyd's whereabouts (355). He comes to learn that Boyd had become a kind of revolutionary, was killed in a gunfight and memorialized in various corridos, and Billy seeks his body so as to return it to New Mexico. Billy exhumes his brother's body and is ambushed by four horsemen, who desecrate Boyd's remains and stab his horse in the chest (396). A band of gypsies help the horse recover (412), and the novel ends with Billy chasing away an old dog (423), obliquely witnessing the light given off by the first atomic bomb explosion, and sitting and weeping in rain as "the right and godmade sun did rise, once again, and without

---

4. Parenthetical references are to Cormac McCarthy, *The Crossing* (New York: Vintage, 1995).

distinction" (426).[5] *The Crossing*, then, tells the story of three tragic and violent crossings bound together and experienced by Billy Parham.

In terms of analyzing the novel for its ideas and presuppositions regarding God, creation, providence, and evil, one could consider the plot itself, filled as it is with violence, misfortune, and unwise decisions but also with many moments of care, hospitality, and charity. Alternatively, one could consider the narrator's characterization of the events of the plot and their causal relation, or the narrator's depiction of nature, which many studies of McCarthy have recently highlighted.[6] Finally, one could consider the perspectives of the characters themselves, which is the primary approach adopted here.

The novel's three crossings are interwoven with four dense meditations on God, creation, evil, providence, and destiny offered by some of the characters whom Billy meets. These reflections are striking given their length, complexity, and noticeable contrast with the otherwise sparse prose of the quotidian conversations between the characters. Their presence in the novel has led one commentator to remark:

> Thus we may read *The Crossing* (the title itself has multiple meanings, inherently spiritual), with its wise old men and women who give warnings or gifts, its unaccountable, vaguely angelic strangers who tell complex stories demanding exegesis or symbolic interpretation, its moments of sudden illumination leading to supra-rational states of awe or even majestic terror, as a book of revelation itself, a mystical text in the guise of a western adventure.[7]

---

5. The light that awakens Billy as he sleeps in the desert seems to be the "Trinity" nuclear test conducted in New Mexico on July 16, 1945. See Alex Hunt, "Right and False Suns: Cormac McCarthy's *The Crossing* and the Advent of the Atomic Age," *Southwest American Literature* 23, no. 2 (April 1998): 31–37.

6. From a growing literature, see Wallis R. Sanborn III, *Animals in the Fiction of Cormac McCarthy* (Jefferson, NC: McFarland, 2006); Steven Frye, "Cormac McCarthy's 'World in the Making': Romantic Naturalism in *The Crossing*," *Studies in American Naturalism* 2, no. 1 (Summer 2007): 46–65; Gabriella Blasi, "Reading Allegory and Nature in Cormac McCarthy's *The Road*: Towards a Non-anthropocentric Vision of the Language of Nature," *Arcadia* 49, no. 1 (2014): 89–102; K. Wesley Berry, "The Lay of the Land in Cormac McCarthy's Appalachia," in *Cormac McCarthy: New Directions*, ed. James D. Lilley (Albuquerque: University of New Mexico Press, 2002), 47–74.

7. Edwin T. Arnold, " 'Go to Sleep': Dreams and Visions in the Border Trilogy," in *A Cormac McCarthy Companion: The Border Trilogy*, ed. Edwin T. Arnold and Dianne C. Luce (Jackson: University Press of Mississippi, 2001), 37–72, here 58–59.

Additionally, three of these conversations are ruminations on past events, their meaning, and the place of God and providence within them.[8] These conversations are in reality more akin to monologues, as Billy essentially listens to other characters making sense of past tragedies in cosmic, metaphysical, and theological terms. The first and shortest instance of these monologues occurs with Don Arnulfo before Billy's first crossing, and each of his crossings has one such monologue: (1) from an ex-Mormon-turned-priest-turned-ex-priest, (2) from a former revolutionary who is now blind, and (3) from a gypsy who is hauling the wreckage of a plane down a mountain. In what follows I will consider these four discussions in order to show that there is a fairly consistent theological worldview put forth by the characters, which can also be seen in the novel's final pages. This theological worldview includes an inscrutable God who continually creates and weaves ephemeral beings into and out of existence, bends the course of history to his own mysterious will, and yet who cares and provides for all of his creatures, whether righteous or unrighteous. Additionally, this universal determination and care for good and evil alike is actually the form of God's grace and blessing for his creatures.

DON ARNULFO, OR THE OLD MAN

Before Billy makes his first crossing, he meets with an old man named Don Arnulfo in the town of Animas, New Mexico, in order to consult Don regarding his knowledge of wolves and how to trap them (42–49). In the course of their conversation, Don Arnulfo tells Billy that the wolf "knows what men do not: that there is no order in the world save that which death has put there" (45) and that "if men drink the blood of God yet they do not understand the seriousness of what they do" (45). There is a disconnection between the world of human beings and their acts, ceremonies, and

---

8. Charles Bailey helpfully notes, "The novel's three crossings are divided into four artistic parts, each presenting a storyteller, an Ancient Mariner whom Billy serves as wedding guest," and, "Each narrates a different story, but each has the same message. And the message of the four storytellers (from McCarthy's perspective, the message of all storytellers) is, not incidentally, about time." See Charles Bailey, " 'Doomed Enterprises' and Faith: The Structure of Cormac McCarthy's *The Crossing*," *Southwestern American Literature* 20 (Fall 1994): 57–67, here 58. We would add that the messages of the four stories are also united in their understandings of God, history, and evil.

sacraments, and the world of nature, with its storms blowing and trees twisting in the wind, a world "of all the animals that God made go to and fro yet this world men do not see" (46). Human beings can only see "the acts of their own hands" and the things they name, and so they are estranged from the immediate world of creation and nature is "invisible" to them. As Billy is leaving, Don Arnulfo tells him that the scent Billy has for the wolf trap will not work and that instead "the boy should find that place where acts of God and those of man are of a piece. Where they cannot be distinguished" (47). After Billy asks about this type of place, Don Arnulfo replies that these are places where iron is already in the earth and that fire has already burned, for "it was at such places that God sits and conspires in the destruction of that which he has been at such pains to create." Don Arnulfo then adds, "y por eso soy hereje" ("and for that I am a heretic") (47). The old man's enigmatic instructions prove effective, for Billy eventually catches the wolf with a trap laid in a campfire pit filled with "ashes and charcoal and fresh bones" (50).

After trapping the she-wolf, Billy decides to return her to Mexico instead of collecting the bounty on her hide. The wolf is then taken from Billy to be used in a dog-fighting pit, and Billy kills the mangled and battered wolf in an act of mercy. After removing and burying the wolf, Billy attempts to imagine her vision of the world and sees: "Deer and hare and dove and groundvole all richly empaneled on the air for her delight, all nations of the possible world ordained by God of which she was among and not separate from" (127).

In his discussion with Don Arnulfo and in his vision of the world of nature, there are representations of God, creation, and providence: God has made all the animals that come to and fro, and the wolf belongs to all "nations of the possible world ordained by God." As for the nature of this providence, however, the wolf is aware that the "only order in the world is death," an awareness that escapes human beings. Additionally, the actions of God and human beings only seem to coincide in places where "God sits and conspires in the destruction" of what he has made. When Billy asks about this place, the image the Don invokes is that of fire, which is both natural and harnessed by humans, and is indeed the place where Billy catches the she-wolf.[9] In this brief conversation there is astonishment at the riches and beauty of creation; the sense that providence, the order of the world, is finally death; and the suggestion that God not only creates but also participates in the destruction of what he has created.

THE EX-MORMON-TURNED-EX-PRIEST

The second vignette is more convoluted and involves a long story within a story (137–59).[10] After burying the wolf, Billy briefly wanders around the sierras and barrancas around the Bavispe River in the state of Sonora and comes into the depilated town of Huisiachepic. As he passes the ruins of the church, he is invited inside by a man with sandy hair, pale skin, and blue eyes. "You are lost," the man informs Billy, in one of the many lines throughout the novel that suggest Billy's displacement and separation from his home and from those around him. The day of the week turns out to be Sunday, and so in this ruined church, on a Sunday, only the man and Billy stand before God.

The man states that he was a Mormon, then converted to Roman Catholicism, and then became himself.[11] He says that he has been the custodian and caretaker of this ruined church for the past six years and that the church was ruined in an earthquake in 1887.[12] The ex-Mormon came to the town and the church "as a heretic fleeing a prior life" (141), and precisely because of the devastation of the church:

---

9. An alternative viewpoint regarding the Don comes from the woman who takes care of him and who tells Billy that the Don is a "brujo," that people say "God has abandoned this man" for his pride, that he thinks that he "knows better than the priest" and "better than God," and that in reality faith is everything (48–49).

10. This conversation is sometimes taken to be the novel's center and has received a great deal of critical attention. See Matthew Potts, *Cormac McCarthy and the Signs of Sacrament: Literature, Theology, and the Moral of Stories* (London: Bloomsbury, 2015), 152–56; Petra Mundik, *A Bloody and Barbarous God: The Metaphysics of Cormac McCarthy* (Albuquerque: University of New Mexico Press, 2016), 141–59; Edwin T. Arnold, "McCarthy and the Sacred: A Reading of *The Crossing*," in Lilley, *Cormac McCarthy: New Directions*, 215–38, here 224–26; James Keegan, " 'Save Yourself': The Boundaries of Theodicy and the Signs of *The Crossing*," *The Cormac McCarthy Journal* 1, no. 1 (Spring 2001): 44–61.

11. Consistent with McCarthy's care for historical and geographical detail, Mormon colonies were indeed founded in the states of Sonora and Chihuahua in the 1880s, most of which were evacuated in 1912.

12. In 1887 there was an earthquake around the town Bavispe that killed forty-two people and destroyed the town church, San Miguel de Bavispe.

I was seeking evidence for the hand of God in the world. I had come
to believe that hand a wrathful one and I thought that men had not
inquired sufficiently into miracles of destruction. Into disasters of
a certain magnitude. I thought there might be evidence that had
been overlooked. I thought that He would not trouble to wipe away
every handprint. My desire to know was very strong. I thought it
might even amuse him to leave some clue. (142)

The ex-Mormon was looking for a clue behind this devastation and
explains, "What I wanted to know was his mind. I could not believe He
would destroy his own church without reason" (142). Billy conjectures
that perhaps the townspeople had done some wrong, and the ex-Mormon
agrees with this initial premise: maybe the people themselves "goaded"
God's "hand against it," as with the cities on the plains (a reference to
Gen 19:19).[13] But the man tells Billy that he did not find anything in the
rubble of the town that would suggest such wickedness, no clue as to the
meaning of this event, but that he instead found "Nothing. A doll. A dish.
A bone" (142).

The ex-Mormon then tells Billy that he came to this church to retrace
the steps of a man from Caborca. Before telling the sad story of the man
from Caborca, the ex-Mormon tells Billy that all corridos, all stories, all
tales, finally tell one story. "So everything is necessary. Every least thing.
... And whether in Caborca or in Huisiachepic or in whatever other place
by whatever other name or by no name at all I say again all tales are one.
Rightly heard all tales are one" (143). When still a child, the man from
Caborca's parents were killed in a church while the child was spared; he
then grew up, got married, and had a son of his own. He left the child with
his uncle in Bavispe as the man had some business in another town. While
he was away there was an earthquake, and the boy died under some fallen
rubble. The man returned to Bavispe, saw the devastation, and took the
dead boy back to his mother in Huisiachepic, as a kind of tragic perversion
of his promise to bring her a gift when he returned. The man began to roam,

---

13. "And it came to pass, when God destroyed the cities of the plain, that God remembered
Abraham, and sent Lot out of the midst of the overthrow, when he overthrew the cities in
which Lot dwelt" (Gen 19:29 KJV). The *Cities on the Plain* is the third book in the border trilogy.

and it is unclear what became of his wife. The man from Caborca came to believe that he had been elected by "the hand of Providence" as he has been spared from disaster twice. He became a heretic, then became a message carrier in the capital, and he came to believe that there was another order in the world. The man from Caborca did not cease to believe in God, but "It was rather that he came to believe terrible things of Him" (148). Now lonely and old, the man from Caborca began to pray and to dream of God (149). The ex-Mormon explains,

> Who can dream of God? This man did. In his dreams God was much occupied. Spoken to He did not answer. Called to did not hear. The man could see Him bent at his work. As if through a glass. Seated solely in the light of his own presence. Weaving the world. In his hands it flowed out of nothing and in his hands it vanished into nothing once again. So. Here was a God to study, A God who seemed a slave to his own selfordained duties. A God with a fathomless capacity to bend all to an inscrutable purpose. Not chaos itself lay outside that matrix. And somewhere in that tapestry that was the world in its making and in its unmaking was a thread that was he and he woke weeping. (149)

The man returned to Caborca and took up residence in the church of La Purísma Concepción de Nuestra Señora de Caborca, the same church where his parents were killed. The man took his Bible, entered into the ruined church, and became a hermit. The people of the town came to watch the man, unsure whether he was a saint or mad, and they watched the man flip through the pages of his Bible and argue aloud with God. This man wanted to establish a *colindancia*, or boundaries, with his Maker, to declare what territory belongs to him and what territory belongs to God, but the ex-Mormon points out that "with God there can be no reckoning" (151). The townspeople sent for a priest, and the priest came to speak with him but remained outside the church, thereby sacrificing "his words of their power to witness" (152). The priest stood outside of the church and spoke to the man of the goodness and love of God, and the man and the priest continued to argue.

The man from Caborca began to sense that he had been outwitted by God and that "In the end it seemed" that God had "turned even the old man's heretical usurpations to his own service" (156). The man saw that he was "indeed elect and that the God of the universe was yet more terrible than men reckoned" (156). The priest was deeply shaken and altered by his encounter with this man and finally joined the man in the ruined church. The man from Caborca told the priest what he had learned, that "It is God's grace alone that we are bound by this thread of life" (156). Despite their now-shared space, there was a still a difference between the priest and the man. When the man was dying the priest thought that he wanted absolution and began to administer last rites, but the old man rejected this gesture and told the priest "save yourself" (157). While dying the man told the priest "that he'd been wrong in every reckoning of God and yet had come at last to an understanding of Him anyway" (157). The man saw that "the path of the world is one and not many and there is no alter course in any least part of it for that course is fixed by God and contains all consequence in the way of its going" (158). In the end the man from Caborca was buried in the churchyard.

"Who was the priest?" the ex-Mormon asks. He explains that in the end the priest was not really a priest, but just an advocate of "priestly things" and that the priest in the story is the ex-Mormon himself. The ex-Mormon tells Billy that he came to see what the hermit could not: "That God needs no witness. Neither to himself nor against" (158). God does not need priests to witness for him, nor heretics to witness against him. In fact, the priest understands that "To God every man is a heretic" and that "The heretic's first act is to name his brother. So that he may step free of him" (158). He tells Billy, "Every word we speak is a vanity," and yet we must bless with every breath. The ex-Mormon concludes his tale of tragedy told in a ruined church by saying, "In the end we shall all of us be only what we have made of God. For nothing is real save his grace" (158).

Such a complex tale within a tale has understandably elicited a host of different interpretations. Matthew Potts views this story as the encounter and conflict between two modes of natural theology, with the ex-Mormon being a kind of pantheist and the man from Caborca a kind of gnostic, both of which stand opposed to revealed theology.[14] Steven Frye offers a Hegelian reading of the characterizations of God and history throughout

---

14. Potts, *Cormac McCarthy and the Signs of Sacrament*, 154–55.

the novel, which is especially manifest in this vignette.[15] James Keegan has noted and explored the tale's resonances with the book of Job, as the priest comes to comfort the suffering man from Caborca who stands in the devastated church arguing with God and who finally arrives at some understanding of God.[16] Edwin Arnold maintains that this tale reflects Jacob Boehme's mystical philosophy of the "matrix" as the source of all being, his anthropology, and his view of the relationship between good and evil.[17] Petra Mundik has perhaps offered the most complex account of this tale. She argues that the man from Caborca moves from belief in "a lower-order creator of the cosmos" to "an ineffable Absolute," while the ex-Mormon moves from a kind of realism or empiricism (evident in his initial search for material things in the ruined church) to idealism when he realizes that there is only one tale, that history is essentially one, and that the material world is an illusion.[18] Each of these interpretations is illuminating in its own way, and yet we should add that several themes from the earlier monologues are repeated: a God who creates from nothing and vanishes his creation into nothing and who ceaselessly weaves the world into existence and into nonexistence; a God who follows his own self-ordained duties and bends all to an inscrutable purpose, as even this man from Caborca is part of God's providential weaving and bending of all things; the fixed nature of history; that all human beings who are both elected and nonelected and stand as heretics before God may still be buried in the churchyard; and that this ephemeral and tragic providential order springs nonetheless from the grace and blessing of God.[19]

---

15. Steven Frye, *Understanding Cormac McCarthy* (Columbia: University of South Carolina Press, 2009), 122–32.

16. Keegan, " 'Save Yourself,' " 44–61.

17. Arnold, "McCarthy and the Sacred," 224–26.

18. Mundik, *Bloody and Barbarous God*, 141.

19. The similarities to the weaver god of Hermann Melville's *Moby-Dick*, chapter 102, "A Bower in the Arsacides," have been noted: "Oh, busy weaver! unseen weaver!—pause!—one word!—whither flows the fabric? what palace may it deck? wherefore all these ceaseless toilings? Speak, weaver!—stay thy hand!—but one single word with thee! Nay—the shuttle flies—the figures float from forth the loom; the freshet-rushing carpet for ever slides away. The weaver-god, he weaves; and by that weaving is he deafened, that he hears no mortal voice; and by that humming, we, too, who look on the loom are deafened; and only when we escape it shall we hear the thousand voices that speak through it." See Herman Melville, *Moby-Dick or The White Whale* (Boston: C. H. Simonds, 1922), 422–23; Frye, *Understanding Cormac McCarthy*, 127–28.

THE BLIND FORMER REVOLUTIONARY

In his second crossing Billy encounters a blind former revolutionary, whose wife relates to Billy some of the poignant tragedies that have befallen them both with occasional interjections from her husband (274–94). Her tale is long and convoluted and filled with the wisdom and philosophies of different characters, and is followed by the blind revolutionary himself meditating on these misfortunes, the meaning assigned to them by others, and his own understanding of their metaphysical context. A variety of themes are discussed: light and darkness (both physical and metaphysical), sight and blindness, evil and righteousness, and the place and rôle of God in creation and history.

While this tale and these meditations are worthy of extended analysis, here we can only note several reflections relevant to our own purposes. After relating how the former revolutionary lost his eyes in a horrific act of violence from a German supporter of Victoriano Huerta named Wirtz, the wife adds that this event happened twenty-eight years ago and that much has changed and yet everything is the same. The blind man then speaks up and says, "Nothing had changed and all was different. The world was new each day for God so made it daily. Yet it contained within it all the evils as before, no more, no less" (277–78). In a retold conversation with a friend, the blind man says, "The light of the world was in men's eyes only for the world itself moved in eternal darkness and darkness was its true nature and true condition" (283). The blind man then says that "he could stare down the sun and what use was that?" (283) as the narrator notes that they sit quietly while "The sun shone upon them" (283).

The wife of the blind man has also suffered tremendously, as becomes clear when she relates the story of a young girl whose two brothers and father were murdered by a group of Huertistas. As her mother had died many years ago, the young girl wandered through the streets that night holding her father's hat and came to the town church, which was "empty" (287). In this bare church the town's sepulturero, or gravedigger, came to comfort her:

> He said that while one would like to say that God will punish those who do such things and that people often speak in just this way it was his experience that God could not be spoken for and that men

with wicked histories often enjoyed lives of comfort and that they died in peace and were buried with honor. He said that it was a mistake to expect too much of justice in this world. He said that the notion that evil is seldom rewarded was greatly outspoken for if there were no advantage to it then men would shun it and how could virtue then be attached to its repudiation? (288)

The gravedigger's final words of solace to the girl were to remember the dead, their faces, to speak their names, and to "do this and do not let sorrow die for it is the sweetening of every gift" (288). Billy later asks the blind man what he thinks of the sepulturero's views. He responds by adding that much of what the sepulturero said is true, "that every tale was a tale of dark and light and would perhaps not have it otherwise" (292). Yet he claims that the sepulturero's understanding is incomplete: that the power of immense evil is such that human beings will ignore it; that "the order which the righteous seek is only order," while "the disorder of evil is in the fact the thing itself"; that "the righteous are hampered at every turn by their ignorance of evil to the evil all is plain, light and dark alike"; and that the righteous man "will seek to impose order and lineage upon things which rightly have none" (293).

The blind man admits with the sepulturero that "Quizás hay poca justicia en este mundo" ("Perhaps there is little justice in this world"), but goes on to say that the reason for his lack of complete understanding is not found in the world itself, but in the "perilous" "picture of the world" (293) that all human beings entertain. The truth, the blind man tells Billy, is that "The world which he imagines to be the ciborium of all godlike things will come to naught but dust before him. For the world to survive it must be replenished daily. This man will be required to begin again whether he wishes to or no" (293). The world and history as the "ciborium of all godlike things," whether one takes the reference to a ciborium either architecturally or eucharistically, will also turn to dust. He also says, "Ultimamente sabemos que no podemos ver el buen Dios. Vamos escuchando. Me entiendes, joven? Debemos escuchar" ("Ultimately we know that we cannot see the good God. We listen. Do you understand me, young man? We have to listen"; 292). The narrator continues, " 'Lo que debemos entender,' said the blind man, 'es que ultimamente todo es polvo. Todo lo que podemos

tocar. Todo lo que podemos ver. En esto tenemos la evidencia más profunda
de la justicia, de la misericordia. En esto vemos la bendición más grande
de Dios' " ("What we have to understand is that everything is finally dust.
Everything that we can touch. Everything that we can see. In this we have
the deepest proof of justice, or mercy. In this we have the greatest blessing of God") (293). These words understandably surprise Billy, and so he
asks the blind man,

> why this was such a blessing and the blind man did not answer
> and did not answer and then at last he said that because what can
> be touched falls to dust there can be no mistaking these things
> for the real. At best they are only tracings of where the real has
> been. Perhaps they are not even that. Perhaps they are no more
> than obstacles to be negotiated in the ultimate sightlessness of the
> world. (294)

THE GYPSY

During his third crossing, as he is carrying Boyd's remains back to the
United States, Billy runs across a group of gypsies moving the remains
or "skeleton" of an airplane (401–14). When Billy asks about the wreckage's destination, one of the gypsies tells him that the ruined airplane has
three histories, and Billy responds that he would like to hear the true one.
The gypsy explains, in what seems to be the first history, that there were
actually two airplanes that were lost in the mountains in 1915, and both
had young Americans for their pilot. The second history appears to be
the disastrous attempt to retrieve one of the planes at the request of the
father of one of the dead pilots. The gypsy and another man accepted the
undertaking, and the gypsy realized that the expedition raises the "question of identity" (405), for the two men cannot and do not know whether
the plane they found and attempted to remove from the mountains was
indeed the correct plane. This plane was eventually lost in a river during
transit, and thus "as is so often the case God had finally taken a hand and
decided things himself. For ultimately both planes were carried down from
the mountain and one was in the Rio Papigochic and the other was before
them. Como lo ve" (406).

Reflection on God, providence, and history continues as the gypsy considers the significance of this series of events. The gypsy muses, "God will not permit that we shall know what is to come. He is bound to no one that the world unfold just so on its course" (407), and even those who are able to discern the future may unknowingly cause God to "wrench the world from its heading and set it upon another course altogether" (407). The gypsy also thinks that God did indeed decide which of the two planes the gypsies would now carry but does not believe "that by this act God had spoken to anyone" (410). Additionally, the gypsy claims that too much importance is often given to the past and its artifacts, for "the past was little more than a dream and its force in the world greatly exaggerated. For the world was made new each day, and it was only men's clinging to its vanished husks that could make of that world one husk more" (411).

The third history of the plane's wreckage seems to be humanity's general and continual attempt to render intelligible to itself the course of history from the ruined artifacts of the past that surround it. Such a universal history not only includes Billy's own present journey to return home his brother's bones but also the past stories of the ex-priest and the man from Caborca, their indwelling of ruined churches, and their impulse to make theological and historical meaning in the wake of tragedies. The gypsy explains that "the history each man makes alone out of what is left to him. Bits of wreckage. Some bones. The words of the dead. How make a world of this? How live in that world once made?" (411). This history is exemplified in a grieving father's wish to gather the remnants of a plane, in a grieving young man's wish to return home his brother's bones, and yet the gypsy is clear that these artifacts are unable to create a world that one could meaningfully and stably inhabit.[20]

PILGRIMS AT NIGHT AND THE RISING SUN

One of the clearest portraits of a God solely of creation and providence and creatures as temporary assemblages of dust in an eternal world comes in a dream near the end of the novel.

---

20. We should point out, however, that the depth and enigmatic beauty of the gypsy's reflections are humorously deflated when Billy soon runs across an American cowboy following the gypsies who tells him, "That airplane come out of a barn on the Taliafero Ranch out of Flores Magon" (418).

He slept that night in his own country and he had a dream wherein he saw God's pilgrims laboring upon a darkened verge in the last of the twilight of that day and they seemed to be returning from some deep enterprise that was not of war nor were they in flight but rather seemed coming from some labor to which perhaps these and all other things stood subjugate. A dark arroyo separated him from the place where they were going and he looked to see if could tell by the nature of their implements what it was that they had been about but they carried none and they toiled on in silence against a sky that was darkening all around and then they were gone. When he woke in the round darkness about he thought that something had indeed passed in the desert night and he was awake a long time but he had no sense that it would ever return again. (420–21)

The dream contains a variety of themes: Billy's acute sense of separateness from others; that labor and toil seem to have no point; the foreboding intimation of unknown providential forces; and even that this mysterious God passed in the desert when Billy was sleeping, and yet there is no indication that this God might return.[21] The view of creation and human life present is that of pilgrims toiling and laboring in the twilight seemingly without purpose and on the edge of a precipice until darkness falls and the pilgrims are gone.

The final lines of the novel balance the night and the disappearance of God's pilgrims with the light of the rising sun. After chasing away a three-legged dog, a response different from the previous care Billy exhibited with his own dog and the she-wolf, Billy sits on the road, takes off his hat, "and bowed his head and held his face in his hands and wept. He sat there for a long time and after a while the east did gray and after a while the right and godmade sun did rise, once again, for all and without distinction" (426).

There have been different opinions on how to understand these final lines, but the more convincing interpretations recognize the twofold biblical allusion. In the context of Jesus' intensification of the Mosaic law in

---

21. The language of labor and toil has resonances with the curses given to Adam (Gen 3:17–19) and to Cain (Gen 4:11–12) and to the vanity of work and labor (Eccl 1:3).

the Sermon on the Mount, he tells his listeners: "But I say to you, Love your enemies and pray for those who persecute you, so that you may be children of your Father in heaven; for he makes his sun rise on the evil and the good, and send rains on the righteous and the unrighteous" (Matt 5:44–45 NRSV). In the very different context of the proclamation that all is vanity, in Ecclesiastes 1 the Teacher asks: "What do people gain from all the toil at which they toil under the sun? A generation goes, and a generation comes, but the earth remains forever. The sun rises and the sun goes down, and hurries to the place where it rises" (Eccl 1:3–5 NRSV). Given the seemingly twofold reference, the issue becomes where to place the accent. Georg Guillemin points out the resonances with Ecclesiastes, its declaration of *vanitas*, and notes that Ernest Hemingway, one of McCarthy's influences, used this passage from Ecclesiastes as the second epigraph in *The Sun Also Rises*.[22]

More frequently in the literature, however, Matthew 5:45 is taken as the interpretative center of gravity. Edwin Arnold, for instance, sees the ending as both "devastating and strangefully hopeful," and suggests that the ending recalls "Christ's description of the common grace of God, offered 'without distinction' to all. It recognizes the shared need of all for God's mercy because the external world is a place of evil and hatred and injustice, but it also emphasizes the need for human charity and sacrifice, and ultimately for love, compassion, and forgiveness."[23] Arnold adds that this event does not actually appear to hold much transformative power, as Billy seems just the same at the outset of *Cities of the Plain*, the next book in the border trilogy, and yet Billy quickly shows his readiness and ability to love. Dianne Luce agrees with Arnold that the novel's ending is primarily a reference to Matthew 5:45, notes the secondary resonance with Ecclesiastes, and concludes that the ending is finally affirmative: the sun rises "to make the

---

22. See Georg Guillemin, *The Pastoral Vision of Cormac McCarthy* (College Station: Texas A&M Press, 2004), 156.

23. Arnold, "McCarthy and the Sacred," 231, 233. See also Arnold, "Go to Sleep," 62–64, where he underscores the darker moments of the novel's last pages, especially in the context of the first atomic bomb explosion: "This, I think, is the revelation Billy experiences in this instant of fear, confusion and abasement. The naïve, magical joy of his first vision of the dancing wolves is forever replaced by a darker, more profound understanding of human vanity, an arrogance so great that it threatens the fundamental pattern established by the creative god, a destruction in which that god itself now seems willing to 'conspire'" (63–64).

world anew despite man's enactment of a destructive false dawn, suggesting that the tale of the world continues to unfold, flowing from the hands
of the weaver god in a web which enfolds and contains man's desires and
tantrums, 'Not chaos itself ... outside of that matrix' (149)." She also argues
that this view helps to explain elements of the earlier metaphysical monologues in the novel: "The Priest's observation that 'Every word we speak
is a vanity. Every breath taken that does not bless is an affront' (158) may
contain an oblique criticism of Ecclesiastes' lament about the vanity of the
world and of its complaint that omits to bless."[24] Mundik likewise claims
that the ending sounds a "hopeful note, the sunrise serving as a reminder
that although the manifest world as depicted in the novel may be a place of
darkness soteriological hope may be found in the light that shines 'for all
and without distinction' (426)."[25] For Mundik, however, the overall context
of the ending is McCarthy's perennial philosophy, which for her means the
broader context of Gnosticism, and thus the contrast between a malicious
and clumsy creator god and a higher, alien God of grace.

The position taken here is that the truth of the novel's last lines can
indeed be found in the conjunction of the verses from Ecclesiastes and
Matthew. However, the hermeneutic emphasis should lie on the Teacher's
message, under which Jesus' teaching is then subordinated. This particular
conjugation of Ecclesiastes and Matthew helps to explain how there can
be talk of grace, mercy, and blessing within these profound meditations
on God's inscrutable yet inescapable designs for the course of history and
the ephemeral quality of his creatures, who are all equally subjected to
this history of arising from dust and returning to it. Grace, mercy, and
blessing are enfolded into the outlook of Ecclesiastes, for "All are from dust,
and all turn to dust again" (Eccl 3:20 NRSV), and yet the sun and rain fall
on all creatures during their brief tenures. Within this one tale of death,
of the sun rising and falling on all without distinction, of all coming from
and returning to dust, there can be no separation of oneself from others
into elect and nonelect, heretical or nonheretical. The sun and rain fall
on the righteous and unrighteous, and this universal providence is itself

---

24. Dianne C. Luce, "The Road and the Matrix: The World as Tale in *The Crossing*," in Arnold and Luce, *Perspectives on Cormac McCarthy*, 195–219, here 212, 218.

25. Mundik, *Bloody and Barbarous God*, 199.

God's grace. Indeed, there are continual references in *The Crossing* to the rising and the setting of the sun, to the rain falling and stopping, and to the wind passing as well, which is evocative of the Teacher's pronouncement that "all is vanity and a chasing after the wind" (Eccl 1:14 NRSV). In this way the elements of affirmation, positivity, and hope in the novel's closing lines are not offered in the context of soteriology, but that of providence. The form and limit of grace is providence itself: the sun and rain fall on the righteous and unrighteous, and they do so continually as generations arise and vanish.

The primary advantage of this interpretative decision is its consistency with the portraits of God, creation, providence, and evil throughout the rest of the novel and with the four metaphysical monologues. By combining these verses and yet privileging Ecclesiastes, there emerges the picture of a sun that rises on the just and unjust, goes down on the just and unjust, and that all of humanity's labor under the sun profits it not, for "a generation goes, and a generation comes, but the earth remains forever" (Eccl 1:4 NRSV). There is, then, one tale for all, and this one tale for all is indeed death, as part of the weaver God's making and unmaking of his creation. Thus Don Arnulfo can say that death is the only order of the world and that there are places where God and human beings cooperate in the destruction of what God has made. Thus the ex-Mormon can tell Billy that God does not need a witness for himself or against himself, for all are included and subject to his unknowable purpose; that no one is elect, for no one is not elect; that all are heretics before God, and thus the heretic's first act is to condemn someone else; that "Every word we speak is a vanity" (158); and that "Every breath taken that does not bless is an affront" for "nothing is real save his grace" (158). Thus the blind former revolutionary can say that the ultimate justice, mercy, and blessing of God is that everything is dust, even the "ciborium of all godlike things," and that "for the world to survive it must be replenished daily" (293). Thus the gypsy can tell Billy that none can escape the course set for them by God; that the quick vanishing of all things into the past means that their significance quickly vanishes too; that in this ephemerality even the "witness could not survive the witnessing" (410–11); and that "the world was made new each day" (411). Thus Billy can dream of the appearance, journey, and disappearance of "God's pilgrims," who have

no discernable purpose or plan of their own. Thus after all of the tragedies and deaths suffered, all the "doomed enterprises" undertaken and
undergone, "the right and godmade sun did rise, once again, for all and
without distinction" (426), just as the "godmade sun" had risen the day
before and will rise the day after.[26]

CONCLUSION

What, then, could evil be in this world and history formed solely of God,
creation, and providence? The ex-Mormon tells Billy that in the course of
history there is no favoring, no elect, and that the movement of armies
is no different from grains of sand passing in the desert (148). The harm
and evil that we suffer and the harm and evil that we inflict are merely
part of God's weaving and care of the one order of the world, which is
death. Or, as Timothy Parrish notes, McCarthy's Western novels seem to
take place "beyond good and evil, as well as the fable of national destiny,
even if such questions are parts of the total story that McCarthy relates."[27]
Without resources from beyond creation and providence as read through
Ecclesiastes, evil is no longer the malicious or absurd loss or destruction
of a real or potential good, no longer an irrational resistance to the perfection of the Creator and the well-being of creatures, but simply the one
course of the world fixed by God, who is equally gracious to righteous and
unrighteous alike.

What *The Crossing* gives us, then, is a stark cautionary tale for what
can possibly occur with strong accounts of creation and providence that
are shorn of covenant and of wisdom. It is true that all life ends in death,
and all things that are created are destroyed, and yet this loss seems to
mean nothing to the weaver God, for more creatures will be spun and
unspun as the sun will rise again. There is no covenant between this God

---

26. A similar yet more positively phrased interpretation of this perspective is given by
Boyd's girlfriend: "He asked if God always looked after her and she studied the heart of the
fire for a long time where the coals breathed bright and dull and bright again in the wind
from the lake. At last she said that God looked after everything and that one could no more
evade his care than evade his judgment. She said that even the wicked could not escape his
love. He watched her. He said that he himself had no such idea of God and that he'd pretty
much given up praying to Him and she nodded without taking her eyes from the fire and
said that she knew that" (324-25).

27. Timothy Parrish, "History and the Problem of Evil in McCarthy's Western Novels,"
in Frye, *Cambridge Companion to Cormac McCarthy*, 67-78, here 77.

and his creatures, no faithfulness envisioned or demanded between the two. Equally, there is no wisdom in this God's providence, for this God bends all to an inscrutable purpose, but with no rhyme or reason beyond the weaving itself, nor is there the sense that there are elements of history and human being and action that resist even God's providential care. Hence the Creator's intervention on behalf of and for his creatures in the incarnation, the calling and commissioning of the apostles, the mission and suffering of the church, and the final judgement and restoration of all that is good within creation, all are absent.

10

—

"THE APPEARANCE OF RECKLESS DIVINE CRUELTY"

Animal Pain and the Problem of Other Minds

Marc Cortez

In his justly famous *The Problem of Pain*, C. S. Lewis devotes a chapter to an issue that has received increased attention recently in discussions of the problem of evil: animal suffering.[1] According to Lewis, animal suffering constitutes a significant challenge in Christian accounts of evil because it resists some of the traditional theodicies. As Lewis explains: "The problem of animal suffering is appalling; not because the animals are so numerous ... but because the Christian explanation of human pain cannot be extended to animal pain. So far as we know beasts are incapable either of sin or virtue: therefore they can neither deserve pain nor be improved by it."[2] Yet if animal suffering is neither punishment (i.e., the just consequence of sinful behavior) nor discipline (i.e., something used for the purpose of

---

1. See, for example, Matthew Scully, *Dominion: The Power of Man, the Suffering of Animals, and the Call to Mercy* (New York: St. Martin's, 2002); Christopher Southgate, *The Groaning of Creation: God, Evolution, and the Problem of Evil* (Louisville: Westminster John Knox, 2008); Michael J. Murray, *Nature Red in Tooth and Claw: Theism and the Problem of Animal Suffering* (Oxford: Oxford University Press, 2008); Andrew Linzey, *Why Animal Suffering Matters: Philosophy, Theology, and Practical Ethics* (New York: Oxford University Press, 2009); Nicola Hoggard Creegan, *Animal Suffering and the Problem of Evil* (Oxford: Oxford University Press, 2013); Trent Dougherty, *The Problem of Animal Pain: A Theodicy for All Creatures Great and Small* (New York: Palgrave Macmillan, 2014); Ronald E. Osborn, *Death before the Fall: Biblical Literalism and the Problem of Animal Suffering* (Downers Grove, IL: IVP Academic, 2014); Faith Glavey Pawl, "The Problem of Evil and Animal Suffering: A Case Study" (PhD diss., Saint Louis University, 2014).

2. C. S. Lewis, *The Problem of Pain* (San Francisco: HarperSanFrancisco, 2001), 133.

soul forming), how is it just for God to allow animals to suffer? Of course, we could account for this by modifying our understanding of animals such that they become capable of either sin or soul formation, but we are going to pursue a different set of questions in this paper.[3] If we cannot account for animal suffering by appealing to their own sin or formation, an evolutionary understanding of creation makes it difficult to appeal instead to animal suffering as a consequence of human sin and/or formation. We must somehow account for the justice of allowing animals to suffer and die for the countless millennia *before* the advent of human sin. This is often referred to as the evolutionary problem of evil.

We could simply respond, as theologians often have, that our belief in the existence and goodness of God is fundamental and that we are therefore justified in denying the problem from the outset. So Lewis contends, "From the doctrine that God is good we may confidently deduce that the appearance of reckless Divine cruelty in the animal kingdom is an illusion."[4] But there is another way of arguing that the evolutionary problem of evil is an illusion, one that Lewis also pursued. Maybe God *does not* allow animals to suffer because animals *cannot* suffer. Or, said rather differently, maybe animals lack whatever capacity or capacities are necessary to experience the world in ways that can rightly be described with a term such as "suffering." If that is the case, then there is no problem of animal suffering because there is no animal suffering.

To many this will sound rather counterintuitive. Anyone who has stepped on a dog's paw in the middle of the night has received immediate and rather loud confirmation that animals can and do suffer. However, René Descartes famously offered a rather different view of animals, contending that although they often exhibit behaviors that we associate with pain and suffering in humans, animals themselves cannot suffer. Although Descartes's view is often dismissed in light of modern research on the mental life of animals, several modern thinkers have argued for a more nuanced form of this position, which is occasionally referred to as the

---

3. For examples of those who pursue a kind of soul-forming theodicy for animals, see Southgate, *Groaning of Creation*; Dougherty, *Problem of Animal Pain*; Pawl, "Problem of Evil." Lewis also explores the possibility, though he roots the possibility of animal redemption more closely in their role in the eschatological identity of human persons (*Problem of Pain*, 143–47).

4. Lewis, *Problem of Pain*, 133–48.

neo-Cartesian position. Andrew Linzey points out that something like this view of animals prevails among many today.[5] Consequently, the idea that animals cannot suffer holds a broader range of support than one might expect.[6]

In this essay, then, we will take a closer look at the problem of animal suffering, focusing specifically on what we will call the no-animal-suffering position.[7] In the first section, we will unpack the evolutionary problem of evil further, seeking to understand some of the intuitions that lead people to think that animal suffering constitutes a significant problem for belief in God. The second section will then explain the no-animal-suffering position, summarizing four ways in which someone might deny the reality of animal suffering. Finally, the third section will draw on the clear parallels between the discussion of animal suffering and earlier debates about the problem of other minds, arguing that if we correlate the two discussions, we will see that advocates of the no-animal-suffering position face a difficult challenge if they want to deny animal suffering without denying human suffering and without undermining the very arguments they used to justify the no-animal-suffering position in the first place.[8]

Before we move on, however, it will help if I clarify how I will be using the terms "animal," "pain," and "suffering" throughout this discussion. Regarding the former, although I realize that there is an important sense in which humans should be classed among the animals, I prefer the term "animal" to the far less elegant "nonhuman creature" and will use it throughout with that meaning in mind. Additionally, Faith Pawl rightly notes the difficulty of attempting to deal with "animal suffering" in the singular, as though we can simply equate a baboon's experience with that of a jellyfish.[9] She thus focuses her discussion specifically on baboon suf-

---

5. See esp. Linzey, *Why Animal Suffering Matters*, 9–29.

6. In addition to C. S. Lewis, see, for example, Peter Harrison, "Theodicy and Animal Pain," *Philosophy* 64, no. 247 (1989): 79–92; Roger Scruton, *On Hunting* (South Bend, IN: St. Augustine's, 2002); Murray, *Nature Red in Tooth*, 41–72; Stewart Goetz, "The Argument from Evil," in *The Blackwell Companion to Natural Theology*, ed. William Lane Craig and J. P. Moreland (Cambridge, MA: Blackwell, 2009), 449–97.

7. Murray, *Nature Red in Tooth*.

8. Although there is a clear connection between the question of animal suffering and ethical issues related to animal rights and the proper treatment of animals, I will not be addressing those issues here.

9. Pawl, "Problem of Evil."

fering. Even if we do not want to narrow the discussion to that extent, it does seem useful to focus primarily on relatively well-developed mammals (e.g. primates, elephants, dolphins), those who seem to have the kinds of biological structures most commonly associated with pain and suffering. After all, if we were to conclude that even these kinds of animals are not capable of suffering, it would seem reasonable to extend that conclusion to the rest of the animal kingdom. This does mean, though, that the conclusion of this argument will only have application for these kinds of animals. Whether we should say that things like jellyfish and crickets also suffer will be a subject for another day.[10]

Our other terms, "pain" and "suffering," are far more difficult, since there is little agreement about how best to use those terms.[11] Yet many find it useful to take the definition of pain offered by the International Association for the Study of Pain as at least an adequate starting point: pain is "an unpleasant sensory and emotional experience associated with actual or potential tissue damage, or described in terms of such damage."[12] We could quibble with various aspects of the definition, particularly the focus on "damage," yet it suffices to establish that I will be using "pain" to refer to an experience that has a particular kind of *feel* (i.e., *qualia*), one typically viewed as at least potentially detrimental and negative. "Suffering," on the other hand, will refer to any state that includes an experience of pain and that involves a lack of flourishing on the part of the creature experiencing the pain. Assuming that plants are not capable of experiencing pain, then, this definition means I would not describe the destruction of a plant as *suffering* despite the fact that it clearly involves a lack of flourishing. And, as these definitions suggest, it may be entirely possible for someone to experience pain without being in a state of suffering, if that pain were somehow intrinsically related to bringing about the flourishing of the creature involved.

---

10. For an example of someone who thinks that we should extend the idea of animal suffering to include insects as well, see Dustin Crummett, "The Problem of Evil and the Suffering of Creeping Things," *International Journal for Philosophy of Religion* 82, no. 1 (2017): 71–88.

11. For a very helpful discussion as it relates to animal suffering, see Dougherty, *Problem of Animal Pain*, 25–30.

12. International Association for the Study of Pain (2012).

ANIMAL SUFFERING AND THE
EVOLUTIONARY PROBLEM OF EVIL

The problem of animal suffering as it relates to the problem of evil derives from four common intuitions. To illustrate these, consider the following scenario made famous in William Rowe's argument against the existence of God.[13] Suppose that a lightning strike causes a fire in some forest; and suppose further that in the resulting fire, a fawn is trapped under a falling tree such that it cannot escape from the oncoming fire, is horribly burned, and spends the next three days dying in terrible agony. Finally, to clearly locate this scenario in the context of the *evolutionary* problem of evil, suppose further that this takes place before the evolution of modern humans. The question that arises from this scenario is whether God would be justified in allowing this kind of suffering to take place. If not, then the theist has a problem.

The argument derives its power from the combination of four intuitions, which Rowe believes (rightly, I think) are widely shared.

1. *Animals can experience pain.* Unlike things like rocks and trees, most people believe rather strongly that at least some animals can experience pain. This may stem directly from our experiences with animals in pain, the assumption that at least some animals have sufficiently developed neurophysiologies to be able to feel pain, or the result of a more analogical move in which we extrapolate from our own experiences to what we think animals are likely to experience in similar situations (more on that in a moment).

2. *Animals can suffer.* Most also think that an animal's experiences of pain can at times be sufficiently intense, prolonged, and detrimental to the animal's well-being to qualify as *suffering*. Indeed, I think it safe to say that most people would find it hard to describe the fawn's experience as anything short of extreme suffering. Thus, we typically think that animals are able to experience more than just momentary kinds of pain

---

13. William L. Rowe, "The Problem of Evil and Some Varieties of Atheism," *American Philosophical Quarterly* 16, no. 4 (1979): 335–41.

(e.g., a pinprick), or even a prolonged periods of pain that do not actually harm the animal in any significant way (e.g., that ongoing ache in my left shoulder). If that was all the fawn was experiencing, few would find this scenario anywhere near as troubling.

3. *Purposeless suffering is bad.* According to this intuition, *needless* or *purposeless* suffering is an evil that should be avoided or alleviated whenever possible. Here it is important to see that this intuition does not necessarily include the idea that all forms of suffering are intrinsically evil. Instead, it allows for the possibility that even some significant and extended forms of suffering could be used to accomplish some beneficial end. Yet the "beneficial" part of that statement requires us to think of those sufferings as purposeful. Any suffering that has no benefit (purpose), on the other hand, is intrinsically bad.[14]

4. *Moral beings have an obligation to alleviate purposeless suffering.* The final intuition flows rather naturally from the common conviction that good people have a moral obligation to alleviate or avoid evil whenever possible. If purposeless animal suffering qualifies as such an evil, then any moral being has the obligation to avoid or alleviate that suffering whenever possible. Suppose, for example, that we tweaked the scenario such that the trapped deer were slowly burning to death in the field next to your house. These shared intuitions would lead most to think that you have an obligation to do something to alleviate the deer's sufferings and that it would be morally wrong for you simply to allow the deer's sufferings to continue.

If we grant the legitimacy of these four intuitions, they constitute a rather significant challenge to the goodness or existence of God. The scenario of the fawn seems to involve real pain and suffering that does not

---

14. This, in turn, is probably funded by an additional assumption that intense, prolonged, and detrimental pain is never a good that should be pursued in its own right. I realize that this raises questions about masochistic behavior, but I will set those aside for now.

itself seem to contribute to any greater purpose. Additionally, Rowe argues that even if we could imagine a scenario in which the fawn's suffering served some greater purpose, that would only resolve the problem if the fawn's suffering were somehow intrinsic to the accomplishment of that greater purpose such that the latter could not be accomplished without the former. And he is pessimistic about the likelihood that we will be able to come up with any such scenario that goes beyond mere logical possibility. Yet God not only fails to avoid or alleviate *this* situation, but countless others as well. Consequently, according to Rowe, the most reasonable conclusion to draw from this is that God either is not good or does not exist.

With this argument in mind, we can anticipate many of the various strategies people have pursued to deal with the problem of animal suffering. We could attack the fourth intuition as it relates to God by denying that God can have any sort of obligation to his creatures, yet I think few would find that to be a satisfying explanation of this particular problem. The most common arguments involve the third assumption, with people offering a wide array of arguments for how animal suffering might serve some greater purpose despite the appearance of the contrary. Yet those arguments would be entirely unnecessary if we could dispatch with either of the first two intuitions. In the following section, then, we will consider four ways that people have tried to argue against the intuition that animals can feel pain and/or suffer in any morally significant way.

NO ANIMAL SUFFERING: FOUR OPTIONS

The fundamental idea driving all of the no-animal-suffering position arguments is the fact that we cannot actually know with any real certainty what an animal experiences. As Lewis argues, the inner life of animals is ultimately "outside the range of our knowledge" such that anything we might say about animal pain is purely "speculative."[15] Thus, as Thomas Nagel argued in his famous article, we cannot really know what it's like to be a bat.[16] The problem is not merely a lack of information, as though further study could eventually generate the necessary data for us to truly know how a bat experiences the world. No matter how closely we analyze

---

15. Lewis, *Problem of Pain*, 134.
16. Thomas Nagel, "What Is It Like to Be a Bat?," *Philosophical Review* 83 (1974): 435–56.

the bat, we would still only know what it's like for a human to have the experience of learning about a bat.

This suggests that the argument will be difficult to resolve on the basis of the scientific evidence and/or observable data alone. So even if we established that the neurophysiology of some animal closely approximated that of a human, and even if that animal behaved in ways that we tend to associate with pain or suffering in human persons, we still would not know whether that animal's actual *experience* corresponds to our own in relevant ways. From this Harrison concludes, "No strict argument can be mounted for or against the existence of animal pain. Indeed, it is difficult to see what form such an argument might take, for it is the essence of pain that it is a private experience."[17]

If this is the case, then everything we think we know about animal "pain" and "suffering" needs to be reconsidered, since we have no idea what it would be like for an animal to have those kinds of experiences. That we *think* we do simply means that we have projected onto the animal our own experiences of pain and suffering. According to Michael Murray, it is our decided tendency to anthropomorphize objects that explains why we so quickly assume that animals can suffer.[18] Just as we tend to find meaning in random patterns (e.g., faces in clouds) and personify inanimate objects, so we tend to think of animals as having experiences that mimic our own. Yet this anthropomorphic tendency tells us far more about how humans experience the world than about the world itself.

Consequently, the following no-animal-suffering options all focus on different ways of explaining how we might think of animals as not experiencing pain and/or suffering regardless of whether there is some significant continuity between animals and humans with respect to biology and/or behavior.[19]

Option 1: No animal mentality. The simplest solution would be just to deny that animals have any kind of "inner" mental life. Just as a robot might be capable of mimicking complex behaviors (e.g., pain behaviors) without have any corresponding mental states, so we might envision animals to be

---

17. Harrison, "Theodicy and Animal Pain," 81.

18. Murray, *Nature Red in Tooth*, 71–72.

19. In this summary, I am indebted to Murray's helpful taxonomy (*Nature Red in Tooth*, 52–58), though my four categories differ from his slightly.

more like organic machines than human persons. This is typically referred to as the *Cartesian* position based on Descartes's infamous suggestion that animals are mere automata.[20]

This option provides the easiest response to the problem of animal suffering since the complete lack of an inner mental life entails the impossibility of either pain or suffering. Although the fawn in our case study might be exhibiting the outward behaviors that we associate with pain, she is not experiencing any pain sensations, and she is not even thinking about the fact that she is on fire. She has merely been hard-wired to act the way she is when her body is burning, much like a robot might be programmed to cry out for help if its limbs were crushed by a car. Indeed, some of Descartes's followers developed this argument with the problem of evil clearly in mind, maintaining that since a good God would not allow innocent animals to experience pain, they must not be the kinds of creatures capable of having the kind of mental life necessary for such experiences.[21]

Option 2: No phenomenal experience. Few find the kind of strong skepticism required for the first option palatable. Although it is notoriously difficult to refute such arguments convincingly (at least it is if you grant the legitimacy of the skeptical starting point), most affirm that the neurophysiological and behavioral complexity of advanced animals strongly suggests that they do in fact have a robust mental life.[22] Consequently, positions commonly labeled as *neo*-Cartesian focus on distinguishing between the lower level of mentality possessed by animals (frequently referred to as *sentience*), and some higher aspect of mentality not possessed by animals that is necessary for pain and/or suffering. As Murray notes, "Central to neo-Cartesian explanations is the idea that nonhuman creatures, even if sentient, lack some human characteristic essential to conscious suffering."[23]

---

20. René Descartes, *A Discourse on Method*, trans. Elizabeth S. Haldane and G. R. T. Ross (Mineola, NY: Dover, 2003), 38–39. Descartes himself pointed the way to what has become the most common way of dealing with animal suffering. In some of his later letters, Descartes distinguished between *sensation* and *thought*, arguing that while animals were capable of experiencing things such as fear and joy, they cannot think about the fact that they are experiencing such things (see Murray, *Nature Red in Tooth*, 50–52).

21. Murray, *Nature Red in Tooth*, 50.

22. See esp. David DeGrazia, *Taking Animals Seriously: Mental Life and Moral Status* (New York: Cambridge University Press, 1996).

23. Murray, *Nature Red in Tooth*, 43.

Our second option draws on this neo-Cartesian distinction to affirm that animals have a real and vital mental life—that is, they have real sensory experiences and mental states that shape their behaviors in meaningful ways—but denies that the mental life of animals includes any kind of phenomenal experiences. In this scenario, our fawn is capable of receiving sensory input about her body being on fire that contributes to her having a mental state that includes this information along with the notion that it would probably be best if her body were no longer on fire, but without the further requirement that she also be in some phenomenological state in which she *feels* what it is like for her body to be on fire. She thus has a real mental life, but not one that includes the qualitative aspects of what we think of as pain.

Option 3: No higher-order access. Both of the first two options deny that animals have the same kinds of phenomenal experiences as humans. In each case, although the fawn appears to be in pain, she is not experiencing anything that would correspond to the feeling of pain in a human person. With this option we turn to the possibility that an animal might actually experience pain (i.e., the qualitative feeling of being in pain) while denying that animals are capable of experiencing their pain as suffering. Since this position contends that the real issue in the evolutionary problem of evil is that of animal *suffering*—that is, not just animal *pain*—they maintain that this is sufficient to resolve the problem.

People have offered various ways of developing this approach, but the common element in all of them is to contend that real suffering requires that a creature have some kind of higher-order access to its own suffering. This is probably the best place to locate Lewis's own position regarding animal suffering. Lewis distinguishes "sentience" from "consciousness," and he argues that a mere succession of sensory experiences does not qualify as suffering.[24] Although he does not explain this intuition, the idea seems to be that even a serious pain would not qualify as suffering if it only happened for a moment. Consider, for example, that I have a sudden, shooting pain down my left leg, but one that only lasts for a fraction of a second. While that would be momentarily unpleasant, few would view that as involving real suffering. Now suppose that I experience another

---

24. Lewis, *Problem of Pain*, 135–38.

shooting pain moments later, but that I also have a mental condition that renders me incapable of forming short-term memories. Since I have no memory of the first shooting pain, the second occurs to me as an isolated experience, which would again not seem to qualify as suffering.[25] According to Lewis, as long as these remain disconnected sensory experiences, they qualify only as sensations and not as suffering. Instead, in order to be able to say that I suffer, I need to be aware of myself as a continuously existent self who can be the owner or subject of those conscious experiences. Lewis contends that only humans (and maybe just a few of the higher animals) are capable of becoming these higher-order selves.

Rather than focusing on the necessity of a stable self, people more commonly distinguish instead between lower-level conscious experiences and higher-level thoughts about those experiences.[26] Suppose that our fawn has a real mental life that includes the kind of phenomenal experiences that we associate with pain, which entails that she is having the fawn-equivalent experience that we associate with the feeling of being on fire, but she is incapable of forming higher-order thoughts about the lower-order conscious experience of being on fire. There is a sensory experience, but nothing is thinking about the fact that it is having that sensory experience. Without some conscious subject reflecting on the painful experience, it is difficult to conceive of what it means to say that something is actually suffering in this scenario.

On both accounts, then, the argument is that animals cannot truly suffer because they are not capable of achieving the kinds of higher-order states necessary to have *access* to their pain states and be aware of themselves as suffering. Consequently, according to this argument, without a suffering subject, there is no suffering.

Option 4: No negative evaluation. Murray offers a final neo-Cartesian option when he contends that it is entirely possible to affirm that an animal might experience pain, and have higher-order access to the fact that they

---

25. Peter Harrison offers several additional commonly discussed thought experiments designed to reinforce the idea that continuity of consciousness is necessary for real suffering ("Theodicy and Animal Pain").

26. Although higher-order thought theories are typically associated with functionalist views of consciousness, Murray rightly points out that the approach is amenable to both functionalist and nonfunctionalist interpretations (*Nature Red in Tooth*, 53).

are experiencing pain, and yet not have the capacity to formulate negative judgments about that situation.[27] In other words, it is possible that the fawn feels the pain of being burned, is aware that she is feeling the pain of being burned, but is not able to think that this state is undesirable.

Although this might seem to stretch incredulity a bit far, Murray points out that there is at least one situation in which we see something similar in humans. "Individuals who have undergone a prefrontal lobotomy, for example, sometimes report an awareness of familiar pains but paradoxically insist that they no longer find the pain to be undesirable or unpleasant. They claim the pain 'feels' the same, even though it no longer bothers them."[28] Others contend that some painkillers function similarly, not by eliminating the pain itself, but by altering the person's psychological state such that they no longer mind the pain.[29] After dislocating my shoulder in high school, I was given Demerol before the doctor reset the joint. I have a clear memory of being quite fascinated by the fact that I could feel the joint being pulled apart and the ball rubbing up against the socket as the doctor tried repeatedly to find the right position, but at no point was I bothered by any of these sensations. Murray suggests, then, that we should think of pain reception as involving two distinct pathways: "First, it must involve a pathway that allows the subject to detect that a noxious stimulus has been applied. Second, it must involve a pathway that allows the subject to attach a certain measure of importance or significance or affective weight to the stimulus—this is the component which gives pain its undesirable character."[30] He concludes from situations like these that even in human pain reception it is possible to have the first pathway (pain sensation) without the second (pain evaluation).

If we imagine animal mentality as functioning in the same way, we could affirm that they can have sensory experiences like pain, and that they can formulate higher-order thoughts about the fact that they are having these sensory experiences, while denying that they are capable of formulating negative judgments about these states.

---

27. Murray, *Nature Red in Tooth*, 56.
28. Murray, *Nature Red in Tooth*, 56–57.
29. Harrison, "Theodicy and Animal Pain," 86.
30. Murray, *Nature Red in Tooth*, 66–67.

We thus have four different ways of imagining how animals might possess all of the neurophysiological features that correspond to suffering in human persons and be able to exhibit all of the behaviors that we associate with suffering, while still denying that they experience anything that would qualify as suffering in a way that would create problems for the goodness and justice of God. If we could reasonably maintain that one or more of these offers a plausible description of how animals experience the world, we would have good grounds for rejecting the evolutionary problem of evil.

ANIMAL SUFFERING AND THE PROBLEM OF OTHER MINDS

The parallels between this discussion and the debates about the problem of other minds that occupied so much attention in philosophy and philosophical theology in earlier decades should be reasonably clear.[31] Although the problem of other minds focused primarily on the question of whether we are justified in believing that other humans have a conscious life that is relevantly similar to our own, that discussion pursued many of the same questions we have encountered here: To what extent do I have unique (first-person) access to my own phenomenological experiences? Is it possible to extrapolate from those experiences to the conclusion that other creatures have similar experiences? Can scientific (third-person) data ever be sufficient to ground belief in the idea that other creatures have conscious experiences? What role should skepticism and arguments about what is "logically possible" play in our beliefs about the conscious life of other beings? Consequently, although our discussion has focused specifically on the conscious life of nonhuman animals, the overall shape of the debate is largely the same.

It thus comes as somewhat of a surprise that the problem of other minds does not play any significant role in arguments for the no-animal-suffering position, despite the fact that these thinkers are almost certainly aware of the significant body of literature dedicated to the topic. This may

---

31. For good introductions to the discussion, see Anita Avramides, *Other Minds* (New York: Routledge, 2001); Alec Hyslop, "Other Minds," Stanford Encyclopedia of Philosophy Archive, Spring 2016, https://plato.stanford.edu/archives/spr2016/entries/other-minds/.

stem at least partly from the fact that few thinkers seem to be as intrigued today by skeptical arguments about the possibility that the person sitting next to you is actually an empty-headed zombie or craftily constructed android. Instead, most now take our belief in other *human* minds to be fairly well grounded, although they differ on the precise explanations they offer for the reasonableness of that conclusion. Yet, if it is largely accepted that we are justified in believing in the existence of other human minds, why would we not be similarly justified in accepting the existence of other *non*human minds? Or, contrarily, if we think no-animal-suffering arguments succeed, why would we not also apply these arguments to the problem of other minds and generate a similar skepticism about the existence of other human minds?

Although there may be some who are willing to explore the skeptical option, I will take it as more likely that no-animal-suffering advocates would prefer instead to explain why they do not think that their no-animal-suffering arguments should be brought to bear on the problem of other minds in general. To do this, they would need to provide some explanation for why their arguments against animal suffering should not be thought of as having implications for the existence of human minds. In other words, they would need to explain what makes these two situations sufficiently unlike each other that the arguments of one should not be applied to the other.

Yet is it not entirely clear how the no-animal-suffering advocate would go about developing such an explanation without undermining the very arguments she used to support her no-animal-suffering conclusions in the first place. To see this, let's take a brief look at three prominent ways of dealing with the problem of other minds and consider ways in which the no-animal-suffering advocate might explain why these arguments work for the problem of other minds and not for animal suffering.

On the first approach, my belief in other minds is grounded in analogous reasoning. I know that I have conscious experiences, and I know that there are other creatures (humans) who are quite similar to me in important ways (especially in behavior and biology), and therefore it seems reasonable to think that they would have conscious experiences that are analogously similar to my own. Although some of our no-animal-suffering positions might allow for a limited form of the analogy argument,

specifically as it applies to lower states of consciousness, they are all committed to the idea that I *cannot* simply reason by analogy from my own
experience of human consciousness to the conscious life of animals. So the
no-animal-suffering advocate will probably need to argue that the obvious *differences* between humans and nonhuman animals are sufficient to
justify *not* extending the analogy argument to include nonhuman minds.

Without further development, though, such an argument will not
work. Setting aside for a moment the fact that many have raised significant objections to the analogical argument as a resolution to the problem
of other minds,[32] we will assume for the sake of argument that the analogy argument works with respect to human minds. But this requires the
no-animal-suffering advocate to grant the validity of reasoning analogically on the basis of biological/behavioral similarity, which is precisely
what the no-animal-suffering advocate has refused to do in all four of the
no-animal-suffering options. Each of them requires us to believe that even
animals with well-developed neurophysiological structures that exhibit
behaviors that correspond closely to human behaviors somehow lack some
key aspect of consciousness that enables true suffering.

To strengthen the argument here, the no-animal-suffering advocate
will have to avoid general appeals to obvious differences, being more specific about what exactly it is about animal behavior/biology that creates
the relevant disanalogy. For example, Murray has argued that the kinds of
higher order capacities necessary for animals to be aware of their own suffering and/or form negative judgments about their suffering are associated
with the prefrontal cortex, which developed relatively late in evolutionary
history. If this is the case, then we are justified in maintaining that very
few animals (maybe none) have brains that are sufficiently advanced to
provide the capacities necessary for suffering. Yet even this more nuanced
form of the argument runs into problems. Why assume that the capacities
necessary for suffering are possible *only* on the basis the prefrontal cortex?
As many have pointed out, mental states are multiply realizable, meaning
that the nonexistence of one particular physical state does not entail the
nonexistence of the corresponding mental state. So even animals without

---

32. For a classic formulation of these worries, see Norman Malcolm, "Knowledge of Other
Minds," *Journal of Philosophy* 44 (1958): 35–52.

the prefrontal cortex may well be capable of the kinds of mental states necessary for suffering. Additionally, as Trent Dougherty has argued, it is entirely possible (maybe even likely) that we need to understand suffering in more emotion-like and less cognitive terms.[33] This would still allow for there to be an evaluative component in the experience of pain, but one that is shaped largely by our *affective* states. Since emotions are associated with parts of the brain that developed far earlier in evolutionary history, such an account also makes it more likely that a broader range of animals are capable of suffering.

A second option for dealing with the problem of other minds arose in response to some of the objections to the analogical argument I alluded to above. Rather than reasoning analogically on the basis of a single data point (my own conscious experiences), this approach contends that our belief in other minds is justified as an inference to the best explanation. My belief in other minds thus functions more like a theory that I posit as the best explanation for the observable data of how I see people behave in response to environmental stimuli.

Although something like this is now the most common way of dealing with the problem-of-other-minds worries,[34] it is hard to see how this helps the no-animal-suffering advocate. Most of those who affirm the reality of animal suffering do so precisely on this basis, maintaining that their position is not based on an anthropomorphic appeal to analogy, but is simply the best way of explaining the observable data that we have regarding animal behavior. Cognitive ethology as a field focuses specifically on the task of positing animal mentality as the best explanation of animal behavior.[35]

The likeliest way for the no-animal-suffering advocate to respond to such arguments is to contend that the posited theory (animal suffering) is actually underdetermined by the observable data (animal behavior) because other explanations remain entirely possible. Murray pursues this strategy when he argues that most animal behaviors require only that animals be capable of forming things such as beliefs and desires, which do

33. Dougherty, *Problem of Animal Pain*, 78–86.
34. Hyslop, "Other Minds."
35. See esp. DeGrazia, *Taking Animals Seriously*, 1.

not themselves require that animals be capable of the higher-order states required by neo-Cartesian explanations of suffering.[36] To see this, just consider the instance of blindsight in humans, which involves a condition in which a person is unable to consciously process what they see, often involving only one side of their visual field. In such cases, the person can often still react to the visual stimulus correctly (e.g., correctly selecting a certain object) despite the fact that they have no conscious awareness (higher-order access) of the stimulus. This creates the possibility that all animal behaviors are merely the function of mental states to which the animal has no higher-order access.

However, if we were to grant the legitimacy of such an argument, it is difficult to see why it would not have implications for the problem of other minds as well. Indeed, the most common worry raised against the inference to the best explanation argument in the problem of other minds is that it ultimately fails to account for the phenomenal quality of the mental states experienced by other humans since there are ways to account for the corresponding behaviors without appealing to such phenomenal qualities. Consequently, it would seem that if no-animal-suffering advocates adopt this solution, they will have to jettison what has become the most common way of dealing with the problem of other minds .

A third way people commonly seek to address the problem-of-other-minds worries is to deny the premise that only a first-person perspective provides direct access to a person's mental states. By privileging the first-person perspective, we end up viewing the body as an obstacle, something that prevents us from understanding the "inner" life of the person and that must be overcome through analogical and/or inferential reasoning. This third approach denies the mind/body separation that such assumptions require, maintaining instead that mental states express themselves through the body in such a way that they may be directly experienced by others and serve as a reliable indicator of human mentality. Thus, for example, Fiona Ellis argues the mistake made here is in assuming that an embodied behavior is fundamentally distinct from mental states for which that behavior "provides, at best, dubious evidence."[37] Instead, she argues

---

36. Murray, *Nature Red in Tooth*, 58–69.
37. Fiona Ellis, "God and Other Minds," *Religious Studies* 46, no. 3 (2010): 337.

that we should view at least some behaviors as "mind-involving" such that other persons can directly perceive our mentality at work in and through our bodies.[38] This approach thus resonates with Ludwig Wittgenstein's claim that "the human body is the best picture of the human soul."[39]

Here again, though, it is hard to see how such an approach offers any assistance to the no-animal-suffering advocate. If it is true that certain *human* behaviors are mind-involving such that they can be directly perceived by a third party, on what basis would we maintain that very similar behaviors performed by nonhuman creatures are *not* similarly mind-involving? Although the no-animal-suffering advocate could certainly continue to claim that animal behaviors are simply different and are not mind-involving in the same way, such a claim requires some kind of justification.

CONCLUSION

Given that people have suggested an impressive array of possible solutions to the problem of other minds, we could extend this exploration of correlations between the problem of other minds and animal suffering almost indefinitely. However, by focusing on three of the more common problem-of-other-minds arguments, we can already see the challenge facing the no-animal-suffering advocate. Now, depending on what the no-animal-suffering advocate is trying to accomplish, she might not be terribly troubled by this. Some might view the no-animal-suffering position merely as a logically possible way of resolving the evolutionary problem of evil. If so, then there is no good reason to concern yourself with the problem-of-other-minds worries, since I see no reason that such considerations would raise problems for the logical possibility of the no-animal-suffering position. However, this strategy will only work for responding to a form of the evolutionary problem that stipulates the *impossibility* of God existing in light of all of this animal suffering. Yet William Rowe rightly

---

38. Ellis, "God and Other Minds." It is worth noting here that Ellis rejects the conclusion that this entails a physicalist view of the person, arguing that it is perfectly compatible with more holistic or integrative forms of dualism.

39. Ludwig Wittgenstein, *Philosophical Investigations* 2.4.178. Wittgenstein's own thoughts on the problem of other minds is notoriously complex (see, e.g., M. R. M. Ter Hark, "The Development of Wittgenstein's Views about the Other Minds Problem," *Synthese* 87, no. 2 [1991]: 227–53).

notes that the more significant form of the evolutionary problem focuses on what we can *reasonably* or *plausibly* believe in light of the available evidence.[40] Consequently, it will not suffice to respond with the mere logical possibility that animals might not suffer. Michael Murray agrees, stating that what he is after are explanations that are *"as plausible as not, overall."*[41] Consequently, it seems that we need more than logical possibility here.

As Murray recognizes, though, the extent to which you view some proposal as plausible depends to a large degree on our "justified acceptances," which are those other things that we justifiably accept as true. Since I think most would take belief in other minds as just such a justified acceptance, it seems that no-animal-suffering advocates face the challenge of explaining their position in light of the belief in other minds. On the one hand, they could simply accept that their arguments have implications for the problem of other minds and accept the consequences. That is the possibility we have not explored in this paper, taking it as likelier that no-animal-suffering advocates would prefer not to weaken belief in other minds more generally. On the other hand, no-animal-suffering advocates could provide some explanation for why their arguments against animal suffering do not have troubling implications for other minds more generally. Yet, as we have seen, their own arguments make it difficult for them to offer any such explanation.

The upshot of all this is that, although I do think that animal suffering constitutes a significant theological challenge that needs to be taken seriously today, I remain unconvinced that the no-animal-suffering position offers a viable path forward.

---

40. Rowe, "Problem of Evil," 337.

41. Murray, *Nature Red in Tooth*, 38, italics original.

11

RECENT EVOLUTIONARY THEORY AND THE POSSIBILITY OF THE FALL

Daniel W. Houck

Christians have traditionally affirmed that evil entered God's good creation only because his creatures disobeyed him. In the early church, there was widespread agreement that the sin of Adam brought death and corruption to humanity. This event came to be known as the fall.[1] Recently, however, the doctrine of the fall has fallen on hard times. Since the rise of evolutionary thinking in the nineteenth century and the triumph of the neo-Darwinian synthesis in the twentieth, many people have come to believe that a historical fall is incompatible with the theory of evolution.[2] There are a number of reasons for this. In the nineteenth century and the first half of the twentieth, the fall was thought to represent a "regressive" view of

---

1. Parts of this chapter derive from research I conducted as a resident fellow at the Carl F. H. Henry Center for Theological Understanding of Trinity International University, with a generous grant from the Templeton Religion Trust. I am deeply grateful to Templeton and Trinity. Earlier drafts of this paper were presented at the Chicago Theological Initiative and discussed during a Creation Project lunch. I would like to thank both groups for many helpful suggestions. I would also like to thank Clay Carlson and Jitse M. van der Meer for comments on an earlier draft of this paper. Defects that remain are, of course, my fault alone.
According to N. P. Williams, Methodius of Olympius first used the phrase "the fall." See *The Ideas of the Fall and Original Sin* (London: Longmans, Green, 1927), 73n1. In the post-Augustinian West, the fall was also thought to have brought sin to the rest of humanity.

2. There have been a number of attempts to reinterpret the fall in nonhistorical terms, beginning with Kant in the first book of *Religion within the Limits of Reason Alone*. It is beyond the scope of this paper to discuss these proposals. I take it that even those who would defend a nonhistorical view of the fall could be interested in whether evolution is compatible with a historical fall.

history opposed to "progressive" evolution.[3] More common today, perhaps, is the assumption that because the early chapters of Genesis contain a description of human origins inconsonant with evolutionary theory, the fall (along with a historical garden of Eden, an original couple, and so on) is likewise incompatible with evolution. This assumption is found among Christian critics of evolution as well as scientists critical of the fall.[4]

Nevertheless, the question of the historicity of the fall can be distinguished from whether the early chapters of Genesis should be read as offering a precise description of human origins according to the canons of modern history. And it often is. *The Catechism of the Catholic Church*, for example, teaches that "the account of the Fall in Genesis 3 uses figurative language, but affirms a primeval event, a deed that took place *at the beginning of the history of man*."[5] A leading evangelical theologian, Henri Blocher, argues similarly: "The real issue when we try to interpret Genesis 2–3 is

---

3. "The consenting voice of unbiased investigators in all lands has declared more and more that the beginnings of our race must have been low and brutal, and that the tendency has been upward." A. D. White, *A History of the Warfare of Science with Theology in Christendom* (New York: D. Appleton, 1913), 1:312. For White, the fall was one example of the greater war between science and theology. For a criticism of White's "conflict model" of the relation between science and theology, see Mark Noll, "Science, Religion, and A. D. White: Seeking Peace in the 'Warfare Between Science and Theology,' " BioLogos, August 7, 2010, https://biologos.org/articles/a-d-whites-warfare-between-science-and-theology. This teleological conception of evolution is now generally disavowed by scientists. See Michael Ruse, *Monad to Man: The Concept of Progress in Evolutionary Biology* (Cambridge: Harvard University Press, 1996).

4. The president of the flagship seminary of the Southern Baptist Convention, for example, argues as follows. "If evolution is true, then the entire narrative of the Bible has to be revised and reinterpreted. The evolutionary account is not only incompatible with any historical affirmation of Genesis 1–2, but it is also incompatible with the claim that all humanity is descended from Adam and the claim that in Adam all humanity fell into sin and guilt. The Bible's account of the Fall, and its consequences, is utterly incompatible with evolutionary theory." R. Albert Mohler Jr., "The New Shape of the Debate," *Southern Seminary Magazine* (Winter 2011): 25–26. Jerry Coyne, a biologist and outspoken atheist at the University of Chicago, argues as follows. "The Adam and Eve story continues to plague theologians, for we know from genetics that it's wrong—modern humanity did not all descend from two contemporaneous ancestors—and yet the concept of sin and redemption through Jesus is desperately important to Christians. Without a literal interpretation of the Fall, what sense does Jesus's sacrifice make?" "David Lose Tells Us How to Interpret the Adam and Eve Story," Why Evolution Is True (blog), August 18, 2011, https://whyevolutionistrue.wordpress.com/2011/08/18/david-lose-tells-us-how-to-interpret-the-adam-and-eve-story/. Mohler and Coyne both lump the question of the fall's compatibility with evolution together with reading Genesis as a precise historical description of a primordial pair.

5. *The Catechism of the Catholic Church*, 2nd ed. (Vatican City: Libreria Editrice Vaticana, 1997), §390, emphasis original.

not whether we have a historical account of the fall ... but whether or not we may read it as an account of a historical fall."[6] In line with this perspective, there have been various accounts of the fall, post-Darwin, that admit that parts of the Bible's creation story (Gen 2:7, for example) need to be read in a new light. Karl Rahner and C. S. Lewis are two notable examples of this approach.[7]

That said, there *are* serious objections to the fall in light of evolutionary theory. This chapter engages two of them and suggests a way forward. I begin by briefly discussing the predominant interpretation of the fall in the history of Christian theology, which I will call "the disease view." We then turn to the first objection to the fall—the "objection from natural selection"—which stems from the gradual nature of evolutionary change. Even if there was a state of original justice, it is hard to see how we could have fallen from it. The second objection stems from the legacy of our evolutionary history. It seems that evolution has selected for sinful behavior, including violence, implying that there was no state of original justice. I'll call this the "objection from original violence." These objections create major, perhaps insurmountable problems for the disease view of the fall. I argue, however, that Thomas Aquinas's account of the fall is amenable to modification in such a way that it does not fall prey to these objections.

THE DISEASE VIEW

In order to address the question of whether the fall is compatible with mainstream evolutionary theory, we first need to say a bit more about what the fall is. In general terms, the fall is a "moral catastrophe"—to borrow N. P. Williams's phrase—that separates humanity from God. The nature of the catastrophe has been understood in various ways. In Christian theology, the most common way has been in terms of a disease. For example, in a memorable phrase, Cyprian of Carthage (ca. 200/210–258) claimed that infants

---

6. Henri Blocher, *Original Sin*, 50, cited in Matthew J. Levering, *Engaging the Doctrine of Creation: Cosmos, Creatures, and the Wise and Good Creator* (Grand Rapids: Baker Academic, 2017), 268. Levering endorses Blocher's point here: "Blocher's statement is on point: I think that we can and, indeed, *should* read Genesis 2–3 as an account of a historical fall, since the stories of Adam and Eve make clear that the creator God was not the cause of human sin and death" (268).

7. C. S. Lewis, *The Problem of Pain* (New York: HarperCollins, 2015), 66–67; Karl Rahner, "Original Sin," in *Sacramentum Mundi*, ed. Karl Rahner et al. (New York: Herder & Herder, 1969), 4:328–34.

contract, from Adam, the "contagion of the ancient death" (*contagium mortis antiquae*). The idea is that we were created in health, but Adam's disobedience made us sick; the "contagion" of sin was passed down through the generations. This is also how Augustine thought of the fall. In *The City of God*, he writes that we "were all in that one man ... who fell into sin. ... The particular form in which we were to live as individuals had not yet been created and distributed to us; but the seminal nature from which we were to be propagated already existed."[8] We all preexisted in Adam according to "seminal nature" (*natura seminalis*), and when Adam sinned that nature was corrupted. He thus produced depraved and corrupted children. If he had not sinned, he would have produced righteous children.

A great deal of scholarship has established that the Eastern church fathers differed from Augustine in some noteworthy respects. Gregory of Nyssa, for example, denied that infants who died unbaptized would be condemned, apparently because he thought they were sinless. Nevertheless, there is a significant amount of common ground between Eastern and Western views of the fall. Pier Beatrice sums up the views of Irenaeus, Basil of Caesarea, Gregory of Nazianzus, and John Chrysostom (ca. 347–407) as follows: "We pay the price of his [Adam's] disobedience with physical death and moral frailty."[9] For these influential church fathers, Adam and Eve began existence free from passion directed toward sin and had the possibility of immortality. Both were forfeited by Adam's sin.

Despite their differences over the questions of infant damnation, original sin, and much else besides, the Greek East and Latin West generally agreed that Adam's sin brought at least the desire for sin—concupiscence or passion directed toward sin—to subsequent generations.[10] The idea that a sinful event or series of events at the beginning of history deleteriously altered the structure of subsequent human desire was predominant in the medieval church, all sides of the Reformation, and a great deal of modern theology. This is true despite the diverse accounts of original sin

---

8. Augustine, *Civ.* 14. The Latin is from CCSL 48:395.

9. Pier Beatrice, *The Transmission of Sin: Augustine and the Pre-Augustinian Sources*, trans. Adam Kamesar (Oxford: Oxford University Press, 2013), 166.

10. Of course, there were exceptions. The agreement was widespread, not unanimous. Origen of Alexandria, for example, did not think of the fall as a disease. See Stephen Bagby, *Sin in Origen's Commentary on Romans* (Lanham, MD: Lexington, 2018).

that arose over the years. For example, even "federalist" views of original sin common in Protestant scholasticism—which claim that Adam's sin was counted against or imputed to his posterity—have also maintained that Adam transmitted a corrupted human nature, which explains the universality of sinful action.

For the purposes of this chapter, I am going to abstract from the various accounts that think of the fall as a disease and speak of *the* disease view of the fall. Moreover, I will focus on one aspect of the fall, the change in the structure of human desire. Questions of mortality, death, original sin, and original guilt will be left aside.[11] This is because evolution raises problems for accounts of the fall that do not involve original sin or the lost possibility of immortality.

Here is my definition of the disease view of the fall. A human or humans sin. Therefore—prescinding from any miracle—if they reproduce, they necessarily pass on disordered desires to all their descendants. If they had not sinned, they would have necessarily passed on rightly ordered desires to the next generation. Each generation that refrained from sinning would have necessarily passed on rightly ordered desires.

Let me clarify a couple of things about this definition. By "desire" I mean *habitual* desire. To have habitually rightly ordered desires implies, among other things, that no unchosen impulse can, as it were, pull one away from the good. With rightly ordered desires, we would never feel angry or lustful at the wrong time, for example. The human being with rightly ordered desires would need to deliberately reject the good in order to sin. Fallen humans lack rightly ordered desires, and they can be drawn to sinful behavior without deliberating. On the disease view, unfallen human beings had rightly ordered desires, and they could have passed them on. Not only that, they could have passed on the ability to pass on rightly ordered desires, such that their grandchildren would have had rightly ordered desires if their children remained unfallen, and so forth. Conversely, by falling, they lost rightly ordered desires for the rest of humanity. Traditionally, the fall was the event in which *Adam* forfeited the ability to transmit righteousness.

---

11. For an argument that the orthodox doctrine of original sin does not include original guilt, see Oliver Crisp, "On Original Sin," *International Journal of Systematic Theology* 17, no. 3 (2015): 6. See 5–12 of this article for a constructive development of a "moderate Reformed doctrine of original sin."

Even if Eve had remained upright, humanity would have fallen in Adam—but not vice versa.[12] I take it that this is not essential to the disease view of the fall, so I have left it open whether an individual or group needed to sin in order for the fall to have occurred.

The great advantage of the disease view is the clarity with which one who adopts it can proclaim the goodness of God. God is not to blame for the fall. He created human beings in a healthy state of righteousness; only their disobedience brings sickness. Yet there are two objections that can be raised against it (objections that are typically phrased as though they were objections to the doctrine of the fall itself). First we raise the objection from natural selection, then the objection from original violence.

THE OBJECTION FROM NATURAL SELECTION

The first challenge to the fall comes from the "modern synthesis" of Darwin's theory of evolution by natural selection with Gregor Mendel's theory of inheritance.[13] In order to grapple with its theological implications, we need to discuss the basics of the modern synthesis (also known as the "synthetic theory" or "neo-Darwinism"). Synthetic theory is best understood in contrast to Jean-Baptiste de Lamarck, who offered the first scientific theory of evolution. In his *Philosophie Zoologique*, published in 1809, Lamarck proposed that evolution occurs through the inheritance of acquired characteristics.[14] Organisms behave in accordance with pressures exerted by their environments, and they pass on the traits they develop from their behavior. Darwin, by contrast, argued that variations are random with respect to the environment. Organisms with favorable heritable variations will survive and reproduce more successfully on average, leading over time to evolutionary change and the adaptation of populations to their environments. This is the theory of natural selection.

---

12. For example, see Aquinas, *Summa Theologica* I–II, q. 81, a. 5.

13. My comments here on the basics of evolutionary theory are indebted to Francisco J. Ayala and Camilo J. Cela-Conde, *Processes in Human Evolution: The Journey from Early Hominins to Neanderthals and Modern Humans* (Oxford: Oxford University Press, 2017).

14. As Richard Burkhardt points out, the view that acquired traits are heritable was not original to Lamarck and was widely accepted throughout the eighteenth and nineteenth centuries, even by Darwin. "When the names were assigned to the theoretical positions, however, this detail was considered negligible." See Burkhardt, *The Spirit of System: Lamarck and Evolutionary Biology* (Cambridge: Harvard University Press, 1995), 2.

Given that evolution is driven by natural selection, how are favorable variations passed on? Many biologists in Darwin's day assumed that offspring inherited the average of their parents' traits. This "blending" theory of inheritance does not cohere well with natural selection, however. Favorable mutations would be halved in each subsequent generation and eventually dissipate. Darwin never solved this problem. Augustinian monk Gregor Mendel proposed a theory of inheritance through "particulate factors"—later known as "genes"—which won widespread acceptance in the scientific community. Offspring inherit particulate factors from each parent, and the factors separate in the gametes (sex cells). Favorable variants can thus be maintained through the generations.

Geneticists in the 1920s and 1930s combined Mendel's account of particulate inheritance with Darwin's account of natural selection. This is the modern synthesis. By the 1940s, it was the consensus view among biologists. Many would say it still is. In recent years, however, debate has arisen *within* academic biology over whether the evolutionary mechanisms of the modern synthesis—which include not only natural selection but also genetic drift and recombination, gene flow, and founder effect—are sufficient. An "Extended Evolutionary Synthesis" has been proposed to rectify the alleged shortcomings of the modern synthesis.[15] More on that shortly.

What challenge does the modern synthesis pose to the doctrine of the fall? Anglican theologian F. R. Tennant puts it this way: "It is not easy to understand how one act of sin, however momentous, could serve to dislocate at once the whole nature of man."[16] Even if we grant that the first sin was a gross affront to God, it is far from clear how that action could have affected human nature at the biological level, such that sin or at least the disposition thereto would be passed on through the generations. Tennant was writing at the turn of the twentieth century, before the modern

---

15. For an introduction to the debate, see Kevin Laland et al., "Does Evolutionary Theory Need a Rethink?," *Nature* 514 (2014): 161–64. Advocates of the extended synthesis argue that the modern synthesis cannot account for how "physical development influences the generation of variation (developmental bias); how the environment directly shapes organisms' traits (plasticity); how organisms modify environments (niche construction); and how organisms transmit more than genes across generations (extra-genetic inheritance)" (162). Defenders of the modern synthesis argue that it can take these phenomena into account.

16. F. R. Tennant, *The Origin and Propagation of Sin* (Cambridge: Cambridge University Press, 1902), 28. For a summary of the debate at the time, see "Note D: On the Heredity of Acquired Characters," in *Origin and Propagation of Sin*, 176–81.

synthesis was adopted by the scientific community; the problem is arguably more acute today. Yet unfortunately there is a dearth of reflection on the problem among theologians who are both open to evolution and maintain the fall. A quasi-Lamarckian view of inheritance is often assumed. A prominent philosopher-theologian recently argued, for example, that a hypothetical "Neo-Augustine" would have no problem with evolutionary theory. Neo-Augustine could simply argue that the first human beings acquire vices, which "become a part of their make-up—of their genetic structure if you will—to be inevitably handed down."[17] But this is not how we acquire traits, at least according to synthetic theory. The personal vices acquired by the first human beings would not be transmitted to all their descendants unless they had a genetic basis.[18] But if they had a genetic basis, then they were not acquired.

It is worth reformulating Tennant's intuition into an argument. In the argument that follows I'll use the phrase "strictly natural" to refer to traits that are be passed on through the generations in accordance with the disease view of the fall. Here is an argument to the effect that contemporary evolutionary theory is incompatible with the fall. The fall is a volition whereby a human being loses the strictly natural trait of rightly ordered desires (first premise). Every strictly natural trait is transmitted through germline DNA (second premise). Therefore, the fall is a volition that changes germline DNA. This is absurd, because the volition of a human being cannot change its germline DNA.

The first premise follows from the disease view of the fall. The second premise arguably follows from mainstream biology. Traits that do not come from our environments (broadly construed, so as to include culture, nutrition, and so forth), free choices, or whatever immaterial parts we might have come from our DNA.[19] Thus, if a trait were to be inseparably fixed to the human species, it would be transmitted through germline DNA. These

---

17. John Rist, *Augustine Deformed: Love, Sin and Freedom in the Western Moral Tradition* (Cambridge: Cambridge University Press, 2014), 387.

18. Of course, parents can have a bad influence on their children. But the particular vices of the first human beings were not inevitably handed down to all subsequent human beings, as evidenced by the diversity of human cultures and patterns of virtue and vice.

19. This premise has nothing to do with genetic determinism. One might think that the environment and free choice determine all the traits we care about and still accept this premise.

premises seem to lead to the conclusion that the fall would have altered human nature at the genetic level. But particular volitions do not change DNA—and thus the conclusion is absurd. Perhaps at one time it was reasonable to believe that an action corrupted our "seminal nature" (Augustine) or inculcated a transmissible "acquired vice" (Lamarck), but it is not today. Or so the argument goes. What might an advocate of the disease view say in response?

One might argue against the second premise as follows. Not all inherited traits come from germline DNA, contrary to synthetic theory. There has recently been a renewed interest in "soft inheritance," the inheritance of traits through nongenetic processes. The field of epigenetics, for example, studies changes in gene expression during organisms' lifetimes and such changes that are transmitted from parents to children. Warren Burggren has helpfully distinguished intragenerational epigenetics—the study of epigenetic change within an individual's lifetime—from transgenerational epigenetics, "the inheritance of a modified phenotype from the prenatal generation without changes in genes or gene sequence." An example of transgenerational epigenetics is that the offspring of fish who undergo hypoxia (the deprivation of oxygen) are sometimes born with thinner gills as a result.[20] Could the fall have consisted in an epigenetic change? Given the current state of our knowledge, it is not clear that reinterpreting the fall in epigenetic terms would be helpful. First, it is unclear whether transgenerational epigenetic changes last longer than a single generation in humans. It has been argued by Denis Alexander, among others, that this is unlikely.[21] But temporary changes are not strictly natural in the sense required by the disease view of the fall. It is also unclear how a volition could bring about transgenerational epigenetic change.

---

20. Warren Burggren, "Epigenetic Inheritance and Its Role in Evolutionary Biology: Re-evaluation and New Perspectives," *Biology* 5, no. 24 (2016), 2, 10. This is opposed to intragenerational epigenetics, the "modification of gene expression through epigenetic marks (e.g., DNA methylation, covalent histone modification, microRNA action) that results in a modified phenotype, often considered at the molecular/cellular level, within an individual's lifespan."

21. "In mammals it is very unlikely that such long-term environmentally induced epialleles will ever be detected over more than a few generations for the simple reason that the great majority (though not all) of the epigenetic modifications gained during life are wiped from the genome during transmission of parental DNA to the next generation." Denis Alexander, *Genes, Determinism, God* (Cambridge: Cambridge University Press, 2017), 79.

One could also argue against the second premise by appealing to a "preternatural" power possessed by the first humans to transmit rightly ordered desires that has nothing to do with germline DNA.[22] It is unclear, however—or at least it is unclear to me—how the hypothesis that the first humans had transmissible preternatural powers that were forfeited by disobedience to God could be reconciled with contemporary genetics. What *were* these nongenetic, preternatural powers, and how were they to be transmitted? How could one act of disobedience bring it about that they were not? I grant that advances in epigenetics or further development of the concept of "preternatural power" could render the view that the disease view is compatible with genetics plausible.

THE OBJECTION FROM ORIGINAL VIOLENCE

The previous argument against the fall presupposed the possibility of a state of original justice. Even if the first humans had evolved with only good desires, it was difficult to explain how a single action could have reversed the course of evolutionary history and given the next generation of humans evil desires. We can now consider a second, independent objection to the fall. This objection can grant for the sake of argument that the fall is not in tension with natural selection. Even if one action *could* have corrupted human desire in principle, the fact is that at least some of the first humans inherited dispositions to sinful behavior from their nonhuman ancestors—not justice. This is because, as Richard Swinburne puts it, "The desires which cause all the trouble are there in the monkeys and the apes as well. The desires are not caused in us by Adam's sin."[23] We can rephrase and extend Swinburne's argument against original justice as follows.

The doctrine of original justice requires that the first humans could have lived without the desire for sin (first premise). Evolutionary theory indicates that the hominid ancestors of the first humans had desires that—when they are in humans—are for sin (second premise). Therefore, the

---

22. See Nicanor Pier Giorgio Austriaco, "A Theological Fittingness Argument for the Historicity of the Fall of *Homo Sapiens*," *Nova et Vetera* 13, no. 3 (2015): 651–67.

23. Richard Swinburne, *Responsibility and Atonement* (Oxford: Oxford University Press, 1989), 143.

first humans could not have lived without the desire for sin, and the doctrine of original justice is false.

The first premise accords with the traditional view of original justice and the disease view of the fall.

The second premise neither affirms nor denies that nonhuman animals can sin or desire to sin. It claims that there are desires that, even if they are amoral in nonhuman beings, are ordered to sin in human beings. It also claims that the parents of the first humans had these desires.[24] What might they be? There are a wide variety of candidates; for the sake of space it will be convenient to nominate only one: aggressive violence. By "aggressive" I mean "not undertaken in defense."[25] It should be uncontroversial that the desire for aggressive violence in this stipulated sense is a desire for sin in humans. The results of several decades of biological research indicate that the hominid ancestors of the first humans were prone to aggressive violence. The details are contested, to be sure, and there is also a large body of recent research arguing that *cooperation* is a crucial feature of our evolutionary history.[26] Yet it does not seem that this research challenges the claim that violence played a role in our evolutionary history. Given the strict requirement of the doctrine of original justice—that the first humans could have lived without the desire for sin—the ratio of cooperative to violent behavior is not the issue. *Any* desire for aggressive violence among the first human beings would be incompatible with original justice. It may be worth briefly highlighting a summary of some salient literature.

According to Harvard biologist Richard Wrangham and author Dale Peterson, two crucial discoveries since the 1970s shed light on the origins of human violence. The first is that chimpanzees are far more violent than

---

24. I assume that there was a first generation of human beings. Given that human beings now exist but at one point did not, it seems that there must have been.

25. I will not attempt to define violence very precisely here. I take it that it means *at least* lethal violence, though I assume that there are other forms of violence that are sinful, at least when not undertaken in self-defense. Some Christians believe that all human violence is sinful. Though not all go that far, most Christians have believed that violent action not undertaken for defensive purposes is sinful. Thus, regardless of whether unchosen desire for aggressive violence is sinful—that is, regardless of whether one needs to freely consent to a desire for or impulse to aggressive violence in order to be culpable for experiencing it—the desire is ordered to sin, such that *if* one consents to the desire, one is guilty of sin.

26. Martin A. Nowak and Sarah Coakley, eds., *Evolution, Games, and God* (Cambridge: Harvard University Press, 2013).

we had thought. In 1974, a researcher working with Jane Goodall's team at Gombe National Park in Tanzania observed a surprising event. A group of eight chimpanzees left their range and approached the territory of Kahama, another chimpanzee community. They found a member of the Kahama community named Godi eating alone. The eight chimpanzees initiated a vicious attack on Godi: they kicked, clawed, and bit him, and left him for dead. According to Wrangham and Peterson, this was the first time scientists had observed a lethal raid among chimpanzees.

> The attack on Godi ... struck a momentous chord. This sort of thing wasn't supposed to happen among non-humans. Until the attack on Godi, scientists treated the remarkable violence of humanity as something uniquely ours. To be sure, everyone knew that many animal species kill; but usually that killing is directed toward other species, toward prey. Individual animals—often males in sexual competition—fight with others of their own species; but that sort of contest typically ends the moment one competitor gives up. Scientists thought that only humans deliberately sought out and killed members of their own species.[27]

The first discovery was how violent chimps are. The second discovery was how close to chimps *we* are. Scientists discovered in 1984 through DNA hybridization that humans are more closely related to chimpanzees than chimpanzees are to gorillas.[28] The last common ancestor of chimpanzees and humans existed around five million years ago, and since that time chimpanzees have changed very little. (They evolve "conservatively" because their habitat has remained stable.) What all this implies,

---

27. Richard Wrangham and Dale Peterson, *Demonic Males: Apes and the Origins of Human Violence* (New York: Houghton Mifflin, 1996), 6–7.

28. Charles G. Sibley and Jon E. Ahlquist, "The Phylogeny of the Hominoid Primates, as Indicated by DNA-DNA Hybridization," *Journal of Molecular Evolution* 20 (1984): 2–15. Wrangham and Peterson sum up the consensus *before* Sibley and Ahlquist's study as follows. "As for the three African ape species—gorillas, chimpanzees, and bonobos—well, a little common sense combined with some elementary anatomy would indicate that they were tightly associated in their own group. ... Surely, so went the conventional thinking up to 1984, they were all each other's closest relatives, with humans as the special outsiders whose ancestors peeled off first" (Wrangham and Peterson, *Demonic Males*, 38–39). "Sibley and Ahlquist took the two strands of DNA, zipped, heated ... and found that chimpanzees were more closely related to *humans* than they were to gorillas" (40).

Wrangham and Peterson argue, is that the investigation of chimpanzee behavior serves as a "time machine" that takes us back to the dawn of human history.[29] When we see aggressive violence in chimps, we see, in broad strokes, how the earliest humans would have behaved.

Interestingly for present purposes, Wrangham and Peterson claim that their research rules out the doctrine of original sin: "We cloaked our own species' violence in culture and reason, two distinctly human attributes, and wondered what kind of original sin condemned us to this strange habit." There was no fall from peace; we were always "deeply infused with the essence of that ancient forest brain."[30] We *used* to think our aggressive violence was uniquely human, not the product of our prehuman history, but now we know we have always been violent. This, at any rate, is their argument.

Let's grant that the research discussed by Wrangham and Peterson shows that the second premise of the objection from original violence is correct (the hominid ancestors of the first humans had desires that—when they are in humans—are for sin). Why does it follow that the first human beings couldn't have lived without the desire for sin? One could argue that it does not, because God could have supernaturally prevented the first human beings from being affected by the natural course of evolutionary history. That is, God could have prevented the first human beings from experiencing the sinful desires they would have experienced if they had descended from nonhuman animals and did not receive a special gift of grace.[31] Thus the data adduced by Wrangham and Peterson are compatible with the doctrine of original justice.

Moreover, one could argue not only that God could have done this but that we must affirm that he did. God is not the author of (at least) moral

---

29. "The rainforest ape line has changed very little since these two species split around 8 to 10 million years ago. That means that our own rainforest ape ancestor, peeling away from the same line at 5 million years, came out of the chimpanzee-gorilla mold" (Wrangham and Peterson, *Demonic Males*, 45). "To be with modern chimpanzees in an African rainforest is to climb into a time machine. Stepping into the dappled world of these extraordinary apes we move back to glimpse our origins" (47).

30. Wrangham and Peterson, *Demonic Males*, 7; 62.

31. For present purposes it makes no difference whether one holds that a creature can be the principal efficient cause of the rational soul, or that only God can bring a rational soul into existence.

evil.[32] The desire for aggressive violence is a moral evil. Thus, God created the first human beings with the possibility of not experiencing the desire to commit aggressive acts of violence.

There are objections that can be raised against this response to the argument against the fall. One could argue that this appeal to a supernatural gift at the dawn of history carries a whiff of fundamentalism. Even if this hypothesis is not formulated on scientific grounds, doesn't it involve rejecting a plausible scientific hypothesis—the first humans were disposed to violence because their ancestors were—on the basis of the Bible? Isn't this the same sort of argumentation used to defend the special creation of species against evolution in general?

Or one could argue that it would be unfitting for God to use evolution to create (at least the bodies of) the first human beings if he intended to cancel out the effects of that evolution from the beginning. Why not guide evolution to select for the properties the first human beings were always intended to have? (A disposition toward peace, for example.) If that was impossible or undesirable—though it is hard to see *why* it would be impossible for an omnipotent God and hard to see why it would be undesirable on the supposition that God intended us to have these dispositions—why not simply create human beings from the dust, as classical Christian theology has it? If we were intended for peace, why did God apparently make us for war?

I think these questions of fittingness are important. But I will not try to resolve or even address them here. Instead, I will propose an account of the fall that is compatible with different views of whether God restrained our aggressive desires *ab initio*, an account that also allows us to respond to the objection from natural selection.

TOWARD A NEW THOMIST VIEW

It seems to me that Aquinas gives us the resources to move beyond the disease view of the fall. Let me say a couple of words about his views and then sketch an account that is indebted to them. To make a long story short, the fall, for Aquinas, was the event in which Adam forfeited the

---

32. Many theologians have distinguished natural evil from moral evil and argued that God can will the former but not the latter. See Thomas Aquinas, *Summa Theologica* I, q. 19, a. 9, for an example of this approach.

gift of original justice for himself and his posterity, such that he passed on bare human nature instead.[33] The original justice Adam lost had two parts: the will's subjection to God and rightly ordered concupiscence. To have rightly ordered concupiscence involved the habitual right ordering of one's desires. Original sin in infants, correspondingly, involves habitually disordered desires. Unlike Augustine, Aquinas clearly argued that rightly ordered desires were a gift of supernatural sanctifying grace. God could have created human beings without sanctifying grace, but if he had, our desires would have been disordered and our wills not subjected to God.[34]

There are, I would suggest, a number of theological advantages to thinking of sin, nature, and grace along these lines. For one thing, understanding grace as supernatural helps us avoid the arguably absurd claim that God owes human beings the beatific vision by virtue of creating us. The glories of heaven are God's gift to us. Moreover, understanding sin as the lack of a supernatural gift helps us clarify that postlapsarian human beings continue to exist: they continue to possess human nature.

For present purposes, the benefit is that these Thomistic building blocks, as it were, can be used to construct an account of the fall that does not commit us to beliefs that stand in tension with—or at the least do not contradict—mainstream evolutionary theory. Here is that account, which I'll simply call the new Thomist view. A human or humans sin. Therefore— sans miracle—if they reproduce, they necessarily pass on disordered desires to all their descendants. If they had not sinned, God would have given sanctifying grace to their children. If their children obeyed, their grandchildren would have been born in the same grace, and so on. On this account, the first humans were given supernatural grace, but that grace was withheld from later generations. Subsequent humans begin to exist with only human nature—creation's grace, if you like—and as a result have disordered desires.

---

33. For a defense of this reading of Aquinas, see Daniel W. Houck, "Natura Humana Relicta est Christo: Thomas Aquinas on the Effects of Original Sin," Archa Verbi 13 (2016): 76–110. Human nature was not, strictly speaking, corrupted by the fall. If it were, Aquinas argues, the absurd conclusion that human beings would no longer exist follows. For the supernatural status of original justice, see Summa Theologica I, q. 95, a. 1. For Thomas's definition of original sin as the lack of due original justice, see Summa Theologica I–II, q. 82, a. 3.

34. Scriptum II, d. 31, q. 1, a. 2, ad 3. See also Summa Theologica I–II, q. 81, a. 4, a terser presentation of the same view.

This account of the fall is compatible with two different ways of responding to the objection from original violence. The first option is this. The first humans were created in sanctifying grace that restrained all their disordered desires, including the desire for aggressive violence. The second option is this. The first humans were created in sanctifying grace that did not restrain all their naturally disordered desires. The grace was sufficient to give them free will to resist these desires, however. They might have been tempted to commit violent actions, for example, but they could have refrained from actual violence. The first option is more traditional but arguably open to the aforementioned objection that it stands in tension with evolutionary theory. The second option is easier to square with evolution but arguably open to the aforementioned objection that evil is built into creation.

Whether one picks the first or second option will relate to one's view of the nature of sin. Anselm of Canterbury (1033–1109) influentially argued that disordered concupiscence (roughly speaking, habitually disordered desires) is not sinful, that sin is *only* in the rational will. Alternatively, in dialogue with Augustine, other theologians have argued that disordered concupiscence itself is sinful. If one thinks that disordered concupiscence is sinful, then the second option discussed here implies that the first humans were created in sin, despite the fact that they were also created in sanctifying grace. If one takes a broadly Anselmian view, which denies that disordered concupiscence is intrinsically sinful, one could admit that the first human beings had disordered desires—including the previously discussed desire for violence—so long as they had sanctifying grace.

In either case, the new Thomist view denies that the fall affected the DNA of the first humans. It is thus compatible with the story Wrangham and Peterson tell of our prehuman history. Without grace, at least some of us are inclined to aggression. Precisely because it does not need to claim that our DNA has been corrupted, the new Thomist account can also respond to the objection from natural selection. The fall is not the loss of a "strictly natural" trait in the aforementioned sense. We do not need to appeal to the hypothetical possibility of the first human beings sexually transmitting righteousness; we only need to appeal to the hypothetical possibility that God would have continued to bestow the gift of sanctifying grace, the gift of divine friendship. It should be obvious that natural selection is not in tension with the view that the earliest human beings enjoyed friendship with God.

This account raises various objections and questions that I plan on engaging in future work. One important question relates to the problem of evil. We mentioned that an advantage of the disease view is that it is fairly clear that God is not responsible for our fallen condition. Does the new Thomist view change that? One could object that the divine decision to withhold grace from later generations is the *cause* of fallenness. I don't think it needs to be understood that way—though much more work needs to be done to explain why. In brief, I would argue that if the first human beings had obeyed—and they could have—then God would have continued his friendship with the next generation. It seems that this view does not violate the grammar of Christian theology, which "encapsulates the biblical narrative in a *plot* that begins with the goodness of creation, [and] a fall into sin."[35] Human beings are made good: they have the goodness that comes to them by virtue of being human, and they are friends of God. They are the ones who fall away.

---

35. James K. A. Smith, "What Stands on the Fall? A Philosophical Exploration," in *Evolution and the Fall*, ed. William T. Cavanaugh and James K. A. Smith (Grand Rapids: Eerdmans, 2017), 51.

12

—

INTELLECTUAL DISABILITY AND THE SABBATH STRUCTURE OF THE HUMAN PERSON

Jared Ortiz

When he was three, our oldest son, Benedict, was diagnosed with autism. This was *not* a terribly traumatic revelation for us and was, in many ways, a relief, since it helped explain a number of things about our sweet little boy. Since his diagnosis, we have received excellent support and good practical advice, but as I tried to understand more about autism and disability, I found myself increasingly frustrated. Most of the disability literature, both secular and theological, operated on assumptions I found problematic. On one extreme, there are those who argue that the disabled, especially the intellectually disabled, are not in fact persons and that generally it would be better not to let them see the light of day.[1] On the other extreme, there are those who argue that there is no such thing as disability,

---

1. For example, Peter Singer, *Practical Ethics*, 3rd ed. (Cambridge: Cambridge University Press, 2011), says, "Many beings are sentient and capable of experiencing pleasure and pain but they are not rational and self-conscious and, therefore, are not persons. ... Many non-human animals fall into this category; so must newborn infants and some intellectually disabled humans" (85). See also the chapter in the same book, "Justifying Infanticide and Non-voluntary Euthanasia" (159–67). Also see Jeff McMahon, *The Ethics of Killing: Problems at the Margins of Life* (Oxford: Oxford University Press, 2003), particularly the chapter "Animals and Severely Cognitively Impaired Human Beings" (203–31). For a philosophical critique of Singer and McMahon's understanding of persons, see Eva Feder Kittay, "The Personal Is Philosophical Is Political: A Philosopher and Mother of a Cognitively Disabled Person Sends Notes from the Battlefield," *Metaphilosophy* 40, no. 3/4 (July 2009): 606–27.

only difference, because there is no such thing as normal.[2] Proponents of this approach effectively deny that there is such a thing as human nature or, perhaps, unwittingly absorb human nature into the person. The first extreme, thankfully, has few theological supporters. The other extreme, though, has many. The theological version of this extreme claims that disability is part of creation rather than a result of the fall, and so disability is positively willed by God, essential to the identity of the person, and therefore that some disabilities will remain in the resurrection.[3]

Neither of these extremes, in their secular or theological forms, spoke to my experience as the father of an autistic son, nor did they provide theologically satisfying answers to the questions I was asking. I love my son, but recognize that something is not right. Is it possible to love him unconditionally, not want to "fix" him, but also to help him grow and develop? And if so, grow and develop toward what?[4] Can I say, without fear of reprisal, that autism impairs him in some way and is something to be overcome?

---

2. The standard text is Lennard Davis, "Introduction: Disability, Normality, and Power," in *The Disability Studies Reader*, ed. Lennard Davis, 5th ed (New York: Routledge, 2017), 1–16. See also John Swinton, "From Inclusion to Belonging: A Practical Theology of Community, Disability, and Humanness," *Journal of Religion, Disability, & Health* 16, no. 2 (2012): 172–90: "Other than the fact that we may prefer certain looks and feel more comfortable with certain body shapes or ways of thinking, there seems to be no real *norm* for being human" (178).

3. For example, in his *Disabled Church, Disabled Society: The Implications of Autism for Philosophy, Theology, and Politics* (London: Jessica Kingsley, 2010), John Gillebrand, father of a nonverbal autistic son, asks and answers, "If creation had been perfect, rather than very good, would it have included autism, and thence people with autism? I believe the answer would be yes. ... Did the prelapsarian excellence of God's creation include autism? I believe it did. ... Is the existence of autism and other disabilities to be attributed to the fallen nature of humanity as described in the Book of Genesis? I believe not, because I have a general concern about associating disability with ill-health in a medical model of disability, and about the further step of associating ill-health with sinfulness" (56). The rest of the book defends these answers. Amos Yong, *Bible, Disability, and the Church: A New Vision of the People of God* (Grand Rapids: Eerdmans, 2011), is also representative when he says, "But this [conventional understanding of perfection, wholeness, and beauty] requires people with disabilities to internalize a self-understanding that rejects who they are as unacceptable to God or as less fit for participation in the Deity's eschatological blessing. If they are to fit into the 'acceptable' mold, their blemishes, defects, and disabilities will need to be removed. *But what if some disabilities are identity-making in the sense that they are inextricable from who persons are in essence ... ? How might these disabilities be removed without eliminating the person entirely*" (38, emphasis added)? Almost all the major theologians of disability—Nancy Eisland, John Swinton, Stanley Hauerwas, Martin Lloyd Williams, Thomas Reynolds, to name a few—hold to some form of these claims.

4. Those who deny that there are norms for human being, health, and behavior have a difficult time answering this question while remaining consistent. All therapy aims at healing something perceived to have gone awry and setting it right.

It seems almost commonsensical to me to assert that disability is part of the death and disease that results from the fall; yet, I don't see my son as some kind of tragedy. Is it possible to affirm that disability is a sign of our fallen human nature while also affirming that every person is willed by God and precious in his sight? Last, I and many others can attest to the challenges of living with the intellectually disabled, yet we can also attest to how life changing, even mystical, this experience can be. How can we take seriously the real suffering that occurs while also accounting for the mysterious, transformative power that the intellectually disabled so often exert on those who live with them?

I address these questions in two ways: First, I want to retrieve a basic philosophical distinction between person and nature. This distinction allows us to defend the dignity of intellectually disabled persons while also providing a realistic framework for understanding the meaning of disability. And second, I want to deepen this account theologically by exploring the "Sabbath structure" of the human person. This is still rather mysterious to me, but I want to argue that the Sabbath is a constitutive dimension of our humanity that can help account for the transformative power people often experience when living with the intellectually disabled.

PERSON AND NATURE

Let us begin with a brief discussion of person and nature. A nature is *what* something is and determines what it can do. A person is *who* someone is. By nature, humans can walk, talk, think, and laugh, while birds can fly and chirp, and stones can do none of these things. Humans are made up of a body and a rational soul. This is true of human beings at all stages of life and is true whether the body is impaired in some way or the soul never realizes its native capacities. Because human beings have rational natures, they are persons. A person is a *who*. Being a person is not a dignity bestowed by others, nor is it a reality that emerges with the realization of certain capacities or activities. Being a person is a function of what we are rather than what we do.[5] Individual birds or stones are not persons; they are not

---

5. In *The Ethics of Abortion: Women's Rights, Human Life, and the Question of Justice* (New York: Routledge, 2011), Christopher Kaczor makes a helpful distinction between endowment and performance accounts of the human person. "The endowment account holds that each human being has inherent, moral worth simply by virtue of the kind of being it is. By

"whos." Human beings are "whos" who have the capacity (even if never developed or if subsequently hindered by age or accident) to do things, the things that are proper to their human, rational nature. Persons do things by or through their nature. By nature, humans can do human things, but it is the persons themselves who do them.

With this basic account, we can speak of disabilities or impairments as conditions that hinder the exercise of something proper to our nature. It is proper to human nature that our eyes see and our ears hear and our minds think, but sometimes blindness or deafness or autism compromises these operations. It is not proper to human nature to fly, so we are not compromised or impaired by not being able to fly (it is, though, proper for a bird to fly, so if it cannot, then it is impaired in some way). One who has an impairment or disability cannot, to some degree, do what is proper to one's nature, but (and this is the important point) the impaired nature does not make one any less of a person. A disability may shape how a person lives or behaves or develops, but it does not in any way change the fact that we are speaking about a *person* with a disability. A person's a person no matter how impaired. Someone with a disability, like every other person, is composed of a body and rational soul, even if one's physical or rational capacities can never be exercised or exercised only in a limited way. A person is a person by what they are, not what they do.

This kind of account of human beings pushes back against those who would deny the humanity of the disabled based on their (seeming) inability to achieve a certain level of competence or activity. It also pushes back against those who would essentialize disability. It creates space to affirm the goodness of persons and name the things that hinder them. Against those who see only the impaired natural powers and therefore a life not worth living, this account defends the personhood of all human beings in

---

endowment, I mean that the being in question has an intrinsic, dynamic orientation towards self-expressive activity. ... Beings with endowments that orient them towards moral values, such as rationality, autonomy, and respect, thereby merit inclusion as members of the moral community. The performance account ... denies this and holds that a being is to be accorded respect, if and only if, the being functions in a given way. There are numerous conflicting accounts of what this function is, but some of the proposed candidates include: self-awareness, rationality, sentience, desirability, ethnicity, economic productivity, gender, nationality, native language, beauty, age, health, religion, race, ethnicity, fertility, birth, and national origin" (93). See also Peter A. Comensoli, *In God's Image: Recognizing the Profoundly Impaired as Persons* (Eugene, OR: Cascade Books, 2018).

virtue of their rational nature (even if this rationality is never developed). Against those who deny any standard of normality, it asserts a common human nature, the features of which are accessible to human reason and which we all presuppose in our everyday life.[6] Against those who make disability an essential part of the person, this account gives a way of identifying the infinite worth of the person while also recognizing that what is proper to one's nature may be impaired in some way.

DISABILITY AND TRADITIONAL CHRISTIAN ANTHROPOLOGY

Thinking about disability in terms of person, nature, and the things proper to our nature provides a coherent way of approaching the questions I posed in the introduction. Thus far, I have kept this discussion within the realm of philosophy because it is the secular disability literature that has set the terms of the debate, even for theologians of disability. But what I have argued above can also be confirmed and deepened by the traditional Christian doctrines of the image of God, the fall, and incarnation. I will touch on these doctrines briefly by drawing on my own Catholic tradition, but what I offer here is common to most other Christian traditions.[7]

The *Catechism of the Catholic Church* says, "Being in the image of God the human individual possesses the dignity of a person, who is not just something, but someone."[8] To be made in the image of God means that we are persons made for communion with other persons and, ultimately, with God. This capacity for communion is rooted in our rational nature, in our capacities of intellect and will, which are made to know and to love God and neighbor. Only humans have these capacities because only humans are called to this kind of communion with God and others. Every human being is made in the image of God, even if these capacities are impaired

---

6. Sometimes it is hard to imagine how those who strongly deny any sense of a human norm would respond to the widespread use of glasses. I wear glasses to correct my failing sight. I have bad eyesight, and therefore I wear corrective lenses. Without presupposing a norm, we would undermine the work of every doctor, teacher, social worker, psychologist, and anyone else who works for the good of another.

7. For a similar account from a Reformed perspective, see Jennifer Ann Cox, *Autism, Humanity and Personhood: A Christ-Centred Theological Anthropology* (Cambridge: Cambridge Scholars, 2017).

8. CCC 357.

in some way.[9] So, a person with a disability, like every other person, is an inexhaustible and irreplaceable mystery who is willed by God and called to communion with him.[10]

Now, there is a sense in which these capacities are impaired in every single one of us. The *Catechism* teaches, "By yielding to the tempter, Adam and Eve committed a *personal sin*, but this sin affected the *human nature* that they would then transmit *in a fallen state*." All of us, then, have a fallen human nature, one "deprived of original holiness and justice." Note carefully that original sin is different than personal sin; "it is a sin 'contracted' and not 'committed'—a state and not an act."[11] This is helpful to note because much of the disability literature is very critical of the Christian tradition on this point, claiming that Christians have held that disabilities are a punishment for personal sin. This may have been held by some Christians at some times, but, as far as I am aware, it is not the position of any major theologian or of any official teaching of the church.[12] Rather, the church teaches that after the fall our human nature is "wounded in the natural powers proper to it, subject to ignorance, suffering and the dominion of death, and inclined to sin."[13] In other words, the church teaches that the things proper to our nature have been compromised; in particular, our intellect, our body, and our will are all impaired and subject to corruption. This is true of *every* human person.

---

9. See *CCC* 356–61. The Catholic understanding of *imago Dei* has been criticized in the disability literature, most famously by Hans Reinders, *Receiving the Gift of Friendship: Profound Disability, Theological Anthropology, and Ethics* (Grand Rapids: Eerdmans, 2008), 114–15. Comensoli's *In God's Image* is a book-length response to Reinders. For a more concise defense of the traditional Catholic position with reference to Reinders, see Matthew Levering, *Engaging the Doctrine of Creation: Cosmos, Creatures, and the Wise and Good Creator* (Grand Rapids: Baker Academic, 2017), 145–92, especially 173–74.

10. See *CCC* 1700, 1702. Also, John Paul II, *Message on the Occasion of the International Symposium on the Dignity and Rights of the Mentally Disabled Person* (2014), 2, http://w2.vatican.va/content/john-paul-ii/en/speeches/2004/january/documents/hf_jp-ii_spe_20040108_handicap-mentale.html.

11. *CCC* 404, emphasis original.

12. Certainly, the church has always claimed that some personal sin *can* lead to sickness and disease. For example, sexual promiscuity (lust) often results in sexually transmitted diseases, excessive eating of unhealthy food (gluttony) can lead to obesity or diabetes, and a habit of resentment or anger (wrath) can cause high blood pressure and increase the risk of heart attacks. Personal sins *can* lead to sickness and disease (not to mention moral, psychological, and spiritual damage) as a kind of natural punishment. But as far as I am aware no major figure or teaching in the Catholic Church has linked disabilities as such with personal sin.

13. *CCC* 405.

It seems significant to me that for most of Christian history there was no separate category for "disability." In the Latin West, there were names for particular physical and mental diseases and conditions, but there was not a general category equivalent to our "disability." Rather, all human weakness was understood under terms such as *fragilitas* (frailty), *infirmitas* (sickness), and *debilitas* (impairment). Human frailty was a spectrum we all lived on, which means that we are all subject to sickness, impairment, and ultimately death. This is constitutive of human reality after the fall; we are all under the dominion of death, and thus all experience the signs of death.[14] What today we group under the category of "disability" (autism, Down Syndrome, spina bifida, etc.) was for our Christian ancestors common experiences of frailty within the range of fallen human nature.[15] A corollary of this attitude is that the personhood of those with intellectual disabilities was never raised as a problematic question for our forebears because it was not really a question at all: all human beings were persons.

For Christians, though, death and disease are not the final word. Rather, Christ entered our human reality not to abolish death and its signs, but to bear them, and by bearing them, to transform them (Matt 8:17). A beautiful prayer from the early church (likely fifth century) powerfully captures this dynamic:

> Since the marvelous exchange of our reparation has shone forth— that is, since out of the old man a New Man stood forth—mortality was cured by mortality. When the human condition is healed by the created medicine of the human condition itself, and an offspring ignorant of all sin arises from the guilty, sinful generation, then not only does our frailty, taken up by your Word, receive perpetual glory, but also by this marvelous sharing, our frailty is made eternal.[16]

Christ unites himself to our human weakness and transforms it by the power of his divinity. He still bears the marks of the "old man" (mortality,

---

14. See Augustine's famous catalog of human miseries in *Civ.* 22.22.

15. For a philosophical perspective on the same insight, see Alasdair MacIntyre, *Dependent Rational Animals: Why Human Beings Need the Virtues* (Chicago: Open Court, 1999).

16. *Sacramentarium Veronense* 1260, my translation. The critical edition is L. C. Mohlberg, ed., *Sacramentarium Veronense (Cod. Bibl. Capit. Veron. LXXXV [80])* (Rome: Herder, 1955). The text has been turned into a searchable concordance at liturgia.it.

the human condition, frailty), but uses these to heal us. He unites our weakness to his strength, so that it becomes medicine for us. It not only repairs us, but gives us eternal life, a new and divine quality that shines forth from our frailty.

We see this dynamic throughout the New Testament. Death no longer stings, but is the passage to eternal life (1 Cor 15:42–58). Weakness, a sign of our fallen nature, is now a vehicle for Christ's power, for his "power is made perfect in weakness" (2 Cor 12:9). Christ radically identifies himself not with the rich and the powerful, but with the poor and sick, so that they are now a special place of encounter with God (Matt 25:31–46). Paul tells us not just to endure our suffering, but to rejoice in it because it is redemptive: "Now I rejoice in what I am suffering for you, and I fill up in my flesh what is still lacking in regard to Christ's afflictions, for the sake of his body, which is the church" (Col 1:24 NIV).[17] God can and ultimately will heal our wounds (Rev 21:4), but he also "uses" them now to manifest his grace and presence.

The Christian tradition, then, has much to offer the disability literature. It upholds the dignity of each and every person as made in the image of God. Instead of separating out "the disabled" as though they were a different species from "the nondisabled," the Christian tradition relativizes disability by considering it part of the *fragilitas* of fallen human existence. It recognizes that "disabilities" are both not normal and normal: on the one hand, God did not will death and disability for human beings, so these are a falling away from the integrity of our human nature (see Wisdom of Solomon 1:12–15); but, on the other hand, death and disability are now the common lot of fallen humanity, and we are *all* subject to them. Last, in the light of Christ, death and disability are no longer merely negative, but gain a positive connotation since Christ has chosen them as a privileged mode of revelation.

---

17. For an exploration of what this means in the Christian life, with implications for a theology of disability, see Carlo Gnocchi, *The Pedagogy of Innocent Suffering* (Chillum, MD: IVE Press, 2017) and John Paul II, *Salvifici Doloris* (1984), http://www.vatican.va/content/john-paul-ii/en/apost_letters/1984/documents/hf_jp-ii_apl_11021984_salvifici-doloris.html.

THE SABBATH STRUCTURE OF
THE HUMAN PERSON

The traditional Christian teaching on the human person, rightly under-stood, is a helpful (and true) framework for understanding disability. We are now in a place to address in what way we can say that the Sabbath is part of the structure of the human person and how this might shed light on disability. Let me begin by juxtaposing a few passages that bring out some striking parallels between the language used to speak about the Sabbath and the language used to speak about people's experience with persons with intellectual disabilities. In his beautiful book on the Sabbath, Abraham Heschel says, "The Sabbath is a day in which we abandon our plebeian pursuits and *reclaim our authentic state*, in which we may *partake of a blessedness in which we are what we are.*"[18] Similarly, in his Apostolic Letter, *Dies Domini* ("The Day of the Lord"), Pope John Paul II writes, "In honouring God's 'rest', man fully discovers himself."[19] According to these two authors, the Sabbath returns us to our authentic state, where we are what we are, and it allows us to fully discover ourselves.

Compare these comments to the experience of Henri Nouwen, who left his professorship at Harvard to live in a L'Arche community in fellow-ship with intellectually disabled people. Nouwen writes of his experience caring for Adam, a thirty-year-old epileptic who could not talk and could not walk, dress, or eat on his own: "As a spiritual teacher Adam would lead us ever so gently to those inner spaces we prefer to leave untouched, so that each of us could live out our true vocations. In relationship with him we would discover a deeper, truer identity."[20] Here, Nouwen describes his time with this profoundly disabled man in terms remarkably similar to the way the Sabbath is described.

Adam helps Nouwen to slow down and let go of his frenetic concerns, so that he is led to a sacred place where he discovers his true identity. By the very power of his being, Adam does what the Sabbath does because, I want to argue, Adam has become what the Sabbath is. This claim may sound

---

18. Abraham Heschel, *The Sabbath* (New York: Farrar, Straus and Giroux, 2005), 30, emphasis added.

19. John Paul II, *Dies Domini* (1998), 61, https://w2.vatican.va/content/john-paul-ii/en/apost_letters/1998/documents/hf_jp-ii_apl_05071998_dies-domini.html.

20. Henri Nouwen, *Adam: God's Beloved* (New York: Orbis, 2012), 31.

fanciful at first, but no less an authority than Augustine says the same thing about the destiny of the city of God: they will not merely enjoy a Sabbath rest, but they themselves "shall *become* that seventh day."[21] Augustine says that our end is to *become* the Sabbath. The Sabbath, then, defines what it means to be truly human; it is our true identity. Let me expand on this claim and lay out the argument for the rest of the essay.

The Sabbath is God's presence to and within creation. While clearly distinct and set apart from the six days, the Sabbath is nevertheless a constitutive dimension of creation, time, and, most importantly, our humanity. The Lord's Day, the day Christians celebrate the resurrection, fulfills the Sabbath because it brings creation, time, and our humanity to their fulfillment. All human beings, because they are persons made in the image of God, bear the marks of the Sabbath; those redeemed in Christ have the quality of the Lord's Day. Those with intellectual disabilities often show forth these dimensions of our humanity more clearly. Their disabilities often make them more transparent to God so his rest (the Sabbath) and his redemption (the Lord's Day) shine all the more brightly through them. Thus, thinking of the Sabbath and the Lord's Day in anthropological terms can help us address the last question I asked in the introduction: How can we take seriously the real suffering that occurs, while also accounting for the mysterious, transformative power that the intellectually disabled so often exert on those who live with them?

THE SABBATH

Let's begin with the Sabbath itself. The Sabbath is one of the seven days of creation; it is one of the commands or "words" God gave in the Decalogue, and the penalty for violating it is death. Each of these facts tells us something important about how the Sabbath is related to our human nature.

God creates all things in six days and says that they are, altogether, "very good" (Gen 1:31). The pinnacle of these six days is the human being, male and female, made in the image and likeness of God. This creature has both a kinship to the animals, made on the same day, and to God, in whose image and likeness he is made. Human beings are unique because they

---

21. Augustine, *Civ.* 22.30, trans. Henry Bettenson (New York: Penguin Books, 1984), emphasis added.

are the only creatures directly addressed by God (Gen 1:28), which means they are made for relationship with God. But the sixth day of creation is not the end. There is a seventh day, which is set apart, both because God ceased creating on this day (i.e., "rested") and because God hallowed or sanctified it (Gen 2:2–3).

There are a number of ways this seventh day has been understood, but I think two passages from Heschel sum them up nicely: "We look to the Sabbath as our homeland, as our source and destination," and, "The Sabbath is the presence of God in the world, open to the soul of man."[22] In other words, the Sabbath is our origin, our end, and God's abiding presence to and within creation. We come from God and are made for God and are brought to God by communing with his presence manifest in creation. This is similar to what Augustine famously says in his Sabbath-themed opening to the *Confessions*, "You have made us for Yourself, and our heart is restless until it rests in You."[23] We are created, but we are not created for creation. We are made for God, who alone gives us rest, that is, brings us to completion as what we were meant to be. The six days of creation, then, do not find their fulfilment in themselves, but are ordered toward the Sabbath, which brings them to completion.[24]

The Sabbath means that within the mystery of time and, as we will see, our very bodies, God makes himself available to be known and loved. God calls us to an intimate communion, which both the Jewish and Christian tradition speak of in terms of marriage. Heschel says, "Israel is engaged to holiness, to eternity. The match was made long before history began; the Sabbath was a union that no one could disjoin."[25] John Paul II takes up this same theme when he says,

> The divine rest of the seventh day ... speaks, as it were, of God's lingering before the "very good" work (*Gn* 1:31) which his hand has wrought, in order to cast upon it *a gaze full of joyous delight.* ... It is a gaze which already discloses something of the nuptial shape of the

22. Heschel, *Sabbath*, 30, 60.

23. Augustine, *Conf.* 1.1.1, my translation.

24. The author of the book of Hebrews picks up on this element when he says, "There remains, then, a Sabbath-rest for the people of God; for anyone who enters God's rest also rests from their works, just as God did from his" (Heb 4:9).

25. Heschel, *Sabbath*, 52.

relationship which God wants to establish with the creature made in his own image, by calling that creature to enter a pact of love.[26]

God wants to marry his creation. He wants union, oneness with us. The Sabbath represents this relationship; the Sabbath *is* this relationship. It is written into the very fabric of things, but it still needs to be realized, made real by our transforming union with God.

Another way to get at this dimension of the Sabbath is to think about what it means that the Sabbath is part of the Decalogue rather than, say, the ceremonial laws, which are given later.[27] According to the *Catechism*, these "ten words" are "engraved by God in the human heart," and therefore they "teach us the true humanity of man."[28] John Paul II says, "These 'ten words' represent the very pillars of the moral life inscribed on the human heart … *a defining and indelible expression of our relationship with God.*"[29] Observing the Sabbath, then, means that we are acting in accord with our own nature. The Sabbath is not an external law imposed on us for our own good, but is constitutive of our humanity and our relationship with God. It is an indelible mark on our heart that defines who we are. When we live the Sabbath, we learn what it means to be a true human.

Perhaps this helps us understand why violating the Sabbath merits the punishment of death (Exod 31:14–16; 35:2). The Old Testament laws that call for the death penalty are much reviled these days, but I think two observations might help to mitigate our aversion and perhaps even help us understand their logic. First, it seems unlikely that this penalty was ever enforced. As Father Thomas Joseph White suggests, "When studying the punishments of the Torah, it must be kept in mind that the penalties in question may be *objectively merited*, but this does not mean that they are *effectively applicable.*"[30] In other words, even if the punishment is never

26. John Paul II, *Dies Domini*, 11, emphasis original.

27. The Catholic tradition generally holds that the Decalogue was written directly by the finger of God, while the later laws were given by Moses. See CCC 2056; see also Exod 31:18; Deut 5:22; 31:9–24.

28. CCC 2072, 2070. See also CCC 2070, quoting Irenaeus, "From the beginning, God had implanted in the heart of man the precepts of the natural law. Then he was content to remind him of them. This was the Decalogue."

29. John Paul II, *Dies Domini*, 13, emphasis original.

30. Thomas Joseph White, OP, *Exodus* (Grand Rapids: Brazos, 2016), 263.

applied, the law teaches us what we deserve for particular transgressions and thereby reveals a truth about who we are. Why, though, does violating the Sabbath objectively merit death? This leads to the second observation: all the transgressions that call for the death penalty in the Old Testament concern violations of life. The law calls for the death penalty for neglecting worship and committing idolatry (separating ourselves from the source of life), sexual misconduct (occluding the transmission of new life), and various forms of homicide (taking the life of others).[31] It is as if the law is trying to teach us that when we do violence to life we undermine our own life. The law makes explicit what is implicit in our violation of it.

Not observing the Sabbath merits the death penalty because the Sabbath is the ground of existence and the ground of our existence. If the Sabbath law is written into our hearts and defines our relationship with God, we do violence to our very being in violating it. We deny we need rest, we deny we are made for holiness, we deny our origin, and we cut ourselves off from our fulfillment. We undermine our own existence by violating the very observance that keeps us in existence and makes our lives worth living. By our actions, we have effectively proclaimed a sentence of death on ourselves.

THE LORD'S DAY

As the Sabbath was to faithful Jews, so the Lord's Day was to faithful Christians. While there were a variety of practices around the Sabbath and Sunday in the early church, Christians eventually came to see the Lord's Day as, in a sense, the extension and full expression of Sabbath's inner meaning.[32] With characteristic lucidity, Gregory the Great articu-

---

31. Death penalty laws pertaining to worship and idolatry include sacrificing to other gods (Exod 22:20; Lev 27:29), blasphemy (Lev 24:10-16), and violating the Sabbath (Exod 31:14; 35:2; Num 15:32-36). Interestingly, the prophet Jeremiah claims that violating the Sabbath is the cause of the Babylonian exile (Jer 17:19-27). Laws pertaining to sexual misconduct include rape (Deut 22:25-27), adultery (Lev 20:10), incest (Lev 20:11-12), and bestiality (Exod 22:19), among others. Laws pertaining to homicide include murder (Gen 9:6; Exod 21:12-14; Lev 24:17-23) and, interestingly, hitting, cursing, or persistent disobedience of a parent, which is tantamount to a kind of patricide or matricide (Exod 21:15, 17; Lev 20:9; Deut 21:18-21).

32. For the variety of Christian practices and interpretations of the Sabbath and Sunday in the early church, see Willy Rordorf, *Sunday: The History of the Day of Rest and Worship in the Earliest Centuries of the Christian Church,* trans. A. A. K. Graham (Philadelphia: Westminster, 1968). The *CCC* emphasizes that the celebration of the Lord's Day is not an external law imposed on us, but one written into our nature: "The celebration of Sunday observes the

lates the heart of the Christian understanding: "For us, the true Sabbath is the person of our Redeemer, our Lord Jesus Christ."[33] Christ is the true Sabbath.

The early fourth-century Acts of the Abitinian Martyrs gives us a glimpse into what this might mean.[34] Here we have a transcript of the trial of some North African Christians arrested for gathering on Sunday. When interrogated about why they have violated the orders of emperors and caesars, these Christians reply, "We have done this because the *dominicus* cannot cease."[35] The word *dominicus* has a range of meanings. Literally, it means "what is the Lord's" or "what belongs to the Lord," and it can refer to the Lord's Day, the Lord's Supper, and Lord's resurrection, though I think these three meanings cannot be separated. Their reply, then, means that the Lord, Jesus Christ, stands above all other lords, both emperors and caesars. He abides, while they will pass away. But also, this reply means that Christian observance of the *dominicus* cannot cease, that there is a law above and prior to the law of temporal authorities, a law written into creation and into our hearts. When the proconsul presses them further, the martyrs reply with a simple and stunning statement: "quoniam sine dominico non possumus," "Without the *dominicus* we cannot exist."[36] The *dominicus* is the ground of their existence, the sustaining center of their lives. Without the *dominicus*, the world is meaningless, only shifting

moral commandment inscribed by nature in the human heart to render to God an outward, visible, public, and regular worship 'as a sign of his universal beneficence to all.' Sunday worship fulfills the moral command of the Old Covenant, taking up its rhythm and spirit in the weekly celebration of the Creator and Redeemer of his people" (2176).

33. Gregory the Great, *Epistula* 13.1, quoted in John Paul II, *Dies Domini*, 18. It is likely that Jesus himself suggested this interpretation of the Sabbath when he said, "Come to me, all who labor and are heavy laden, and I will give you rest. Take my yoke upon you, and learn from me; for I am gentle and lowly in heart, and you will find rest for your souls" (Matt 11:28–29 ESV).

34. A translation of the Acts of the Abitinian Martyrs can be found in *Donatist Martyr Stories: The Church in Conflict in Roman North Africa*, trans. Maureen A. Tilley (Liverpool: Liverpool University Press, 1996), 25–50. (Note that the Abitinian martyrs preceded the Donatist schism.) The Latin can be found in *Patrialogiae Cursus Completus, Series Latina*, ed. Jacques-Paul Migne (Paris: Garnier, 1844–94), 8:705–15. Joseph Ratzinger also uses this text as a way into his discussion of the Lord's Day in "Resurrection as the Foundation of Christian Liturgy—On the Meaning of Sunday for Christian Prayer and Christian Life," in *Collected Works: Theology of the Liturgy* (San Francisco: Ignatius, 2014), 181–200. I am indebted to his treatment at several points.

35. Acts of the Abitinian Martyrs 10, my translation. Tilley translates *dominicus* as "Lord's Supper" every time.

36. Acts of the Abitinian Martyrs 11, my translation.

sands, an abyss. To be a Christian at all is to celebrate the *dominicus*, "as if a Christian could even exist without the *dominicus*."[37] The *dominicus*, like the Sabbath, is a matter of life and death, and these North African Christians were willing to die before they ceased celebrating it.

But how exactly does Christ fulfill the meaning of the Sabbath? One way we might enter into this mystery is to ponder the symbolism of Christ's rising not on the Sabbath, but the following day. Christ dies on Friday afternoon, the eve of the Sabbath, and rises on Sunday morning, "on the third day." In between, on the Sabbath, Christ rests in the tomb, in the sleep of death. His death is the observance of the Sabbath. Christ rises on Sunday, which is the first day of the week but also, in a sense, the eighth day. So, the Lord's Day is the third day, the first day, and the eighth day. How can we understand the inner logic of these three numbers and their meanings?

In the covenant made on Sinai, the third day is the day of theophany (see Exod 19:11–16). "Accordingly," Ratzinger suggests, "the time description 'on the third day' marks Jesus' Resurrection as the definitive event of the covenant, as the ultimate and real entry into history of God, who lets himself be touched in the middle of our world." This helps us understand why the Lord's Day is also the first and the eighth day. It is the first day because in this new covenant Christ has inaugurated a new creation wherein God is uniquely present, even united, to his creation. The Lord's Day, then, is the first day of the new creation, a new light shining in the darkness. It is also the eighth day because in Genesis the seventh day, unlike all the other days, is not said to have an evening, but was understood to open up into an eternal eighth day. Christ's resurrection marks the entry of time into eternity. Ratzinger says, "Hence theophany has occurred in this event in which one has come back from death or, better put, gone beyond death. It has occurred through the reception of the body into eternity, proving that it, too, is capable of the eternal, capable of divinity."[38] We said above that the Sabbath was our origin, our end, and the abiding presence of God who calls us to communion. We can now see how Gregory can say that Christ is the true Sabbath. In a new and definitive way our Creator has personally

---

37. *Acts of the Abitinian Martyrs* 12, my translation: "Quasi christianus sine dominico esse possit."

38. Ratzinger, "Resurrection as the Foundation," 191–92.

tabernacled among us, united us to himself, and brought our humanity into the Godhead. This is true rest for human beings, our true Sabbath.

Christ's resurrection is the Day of the Lord, and Christians commemorate it each Sunday by celebrating the Eucharist. It is no accident that Sunday is traditionally called "the Lord's Day" because Christians understood that the Lord was in fact coming again in the celebration of the Lord's Supper. This is the insight of the word *dominicus* above, which refers to the resurrection, Sunday, and the Eucharist all at once. Only if the Lord is made present again in the Eucharist can we account for the boldness of the North African martyrs, who cannot exist without it. Ratzinger offers us a keen insight into the identity between the Eucharist and the Lord's Day: "The Eucharist is the present, the now of the Risen One who continually gives himself in the signs of the sacrifice and is our life in this way. *For this reason the Eucharist is itself and as such the Day of the Lord.*"[39] The Eucharist makes Christ present; it makes present his passion and, more importantly, his resurrection. In the Eucharist, Christ comes again, thereby making present the Lord's Day, the day for which we were created.

In the conclusion to the *City of God*, Augustine speaks about the Lord's Day as our ultimate destiny and shows how it completes the Sabbath,

> [In that heavenly city of God] that precept will find fulfilment: "Be still and know that I am God." That will truly be the greatest of Sabbaths, a Sabbath that has no evening, the Sabbath that the Lord approved at the beginning of creation, where it says, "God rested on the seventh day from all his works, which he had been doing; and God *blessed the seventh day* and made it holy, because on that day he rested from all his works, which God had begun to do." *We ourselves shall become that seventh day,* when we have been replenished and restored by his blessing and sanctification. There we shall have leisure to be still, and we shall see that he is God.[40]

The Sabbath is our telos as human beings redeemed in Christ; it is the realization of who God created us to be. The Sabbath is not merely something we observe or an image of what heaven will be like, but is something we

---

39. Ratzinger, "Resurrection as the Foundation," 192, emphasis added.
40. Augustine, *Civ.* 22.30, emphasis added.

are and are destined to become. Even so, for Augustine, the Sabbath is not the end, for just as the Lord's Day fulfills the Sabbath in this life, so too in the next. "The seventh day will be our Sabbath, whose end will not be an evening, but the Lord's Day, an eighth day, as it were, which is to last forever, a day consecrated by the resurrection of Christ, foreshadowing the eternal rest not only of the spirit but of the body also."[41] There is an intrinsic connection between the two days, just as there is an intrinsic connection between our soul and body, and between our bliss in heaven and our bliss in the fullness of resurrection. Our destiny is a journey of the whole person, soul and body, to union with God, a union that transforms us. The Sabbath is written into our hearts, but it is realized in us and completed in the Lord's Day. This journey to the Lord's Day is not an external movement from one place to another or one time to another, but is the transformation of our soul and body as God becomes more and more manifest within them.

THE INTELLECTUALLY DISABLED AS THE SABBATH AND THE LORD'S DAY

So far, I have tried to show how the most accurate way of speaking about human beings is in terms of person and nature. I have drawn out the meaning and relationship between the Sabbath and the Lord's Day and how these are intrinsic dimensions of our humanity. Now, I would like to turn more directly to persons with disabilities, who help us to see how the Sabbath and Lord's Day can shine through our humanity, not despite but precisely because of their impaired natural capacities.

When Henri Nouwen asked what it was like living with Adam, the profoundly disabled man he now lived with in L'Arche, Adam's father, Rex, said, "Adam was our peacemaker. By his quiet presence he always brought us again to a still place in ourselves and created a loving atmosphere in our home." Adam did not accomplish this by any actions; rather, it was a function of his "quiet presence." Nouwen expands, "With Adam I knew a sacred presence and I 'saw' the face of God." Because of his limitations, Adam was a Sabbath, an eschatological reality present in time. What Augustine said above about our ultimate destiny seems just as applicable here: Adam had become the seventh day. Replenished and restored by God, Adam had the

---

41. Augustine, *Civ.* 22.30.

leisure to be still and called others to stillness. Indeed, for Nouwen, being with Adam was like observing the Sabbath. "My daily two hours with Adam were transforming me. In being present to him I was hearing an inner voice of love beyond all activities of care."[42] Being with Adam was a call to rest, to move beyond the activity and cares of the six days of toil. With Adam, he was called to be still and know God.

The sacred presence that Nouwen and others encountered in Adam is within every human being, but with most of us this presence is obscured by sin, distraction, or busyness. Our way of life occludes our being. Those with intellectual disabilities are often simpler, less distracted, less concerned with power and prestige or getting ahead. In fact, their lives are marked by an absence of these things, and perhaps this allows them to be more who God created us to be, that is, more like a Sabbath.

Traditionally, the Sabbath is observed by abstaining from work. In doing this, one imitates God himself, who worked for six days and rested on the seventh. On this day, we are called to refrain from toil, to devote ourselves to holiness, to imitation of God, and to remembering what God has done. "The splendor of the day," Heschel says, "is expressed in terms of *abstentions*, just as the mystery of God is more adequately conveyed *via negationis.*"[43] People with intellectual disabilities live lives marked, in a sense, by abstentions, limits, negated powers. These "abstentions" allow the "splendor of the day" to be expressed more clearly through their presence. They, in a sense, "get out of God's way." Without the tangles of the mind, self-deceit, restlessness, anxiety, and striving, they are more transparent, more weak, and thus God's power is made perfect in them without hindrance or interference. Nouwen says of his friend, "Adam possessed an inner light that was radiant. It was of God. He had few distractions, few attachments, and few ambitions to fill his inner space. Therefore, Adam did not have to practice the spiritual disciplines to become empty for God. His so-called 'disability' gifted him with it."[44]

For many intellectually disabled people, there is a kind of nonresistance to God, a contentment with simply being, an imitation of the gentleness of

---

42. Nouwen, *Adam: God's Beloved*, 27, 53.
43. Heschel, *Sabbath*, 15, emphasis original.
44. Nouwen, *Adam: God's Beloved*, 30.

Jesus: "*a bruised reed he will not break*, and a dimly burning wick *he will not quench*" (Isa 42:3 NRSV). They do not impose themselves on the world but let it be. In fact, often unable to do very much, their expertise is in being. Nouwen says, "Adam's peace is first of all a peace rooted in being. ... Being is more important than doing. ... His gift is his pure *being with us*."[45] This is also the quality of the Sabbath. "There is a realm of time," Heschel says, "where the goal is not to have but to be, not to own but to give, not to control but to share, not to subdue but to be in accord."[46] Precisely because of his disabilities, Adam was a man who lived in accord, who shared himself and gave the gift of peace to those who knew him. Because of his disabilities, Adam was, we might say, a perpetual Sabbath.

We have seen how persons with intellectual disabilities can be a Sabbath. What, though, is different about those who become, as it were, the Lord's Day? I would suggest that this is a quality of the baptized whose presence is christological, or better, eucharistic, and therefore is redemptive for others. To understand this better, we can reflect on the phrase "body of Christ," which has always had three related meanings: Christ's physical body (Heb 10:5), the church (1 Cor 12:12), and the Eucharist (Luke 22:19). Indeed, for many, there is a mystical identity between these three.

According to Augustine, those who are baptized "have become not only Christians, but Christ himself."[47] Incorporated into the body of Christ, the baptized are radically identified with Christ and begin to take on his qualities.[48] They become temples of the Holy Spirit and "partakers of the divine nature" (2 Pet 1:4). This means they have a new and divine source of power within them. This is true of all the baptized. Intellectually disabled persons would have an important quality, in addition to this, one that comes from their impairment: an inability to sin (or, at least, a limited culpability for

---

45. Henri Nouwen, "Adam's Story: The Peace That Is Not of This World," in *Seeds of Hope: A Henri Nouwen Reader*, ed. Robert Durback (New York: Image, 1997), 257–58.

46. Heschel, *Sabbath*, 3.

47. Augustine, *Tractates on John* 21.8, my translation.

48. According to the *CCC*, "The two principal effects are purification from sins [both original and personal] and new birth in the Holy Spirit" (1262). Still, "certain temporal consequences of sin remain in the baptized, such as suffering, illness, death, and such frailties inherent in life as weaknesses of character, and so on, as well as an inclination to sin that Tradition calls *concupiscence*" (1264). Baptism "makes the neophyte 'a new creature,' an adopted son of God, who has become a 'partaker of the divine nature,' member of Christ and co-heir with him, and a temple of the Holy Spirit" (1265).

sin). Thus, cleansed of sin, identified with Christ, and unable to sin, baptized persons with intellectual impairments would be, as John Berkman says in his remarkable essay, "sacramental icons of heavenly life."[49]

But more than just images, the intellectually disabled can communicate God's life to others. Augustine helps us here as well. In a famous sermon, he identifies the church with the Eucharist. "So if you are the Body of Christ and its members," he says, "it is your mystery that has been placed on the Lord's table; you receive your own mystery. ... Be what you see, and receive what you are."[50] The baptized congregation is identified with the consecrated bread and wine, but also called to be transformed by it and offer itself up along with the eucharistic sacrifice.[51] The body of Christ (the church) united to the body of Christ (the Eucharist) offers itself to the Father as an acceptable sacrifice. And just as the sacrifice of Christ's physical body on the cross was redemptive for others, so too is the sacrifice of his ecclesial body in the Eucharist. As Christians—as Christ!—the baptized can become a *dominicus*, a Christ event, which can heal and transform others. This, of course, can be obscured by our sin or neglect, but for the intellectually disabled, whose lives are often more transparent to God, Christ comes again unhindered.

Numbering the intellectually disabled among God's poor will help us to emphasize this point. There is an intimate connection between the Eucharist and the poor, because the same body of Christ present in the Eucharist ("This is my body") is the same body of Christ present in the poor ("the least of these"). Saint John Chrysostom makes this point beautifully:

> Do you wish to honour the body of Christ? Do not ignore him when he is naked. Do not pay him homage in the temple clad in silk only then to neglect him outside where he suffers cold and nakedness. He who said: "This is my body" is the same One who said: "You saw

---

49. John Berkman, "Are Persons with Profound Intellectual Disabilities Sacramental Icons of Heavenly Life? Aquinas on Impairment," *Studies in Christian Ethics* 26, no. 1 (2013): 83–96.

50. Augustine, *Sermon* 272.1, my translation.

51. One can also detect a distinction within the identification: the church is a mixed body of Christ, a body that contains both good and bad, while the Eucharist is an unmixed body of Christ, which has the power to transform the church into what they eat.

me hungry and you gave me no food," and "Whatever you did to the least of my brothers you did also to me."[52]

Henri Nouwen makes a similar point about his experience with Adam in no less striking terms: "God's body and Adam's body are one, because, Jesus tells us clearly, 'Insofar as you did this to one of the least of these brothers of mine, you did it to me' (Matt. 25:40). In Adam, indeed, we touched the living Christ among us." The materially poor and the intellectually poor are, we could say, the Lord's Day when Christ comes again. In their wounded humanity, Christ becomes present, a presence that has the power to heal and transform others. Nouwen says, "Each of us who has touched Adam has been made whole somewhere; it has been our common experience."[53]

Some people worry that this kind of account romanticizes disability and does not respect the reality of disabled persons or the struggles of those who live with them. This is a valid concern, yet the testimonies I draw on come from realistic people who suffer themselves and who share their lives with others who suffer. There is no hiding the real difficulties involved in having a disability or in living with those who are disabled. Seeing Christ in others with the eyes of faith does not mean that we do not see the suffering with our bodily eyes. Experiencing Christ in others does not negate experiencing the pain of the world.

Blessed Carlo Gnocchi, a World War II chaplain who knew suffering firsthand (he nearly died of starvation and cold) and who devoted his life to children suffering the ravages of war (the orphaned and the mutilated), could say in light of faith, "[In the suffering child,] we must see not only a small human redeemer with Christ and in Christ, but also an intercessor and mediator of grace. ... Each suffering child is worthy of being honored and almost venerated." But he also can say quite soberly on the next page, "However, such feelings, inspired by reasons of faith, cannot and must not abolish the pain and the dark anguish that, in the face of a child's suffering, grip every man's heart and tear to shreds both body and soul, above all the

---

52. John Chrysostom, *Homilies on the Gospel of Matthew* 50.3–4, quoted in John Paul II, *Dies Domini*, 71.

53. Nouwen, *Adam: God's Beloved*, 111, 127.

heart, body, and soul of the child's parents." Gnocchi is right when he says, "Christianity neither opposes nor abolishes nature."[54]

Using the framework of the Lord's Day helps to avoid romanticism, for the Lord's Day commemorates and makes present not just Christ in glory, but Christ on the cross. The cross and resurrection cannot be separated. There is real suffering, while, at the same time, there is the mysterious, transformative power of the Resurrection. This explains why both can be present in our encounters with the intellectually disabled.

CONCLUSION

Let me conclude with one last illustrative story. When my son was diagnosed with autism, I reached out to a friend who had worked with the intellectually disabled in L'Arche communities. He wrote to me,

> Two of the few times I have had something like a "vision" have been in the company of, or context of, my work with children with special needs. One was an occasion when a child with devastating physical disabilities appeared to me as Jesus, and in that moment I had no doubt that he well and truly was Jesus. Another occasion was more complex but amounts to sitting in adoration of the Eucharist at a Jesuit retreat house and intuiting all of reality channeled through the heart of another child with a devastating disability. These things are of course impossible to explain, and some people take a very dim view of such talk. But the bottom line, visions or no, is this: That children with special needs are among God's poor and a locus of theophany. Benedict's autism may be a way through which divine realities are instantiated to you of which you can barely dream. But this all begins in seeing him as complete as he is, which is the work of years.[55]

---

54. Gnocchi, *Pedagogy of Innocent Suffering*, 29–30. Both sentiments are on display in this passage as well: "In every suffering child, we must see not only a man precociously called to participate in the human solidarity of suffering, in accord with the tragic law of Adam, but also a little lamb who purifies and redeems, according to Christ's loving law, 'a living sacrifice of innocent humanity for sinful humanity' " (29).

55. Joseph Walsh, email message to author, May 16, 2016.

In this essay, I have endeavored to understand this very experience. Reflecting on our common fallen nature and the variety of human brokenness, I have tried to show how Christ manifests himself through weakness and frailty, indeed, through the weakest and the most frail. This capacity is a Sabbath law written into our hearts, a common feature of our humanity, which shines forth when we become empty for God and is brought to completion in Christ when we become the Lord's Day. This is our destiny in heaven and the resurrection, but this eschatological reality is also available to us now, especially in the intellectually disabled who reveal to us our true humanity and become our teachers in achieving it. Broken bodies and broken minds become Christ's body, "broken for you," a Eucharist, "a locus of theophany," the Lord's Day. In the distressing disguise of the intellectually disabled, we encounter Christ, who comes again to draw us to him and transform us into him. This is the mystery of the gospel, made present in our fallen human nature, and revealed by the least among us.

CONTRIBUTORS

—

Michel R. Barnes has written extensively on the Trinitarian theologies of Gregory of Nyssa and Augustine of Hippo. He is the author of the monograph *The Power of God: A Study of Gregory of Nyssa's Trinitarian Theology*, and coeditor of *Arianism after Arius*. He is presently writing a monograph on Augustine's Trinitarian theology as well as a book on the doctrine of the Holy Spirit in the early church.

Paul Blowers is the Dean E. Walker Professor of Church History at Emmanuel Christian Seminary, Milligan University (Tennessee). Among other works he has written *Salvation's Folly: Visions and Faces of the Tragic in Early Christian Literature* (forthcoming), *Maximus the Confessor: Jesus Christ and the Transfiguration of the World*, and *Drama of the Divine Economy: Creator and Creation in Early Christian Theology and Piety*.

Constantine R. Campbell is professor of New Testament at Trinity Evangelical Divinity School. His publications include *Basics of Verbal Aspect in Biblical Greek*, *Advances in the Study of Greek: New Insights for Reading the New Testament*, and *Paul and Union with Christ: An Exegetical and Theological Study*—the 2014 *Christianity Today* Book of the Year in Biblical Studies.

Marc Cortez is professor of theology at Wheaton College. Many of his books have focused specifically on the significance of Jesus Christ for understanding the nature of humanity, including *ReSourcing Theology Anthropology: A Constructive Account of Humanity in the Life of Christ*, *Christological Anthropology in Historical Perspective*, and *Theological Anthropology: A Guide for the Perplexed*.

Paul Gavrilyuk holds the Aquinas Chair in Theology and Philosophy at the University of St. Thomas, Minnesota. He specializes in Greek patristics, modern Orthodox theology, and philosophy of religion. His works include *The Suffering of the Impassible God*, *The Spiritual Senses: Perceiving God in Western Christianity* (coedited with Sarah Coakley), and *Georges Florovsky and the Russian Religious Renaissance*.

Daniel W. Houck's is senior pastor of Calvary Hill Baptist Church in Fairfax, Virginia, and adjunct professor of theology at the John Leland Center for Theological Studies. An ecclesial fellow at the Center for Pastor Theologians, his research draws on medieval thought to address contemporary issues in theology and science. *Aquinas, Original Sin, and the Challenge of Evolution* is his first book.

George Kalantzis is professor of theology and director of The Wheaton Center for Early Christian Studies at Wheaton College. A cofounder of the Chicago Theological Initiative, Kalantzis is the author or editor of numerous books, including *Caesar and the Lamb: Early Christian Attitudes on War and Military Service*, *"Come, Let Us Eat Together": Sacraments and Christian Unity*, and *Christian Political Witness*.

Han-luen Kantzer Komline is assistant professor of church history and theology at Western Theological Seminary in Holland, Michigan. Her research focuses on early Christian theology, especially the thought of Augustine, and has been published in various journals and collected volumes. Her first book, *Augustine on the Will: A Theological Account*, is forthcoming with Oxford University Press.

Matthew Levering holds the James N. and Mary D. Perry Jr. Chair of Theology at Mundelein Seminary. He is the author or editor of over forty books on topics of dogmatic, sacramental, moral, historical, and biblical theology. Most recently he published *Engaging the Doctrine of Creation*; *Was the Reformation a Mistake?: Why Catholic Doctrine Is Not Unbiblical*; and *Dying and the Virtues*.

David Luy is associate professor of biblical and systematic theology at Trinity Evangelical Divinity School and a codirector of the Chicago Theological Initiative. His research focuses on the historical development and modern appropriation of Reformation theology. He has published *Dominus Mortis: Martin Luther on the Incorruptibility of God in Christ* and has contributed to various journals and encyclopedias.

R. David Nelson is senior acquisitions editor for Baker Academic and Brazos Press, and editor of the quarterly journal *Lutheran Forum*. He is author of *The Interruptive Word: Eberhard Jüngel on the Sacramental Structure of God's Relation to the World, Jüngel: A Guide for the Perplexed*, and, with Charles Raith II, *Ecumenism: A Guide for the Perplexed*.

Kenneth Oakes is assistant professor of systematic theology at the University of Notre Dame. He specializes in modern Protestant thought, as well as contemporary systematic and constructive theology. An expert in the theology of Karl Barth, he has authored *Karl Barth on Theology and Philosophy* and *Reading Karl Barth: A Companion to Karl Barth's Epistle to the Romans*.

Jared Ortiz is associate professor of religion at Hope College. He teaches Catholic studies and is founder and executive director of the Saint Benedict Institute, the Catholic spiritual and intellectual center that serves Hope College. He has scholarly interests in liturgy, Latin patristic thought, and disability. In 2016 he published *"You Made Us for Yourself": Creation in St. Augustine's Confessions.*

Gavin Ortlund (PhD, Fuller Theological Seminary) serves as senior pastor of First Baptist Church of Ojai in Ojai, California. He is the author of several books, including *Anselm's Pursuit of Joy: A Commentary on the Proslogion, Retrieving Augustine's Doctrine of Creation: Ancient Wisdom for Current Controversy*, and *Theological Retrieval for Evangelicals: Why We Need Our Past to Have a Future.*

SUBJECT INDEX

—

A

absurdity, 34

Acts of the Abitinian Martyrs, 231

Adam (biblical character), 22, 23, 86, 124

Adam (L'Arche), 226, 234

Aeschylus, 51–52, 123

Agee, James, 118n11

agnosticism, 72–73

Ambrose, 85n5, 96

animal death
and design, 87–94, 98
and hierarchy, 105–6
history of interpretation, 85n5
and perspectival prejudice, 97–108

animal suffering
definition of, 184–85, 186
and evolutionary problem of evil, 182–83, 186–88, 199–200
as nonexistent, 184, 188–94
problem of other minds, 194–200

Ansell, Billy, 127–29

Anselm of Canterbury, 216

"Apocalyptic Antinomies" (Martyn), 148

apocalyptic imagery, 27, 29, 31

apocalyptic theology
distinctives, 137–38
and dualism, 152
emergence of, 134–35, 135n3, 139–44
on evil, 151–54
new vs. old creation, 145–50, 151, 157–58
and Pauline studies, 155–57
and structures of power, 136
and systematic theology, 135, 135n3, 158

Aquinas, Thomas, 85n5, 214–17

Arndt, Johann, 4

Arnold, Edwin, 171, 177, 177n23

Athanasius, 36, 132n49

atheism, 61

atonement, 63

Augustine (354–430)
on animal death, 86–110
and body of Christ, 236, 237
Christology and evil, 67–68, 67n2, 75n25, 77–79, 75–76, 75n24, 80–83, 80n37, 132n49
critique of Platonism, 52n8
Enchiridion, 68–83, 68n6, 106
epistemic limits of evil, 69–73
on evil, 54n16, 55n20, 59, 67n2, 68n5, 68n6, 117
and experience of evil, 118
on the fall, 204
on natural disasters, 57
ontological limits of evil, 73–76
on original sin, 56, 64
and the problem of evil, 107–8
on Sabbath, 228, 233
on Stoicism, 120
on suffering, 3 4
and vanity, 43, 44–45
works of, 68n3, 68n4 (*see also individual works*)

B

Babcock, William, 68n6

"Ballad of Birmingham" (Randal), 128n36

Banks, Russell, 127–29

Barth, Karl, 144–45, 162

SCRIPTURE INDEX

—

Old Testament

New Testament

Apocrypha